EXILED

40 YEARS AN EXILE

A LONG TIME AWAY FROM KITH AND KIN

THOMAS ANTHONY McNULTY

© Copyright Notice

Published by TMN Publications

ISBN 978-0-9575785-0-0

The Man In The Glass by Dale Wimbrow
www.theguyintheglass.com

Printed by Brunswick Press Ltd, Dublin

Dedicated to all the 'unknowns' who must forever remain anonymous.

But who couldn't have been done without.

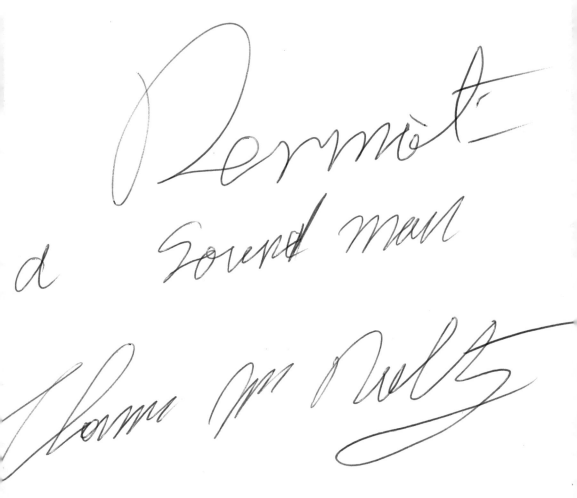

Foreword

by Thomas Anthony McNulty

TO ALL THE families reared in the wee terraced houses in the towns and cities, in the whitewashed cottages and farmhouses of the countryside. to the people who ran the small businesses, and the not so small.

Every section of society was affected by the times they lived through. It brought out the best in familys and communities. For we were all in it together. Ordinary people living through extraordinary times, there was no social barrier to suffering.

My name is Thomas and I was born in January 1949, a couple of miles outside the small market town of Dungannon, County Tyrone. The desire to write this book has been with me for some time, and now seems as good a time as any. This story is about an ordinary Irish family; it could have been any family, caught up in extraordinary times. It tells how history imposed on our lives a situation of which we had no part in the making, but would change the direction of all our lives forever. This is a story of neighbours and neighbours' children.

1

EARLY CHILDHOOD MEMORIES

MY DAD WAS a big man with a lame leg. He was known as Lame Johnny. He was a man of many talents. A fiddle player in a Céilí band, he loved fishing and hunting and reared his own gun dogs, always golden Labradors. Lovely dogs. He kept one or two for himself and sold the rest with pedigree papers. He said they always did better than a litter of pigs! He was always very proud of his first class pedigree dogs. A member of St. Patrick's Hall Social Club in Dungannon and in later years its caretaker, he was paid a wage by the local Dean of the Catholic Church. The Hall, as it was known, had three snooker tables set in three different rooms, and my abiding memories of these snooker tables was the loving care my father lavished on them, with brush and iron to keep them in first class shape for the many games constantly played on them. Card games – Twenty Five, Whist and Rummy – were always being played by some of the town's local characters who always had a friendly word for us 'Wee Macs' when we would come into these smoked filled rooms on an errand for our father.

I remember that old hall fondly, it was a friendly place where one could get an orange mineral or lemonade but never alcohol. My father always frowned upon drink and would turn away members worse for wear because of alcohol; "Come back when you are sober" he'd say. He strongly disapproved of drinking, was a teetotaller himself, just like my mother. Maybe his greatest love of all was playing chess, at which he was respected as "the man to beat" in the whole area. He taught all of us boys how to play at an early age and we all became good chess players quite young. He was also a very good snooker player who was proud to have played and, on occasion, beaten, a man from a local rival club, who later went on to be a world champion. Some of which the local "Dungannon Observers" old copies, can identify to the fact that he won! Unfortunately, he didn't live long enough to see Denis Taylor from the local snooker league become a world champion and a millionaire! His sharp eye for rifle shooting was a local legend and he always had a .22 rifle and a good double-barrelled shotgun. My mother used to tell us of the hard times when he had to sell his beloved shotgun to buy essential things for the family, one of the hardest things he ever had to do. So my father was a good all-rounder, who was a big easy going affable peaceful man. He was well liked and well respected as the "Daddy of the large family of boys and girls out at the Lough". There was a Lough down at the back of our house which was a popular place for fishing and swimming, hence we were known as "the wee Macs from the Lough".

My father married my mother when he was thirty six and my mother was in her early twenties, which was the custom at that time in rural Ireland Over the years she gave birth to twelve children, one year after another, six boys and six girls of which I was the sixth born. Three sons, then two daughters and then myself. Two more boys directly below me, then twin girls and two more girls after that. While my father was easy going and affable my mother was totally different. She was without doubt the driving force behind our family. She was a very single minded person, who, when she put her mind to something would turn heaven and earth to achieve her objective. A very determined and resilient woman, she had a very strong faith in God, the power of the Saints and Our Lady. This was a faith that kept her going through very hard times when there was little or nothing but faith left. She would never give in and if she met with defeat would take it on the chin and go at it again with an even more dogged and sometimes fierce determination! She was not a person to take to fools easily, was a great letter writer and took up many a cause with the unfriendly authorities of that time. She would keep writing back even when turned down repeatedly and sometimes would be rewarded with the odd victory for her stubbornness! A very formidable woman she reared a large family sometimes on little or nothing other than blind faith and her own resilience. She cared for every child that God sent her, and did her utmost to feed, clothe, and keep us all happy – as well as putting a bit of the great faith that she had into each of us. That faith and belief that one can make their way through anything, was to play a vitally important role in the years ahead in all our lives, not least her own. She sometimes mourned the fact that she didn't stay in a little house nearer her own family, in which she and my father had lived in for a few years just after they were married, but the Lough was home and in time she grew very fond and loyal to it. She had good times and hard times there, but it was always home, a home we all loved.

My father bought it off an old uncle of his for £400 which he was always paying back to the bank when he would sell a bullock once or twice a year at Dungannon market. "Oul Jemmy", as we called our father's uncle, had another small farm just about a mile round the road, and the deal was that he'd move to it when he'd finished the building work on it. He never finished it, and lived with us for twenty years and died at the age of 92 after a short illness. He was a big, tall man, a pig butcher, who travelled round the district butchering pigs at the local small farms which were largely for home use. He had a great healthy, long life, liked a drop of whiskey and a bet on the horses which he indulged in when he rode the bike into Dungannon every Friday to collect his pension. My mother and he didn't get on that well but she kept him all those years because none of his own relations would have him. My mother could have done with his bed for some of the children, but she wouldn't turn him out. He was full of pride, and when my mother would row with him, usually over a terrible spitting habit he had, he would bundle up his belongings and state that he had plenty of relations to stay with but he would always be back after a few days and things would be back to normal again. He always took an old clock with him on these departures. I never figured out why because it wasn't worth much. When my father did a major renovation job on the old farm house to accommodate his rapidly growing family, oul Jemmy was very saddened to find himself in the local old people's home. He stayed there and we used to visit him with our father, and one day he cried and said he missed all the children at the oul Lough and asked could he come home. It was the first time he really appreciated all the care my mother gave to him over all the years. When my father told my mother what had happened at the nursing home she sighed and said "bring him home". Oul Jemmy was delighted and lived content and happy with us until he died peacefully in his own bed a few years later. He loved to tell a story about the school inspector coming into his class when he was about ten years old. The inspector found a fault in his copy book, but he pointed out to the inspector how he had made the mistake not himself. When it turned out to be correct his teacher praised him highly, and called him a 'manly boy'. If we had a penny for every time we had to listen to the manly boy story we'd be rich. It was oul Jemmy's favourite party piece. We children all loved him and many were the times he saved us from the wrath of our father when we would put a ball or a stone through one of the little windows of the farmhouse. "It was an accident Johnny", he'd say with the big arms out and us hiding behind him in his bed! My father would say "Jemmy, everything's an accident with you, you never blame them for anything" but he'd save us and later when our father would cool down we would skip back up into the old kitchen and that would be the end of it. Father was like that; when he'd cool down he'd forget all about it. Jemmy had been married, but his wife died very young, and while he had a daughter she only visited him rarely, as she lived in Glasgow. Jemmy went over to visit her a few times but they weren't very close.

2

THE LABRADOR DOGS AND SKIPPER

MY FATHER, AS I said, reared pure bred Labrador dogs for sale. He always had "the papers" for them to prove that they were pure bred. That was vitally important. They would be worth nothing if they hadn't got "the papers" with them as part of the sale. My father kept two Labrador bitches. He later brought a pure bred Labrador dog out from Dungannon to be locked up in one of the sheds under the old loft to get the bitch pregnant when she was in heat. It was very important that no other oul dog or mongrel would ever get at the pure bred bitch when she was in heat, otherwise the pups would not be pure bred and could not be sold for good money. My father used to say a litter of pure bred Labrador pups was better than a litter of pigs to make money! He also had great pride in his pure bred dogs and his old bitch "Lassie" who always had huge litters of eight or nine pups. My father thought the world of her. Me and Joe were nine or ten and always very curious about what the big dog and Lassie got up to when they were locked up in the shed underneath the old loft!

We pulled up a piece of flooring in the loft so we could see down into the shed where the two Labrador dogs were "at it". "Bran" the big dog's name and Lassie were at it alright, all the time! Me and Joe were so very curious that we decided to open the door of the shed where the two dogs were at it and have a proper look. Joe's own dog Skipper, was always near Joe wherever he was. That dog loved Joe as only a boy and dog can love one another. Skipper would have died for Joe. We use to pretend to attack Joe, and Skipper would leap to his defence, growl and bare his teeth. No one would harm Joe with him around. Skipper was a cross breed between a greyhound and a collie. A big, brown, ugly, happy dog, he was Joe's constant companion as a boy.

So as we opened the door of the shed to see more of what was going on, Lassie bolted out of the door and away up the hills beside the old farmhouse. We got the door closed before Bran got out but Lassie was away up the hills with Skipper in hot pursuit. If Skipper got at Lassie we were dead! My father's anger would be so terrible at the loss of his pure bred pups, my life, and Joes just wouldn't be worth living. We'd be better off dead! So me and Joe belted up the hills after Lassie with Skipper catching up on her with every step. God, don't let him catch up and get at her. "Skipper! Come back!" we roared and shouted, but Skipper wasn't interested in anything but the bitch in heat. Skipper was not going to be denied his chance to have his go at Lassie. We ran up the hills and down the other side into a small meadow by the Lough. The dogs had gone out of sight for a little while and when we caught up with them in the small meadow, Skipper was having his way! "Oh no, oh no" we cried! The two dogs had just turned around rear end to rear end as dogs do. Me and Joe caught each of them by the ears and pulled them abruptly apart. We got Lassie, tied a piece of bailer twine around her neck, prayed my father hadn't come home and headed back to the shed to her proper suitor, Big Bran from Dungannon. My father thankfully hadn't come home and we got Lassie back into the shed with Bran without anyone knowing, only me and Joe. We swore each other to secrecy, to tell no-one – not family, not friends – no one. This was life or death. This was a secret no one could ever know. We would just have to wait and see if Lassie got pregnant, and if she did hope that we had got to Skipper in time before he had done the business.

Lassie got pregnant alright, my father was delighted, me and Joe were scared and dismayed. What if Lassie had a pup or pups the image of Skipper? We'll be dead! We'll just have to keep a close eye on her when she comes near her time and try be with her at birth. If there was a big litter and one or two looked like Skipper we would be able to give them away or drown them in a bucket of water and then bury them in a secret grave. It seemed as if Lassie was never going to have those pups, she got bigger and bigger. We knew where she had picked her den to have her litter.

It was summer time and we were off school, my father was working so we had a good chance of being with Lassie at time of birth. I came flying down the lane on my bike one day and Joe was all excited, I knew right away what it was, Lassie was having her litter of pups. She already had three, three lovely golden Labrador pups. Joe looked at me in immense relief, thank god! Three more came straight away, all lovely golden colours, then another one slipped out, we knew she was going to have eight, one more, we watched, hardly able to breathe, "Here it comes, its golden! A beautiful little golden Labrador puppy". Me and Joe started to dance up and down and cheer, you'd have thought Tyrone scored the last minute goal against Kerry in the All Ireland Final. A winner! Skipper looked at us as if we were mad. Joe hugged him with happiness because we might have been dead if there had have been a litter of little Skippers, but Skipper would have been in mortal danger as well! My father was happy with his pure bred puppies and sold them all six weeks later for £8 each, all but one bitch he kept for breeding purposes. About a year or more later, my father was leaning over the old bike he had, his one elbow would be on the saddle, the other would be on the handlebars. He was watching his three Labrador bitches playing in the field in front of the old farmhouse. He shook his head in puzzlement "You know" he said, "there is something strange about that young bitch, only I know for certain that she is a full bred, I would doubt it, I don't know what it is, I cant put my finger on it but I swear there is just something not right. But sure it must just be my imagination, all the people I sold her brothers and sisters to are happy with them, so everything is alright". He got on his bike and headed way up the lane. Me and Joe looked at each other and heaved a big sigh of relief, and it was over at last!

Some months later Skipper was caught worrying sheep, and several of the farmer's sheep died. Skipper was caught red handed in the field and was wounded with a shotgun. He made it home but the farmer tracked him to our house and insisted that Skipper be put down immediately. My father had no choice, took out the shotgun and put Skipper down there and then. When we came home from school my father set Joe down in the old living room and told him what had happened Skipper. Joe cried for days, like he'd never stop. He was broken-hearted over that oul dog, that oul Skipper was Joe's soul mate. I don't think he ever got over it fully, I think even after all that happened him down the years of his life, a part of him still mourns that oul dog Skipper.

3

THE DEATH OF A PROTESTANT NEIGHBOUR

MY MOTHER'S EYES flashed angrily as she turned her wrath on oul Jemmy "Don't you dare speak of old Mrs. Sloan like that" she said "if there's such a place as heaven, and I'm sure there is, old Mrs. Sloan will be in it. She was a good neighbour, a good mother to her family, a good decent Christian woman and how dare you judge her the way you are after doing. If she doesn't get to heaven, then God help you". Oul Jemmy said that he was just quoting the Catholic Catechism, taught by the priests when he was at school. My mother, still angry, said, "I don't care what some book said, if there's such a place as heaven, that lovely old woman, that good old neighbour will be sure to be in it". Old Mrs. Sloan had been our neighbour from just across the Lough all our lives. They were a Protestant family. There were two houses up their lane, George and Old Mrs. Sloan, and Billy the son who had a wife and two children and lived in a new bungalow. Old George played the bagpipes and often played in the still of the summer evenings, with the sound coming across the waters of the Lough, so very clearly. A beautiful sound. We often sat out in the fields at the Lough to listen to George playing the bagpipes. A lovely, quiet Christian family who wouldn't harm anyone.

Mrs. Sloan, who was eighty years of age had taken ill and had died suddenly a few days earlier. The death of a Protestant neighbour was treated with the utmost respect, but differently from the death of a Catholic neighbour. Everyone went to the Wake, then to the Church for the service, then the graveyard for the burial. With the Protestant neighbours death Catholic people went to the grounds of the Church but did not go in. They waited patiently with respect outside the Protestant Church and then rejoined the funeral to the graveyard and the burial. We would be sincerely thanked by the Protestant neighbour for coming to the funeral and for the sympathy and respect shown to their family.

This is what we had done for our neighbour, old Mrs. Sloan, but Jemmy, who was about the same age as old Mrs. Sloan, had been a neighbour of the old woman all of his life. But today my mother was very, very angry with oul Jemmy. He had made a remark about oul Mrs. Sloan and how it was an awful pity that she could not go to heaven because she was a Protestant and only Catholics could get to heaven. My mother had bristled with instant anger. "Don't you dare judge old Mrs. Sloan like that", she had said, "she will be in heaven and that's for sure, she was a good person all her life". Oul Jemmy had quoted from the old green Catholic religion handbook that "only people belonging to the one, Holy, Catholic Apolistic Church could enter the Kingdom of Heaven. My mother, a deeply Christian believer herself, and born into the Catholic church, told oul Jemmy that while she understood what he had been taught, that part of the teaching of the Catholic religion wasn't correct and never ever again was he to say that very wrong unchristian remark about old Mrs. Sloan. You would be judged on how you live your life she told oul Jemmy, not on what is written in some little green religion handbook. Old Mrs. Sloan was a lovely woman who lived a good decent Christian life and would be in heaven. Say a wee prayer for her she told oul Jemmy, and while you are at it say one for yourself, you might have more need for it than old Mrs. Sloan! My mother was way ahead of the Catholic Church, when it came too being a good Christian neighbour. The Protestant families were great neighbours, very helpful, hard working and honest.

4

THE MESSAGE

MY MAMMY WAS after piddling herself. Why did she do that? It wasn't like her. My mammy never did that, but she was after doing it and now she was drying her legs with the towel. I was just about five years old and there was just me and mammy and a couple of the younger ones in the old home. My Dad and all of the older ones were away. My Mammy sat down at the big old table in the kitchen and took a pen and a piece of paper and quietly wrote a wee note. She called me over and said "Now Tommy, I have something very important for you to do, just for me", she said very earnestly. I knew by her that it was very very important; I didn't know what but I just knew it was. She put the note in my hand and closed it with hers. "Now don't lose that message, keep it tightly and safely in your hand," she said calmly, "You know where Mary Rose and John the blacksmith lives don't you Tommy? Yes, I know where they live", I was often there with Mammy and Daddy and my brothers and sisters, they had children the same age as us and one of them was my friend. "Well you take this message in your hand and run all the way up to Mary Rose and give her this note. Away you go now Tommy and don't stop for anything until you get there". I hared away up the lane; I went straight on, up along the hedge in upper Janes field, and over the old iron gate that had a R cast into the middle of it-that meant that Lord Ranfurley owned all the land. On down the little boreen, with its hedges meeting at the top to form a kind of green archway like a guard of honour, and then onto Henry the bread man's short lane and onto his street. His brother Mickey drove Hughes bread van and we often picked up the bread there for our mammy. I climbed on over the little gate beside Henry's byre and duchall and on over a couple of his fields with his black cattle in them, on over an old wooden fence and into the Blacksmith's field. I saw the Smithy's forge in the distance and I leapt the wire fence and into the last field. I could see Mary Rose's house now. I ran fast past the forge. I could hear someone making a lot of noise in there. Out onto the lane, through the garden gate and breathlessly knocked on the door and called "Mary Rose I have a message from my Mammy". Mary Rose came to the door looked at me, took the message out of my outstretched hand. She looked at it, she turned around, grabbed her coat from the coat rack beside her, ran out the door so fast she nearly knocked me down, didn't even say sorry or thanks and ran over to the forge. I heard her say to her husband "I'm away off to Annie Mc' Nulty's, I'll see you in the evening". She didn't wait for an answer and sped away over the fields far faster than me. I ran after her, but I couldn't keep up. She disappeared into Henry the bread man's fields and I couldn't see her anymore. I slowed down then and rested a bit. I had the message given to Mary Rose like my mammy told me to do, so I was happy now.

When I got back to my own house a big black car was on our street, a man in a suit got out of it and took two black cases out of the boot. He looked real swanky with his big black car, fancy suit and his two black suit cases. He was in a hurry and disappeared into our house. My two older sisters, Mary and Angela told me what a good boy I was. They had come home when I was doing "the message". They told me that I couldn't go into the house for the rest of the evening, but one of them went in and got me a farge of bread and jam and a cup of milk for I was hungry and my Mammy had made no dinner for some reason. Me and Joe and Marty played outside. My sisters got them a farge of bread and jam as well. The big black car sat on our street for what seemed like ages. Then the man in the suit came out, only he hadn't a suit on now, he was dressed in white but he had his two suitcases and his jacket over his arm, he also had a big box of chocolates in his hand. I was hoping he'd give me some! He seemed real pleased with himself. He had a happy smile on as he said hello to us boys and then got into his big black car and he was gone, away up the lane and down onto the road. A good while after that Mary Rose called me Joe and Marty into the kitchen – living room of our house. She sat us down and told us we had to be quiet and very good as our mammy was a wee bit sick but with rest and quietness that she would be alright; it was nothing to worry about she assured our anxious faces. We were happy then. Then she said "I have something very important to show you three boys, come on", she said. She herded us quietly into Mammy and

Daddy's room. Mammy was in bed and a bit pale looking. She took my hand in hers and squeezed it, "Thanks son, you're a great wee boy". My Mammy's hands were a bit rough feeling, they always were, but I loved when she took my hand. I felt special. Mary Rose took us over to a cot in the middle of the room; she told me Joe and Marty that we had two baby sisters! She showed us them in the cot. Two funny looking ugly little heads, they smelled funny too! But I already had two sisters, I thought to myself, and they often played hide and seek with me Joe and Marty. They were alright, my two elder sisters, so I was sure these two would be alright too. Someday soon they would be able to play hide and seek too, that would be good fun. In the meantime me Joe and Marty, Mary and Angela would have to play on our own. As I left Mammy and Daddy's room I looked at my Mammy sleeping soundly in her bed, she looked alright now. I was happy. We were told that the man in the suit brought our two baby sisters into the house in his two suitcases. We never questioned that! We just accepted that, that was where they came from.

5

THE GRANVILLE HERO

THE DONAGHMORE CARNIVAL was a big occasion every year, a big marquee was erected in the meadow. "The meadow" being the parish G.A.A. field, all the big show bands of the sixties came to play there to huge crowds. It went on for a week, there was always something big done every year. One year a local character "Honest P.G." was buried alive for the weekend, it was two bob to visit his grave, he got big crowds. There was also a fair day.

One of the events during the fair day was the donkey derby. We got a lend of a donkey from a local farmer who lived near the village of Granville. Hence we called him "The Granville Hero" and entered him in the big race, the donkey derby. The Granville Hero was a big jack donkey, and as luck would have it there was a mare donkey there that was in heat, and the Granville Hero could just not be kept off her. Honest P.G. was Master of Ceremonies and commentator on the big race. When the donkeys were down at the starting line, Honest P.G. was making comments about our very randy Granville Hero. He said "If I had that jack donkey's piece of equipment and the jack donkey had my brains we would be one hell of a team!". The people laughed! Honest P.G. could say anything and get away with it, he was that kind. Nobody ever took offence to anything he ever said. He was so funny.

The race started and we were lucky in that the mare donkey in heat was a great runner. She belted out in the front of the field with The Granville Hero in hot pursuit still trying to mount her. Honest P.G. was laughing his brains out into the mike, "Anyone who backed The Granville Hero each way" he shouted "is onto a sure winner, because while he is a cert for second, he's never going to be first. We took our shoes off and ran in all the races in the sports field in our bare feet, winning a load of the races and prizes. Honest P.G. said that with The Granville Hero coming second, and all the races we won, that the barefooted McNultys from the Lough had had a great day out!

6

THE OLD FARMHOUSE

THE OLD HOUSE where we were reared was one of those long houses, not the cottage type. It had an old wooden door leading into a small box hallway and the right hand door leading directly into the kitchen/living room, which had a big black stove on the left hand side which was the engine of the whole house. From it came the cooking, hot water, heat and was the focal point for the cold winter nights, when we would all gather round it for the craic and the comfort. A big wooden table was set under the back window, out of which you could view the Lough, just one small field away. It was a beautiful view on a summer's day, and a wild and cold one on a winter's stormy day.

It was at this table by the window that my mother would stand and butter the bread, peel the spuds and dish out the food to her large family. She would often give out to us, sometimes angrily, advise us and generally keep us in some kind of order as we would fill up our always hungry bellies. We never rose from that table hungry, for while we had not many of the luxuries of life, we always had plenty to eat from that old black stove and that big wooden table with its covering of flowery oil cloth.

Down off that old kitchen was Mammy and Daddy's room where all of us children were born and spent the first few months of our lives in one of those pedigree prams with its high sides and hood. It was the room where my mother would take us into if we got a sickness or couldn't sleep, and somehow just to be in that bed with Mammy and Daddy was a magical cure for nearly all illnesses. Up the other side of the house were three bedrooms, with little cast iron fireplaces where all us children slept. My father later made a big room out of the barn for us six boys and it had two big double beds and two single beds. My sisters had the other bedrooms and oul Jemmy had the room at the back. Even though the house wasn't that big we did seem to have enough room. I slept in that big room with my brother Joe in a double bed, the eldest Sheamie, and Pat the second eldest, shared the other double bed. Malachy the third oldest and Marty, the youngest boy slept in the two single beds. When the rain and the wind howled up from the Lough and whistled around the gable end of the room, and the rain belted off the window pane, there was no more secure place on this earth to be than that room in that old farmhouse by the side of the Lough in the rural setting in East Tyrone. Each room had a holy picture of some kind or other, and our room had a framed copy of The Easter Proclamation that hung above the beds. Just where it originated from I don't know, but it was always there in my early memories.

My father was a great man for an argument and loved nothing better than a good debate, sometimes very heated with one of his sons, or one of the neighbours, or both! Sometimes it would end with the participants not being on speaking terms for hours or maybe even days. The subject could have been about anything as long as one of the views of it was different from the other. My mother would often have to interfere and sort the argument out, but no matter how much we fought verbally or physically - and sometimes it did end up physically amongst us boys - but never with my father. We would always soon become good friends again. My father used to say that if one of his sons ever hit him it would be the door for him for good, and none of us ever did. He was the boss, even when we were big, strong men and he was wrecked with arthritis. He still carried the respect of being the head of the house and retained that respect right to the end. If we did fall out among each other he'd say "There is a two acre field at the side of this house, get out and sort it out there". It often was sorted out there, with the rest of us cheering on our chosen hero, sometimes ending up with bloody noses and black eyes! That was acceptable as far as us boys were concerned, but when it came to my mother and sisters it was a totally different story. We were taught from a very young age to treat our mother and sisters with the utmost respect. My father treated his little girls like little princesses and it would have been unthinkable for us boys to be any different. We learned that men treated women with the height of respect and that it wasn't a man at all that would lift his hand to hit a girl or a woman. It was a lesson that never left any of us men throughout our lives. If a woman was giving you a hard time you upped and walked away, that was the only line of defence that was permitted. We boys doted on our little sisters. They were really great and grew to be the most loyal friends that we had, even through the most trying of times that were to lie ahead. They were the greatest allies, along with our mother and were a great source of strength and comfort when most needed. We were a large and happy family, even with the strong willed disagreements that would sometimes flare up. We were proud and fiercely loyal to each other and woe betide the outsider who would try to give any one of us a hard time or a raw deal. The loyalty we had for one another was right down to our roots and we would never falter in that loyalty, no matter what the consequences would be. You were either with us or against us.

7

THE THRASHER

WHEN THE THRASHER came to anyone's house in the locality it was a day out for all the neighbouring farmers and farm workers - everyone turned out. The farmer getting the corn thrashed would have his key men who would be asked to be there. Then, when the distinctive roar of that big machine was heard over the countryside it was like the bells of the church, calling people for midnight mass on Christmas Eve, everybody came and answered the call! They brought their own pitchforks with them. Like locusts they seemed to sprout up and out of the hedges like magic. Oul Mick, the bachelor farmer, who lived alone, he was a very squeamish man. He couldn't pull the neck off his own turkey at Christmas, he always came over to our house to get it done for him! He and Matt and Brian who were my father's cousins, took a good sup of drink in the pubs in Dungannon. They could often be seen driving the bikes from one side of the road to the other. Matt and Brian were good friends of my father and mother and they sometimes helped my father to put cattle on the land if he didn't have enough ready cash to do it himself. But my Father wouldn't ask anybody for help very often, as he was, like all countrymen, very proud and independent. Then Jack and Jimmy and George from the big farm down the road, would come striding into the field too. They lived with their sister Nellie, a very well respected and well liked family. When my Mother would send us down to Nellie for a can of buttermilk to make bread with, Nellie would always gather up a dozen eggs and put two or three big pieces of butter in along with the buttermilk. These people were always very good to my Mother and the big family up at the Lough. Then there was John and Tommy who lived in a very tidy cottage near our lane. Tommy had a bicycle shop in Dungannon. John kept the little cottage like something out of a picture postcard. Lena was a lovely woman, very quiet and friendly. These two neighbours came with their pitchforks too, to help.

Then Billy and Willy, two protestant farmers, would turn out to help as well. It was remarkable just how many unmarried men and women, some living on their own, that there was in that part of rural county Tyrone in them years. Yet these men and women all loved us children. Then there was 'The Cat', he lived with John and Tommy and Lena. He was some relation of theirs; 'The Cat' as he was known had been married. He was a builder's labourer, a good hard worker, he worked for my brothers Sheamie's building firm for some time. A very crabbit man, hence his nickname 'The Cat'! He took a lot of drink at the weekend and often came to our house worse for the wear on a Saturday night. My mother would scold him for taking so much drink, but my mother liked him and he loved coming to our house. "Plenty of room in our house" he'd say to my mother. He'd be referring to my mother's house! He was right there, my Mother wouldn't turn anyone away, especially a neighbour. He'd never mention his marriage or his estranged wife, no matter how drunk he was or how often he came drunk down the years, but sometimes he'd keep mumbling to himself drunkenly 'Robbie Burns, Robbie Burns, many a man rocked another man's child and thought he was rocking his own! He quoted the Scotch poet over and over again, we often wondered if this had something to do with his failed marriage! But he came to the thrasher too, all of these old neighbours would come.

My mother's brother Jim would come too, a real good natured man. Him and his best friend Patsy, took more fun out of life than any other two men I knew. Jim played the box, an old button keyed accordion and often came on his Céilí to our house. He loved my mother very much, she loved to see him coming down the lane on his bike. He'd always have sweets when he'd come on his Céilí, but he'd always hide them and tell us he'd forgot to get any. We'd watch his every move until one of us got very brave and start searching him. Then we'd all be onto him like locusts and keep searching him until we'd find the big bag of sweets. He was great craic and our favourite uncle. He'd be working at the thrasher too. Then my mother would come to get us children to help us carry boxes of sandwiches and pots of tea up to the thrasher, for everybody would be very hungry. Everyone would have a good feed, smoke cigarettes and tell jokes and generally chat about everything that was going on in the locality. The best part of the thrasher for us boys was when they were coming down near the bottom of the corn stacks. Me, Joe and Marty and some of the other neighbour's children would have big sticks and would be waiting on the big rats to coming running out of the corn stacks when it came to the bottom! Big fat ones! We'd run after them with the dogs and kill as many of them as we could, it was great craic!!

In the cool of the evening when the work was all done, everybody went back down the lane, and over the fields back to their homes. Great neighbours. No money was paid out on a day like this to our neighbours, nor was any expected, it was just good neighbourliness, and was done with a heart and a half. I loved the day the big, noisy thrasher came to our house and when we heard that old thrasher at some of our neighbours houses we'd be there too, as would all the same neighbours, it was a tradition of the old countryside. Everybody helped everybody else. It was great!!

8

THE THATCH WAS GONE AGAIN

WHEN THERE WAS a storm our house got it worse than anywhere else. Sitting on the edge of the Lough, the wind would gather speed as it drove waves 10ft high and the spray that it took with it from the waves, along with the rain, made our wee old farmhouse - especially with the thatched roof - very vulnerable indeed. My father would put extra strengtheners onto the thatched roof to hold it down tightly and to stop the wind getting under the thatch and lifting it up and blowing it away. Little tufts of the thatch would end up in the front field where it landed after been blown off, like little mounds of hay in a hayfield. My father didn't enjoy thatching, it was a job that had to be done when he couldn't avoid it, like when he couldn't listen to my mother anymore. So then us boys would be sent off to cut sally rods used to pin the thatch down. These would grow wild in the hedges. It was a smart thing when we were out hunting with the dogs to note where the best sally rods were growing, so that when an emergency thatching job arose we would know where to go to get them. It was our job to get sally rods for thatching. "Just get them" my father would say. "I have enough to do". We'd get a sharp knife with our mothers stern warning "Bring that knife back, it's the only sharp knife in the house". We cut the rods about three or four foot long and tied them in bunches of fifty, with twine and land them home triumphantly to my father. The next thing was the material for the thatch. Straw was used by a lot of thatchers, but the reeds or sagans, as we used to call them, grew alongside bogs and Loughs as well. That's what my father thatched with. He'd get out his old sythe, a tool with a huge 3ft blade, a long, crooked, oddly shaped shaft with two handles spaced out for gripping. Mowing with the sythe was an art, hard work, but there was huge skill in doing it well. A good man with a sythe was hugely thought of in the countryside.

My father wasn't good at it, he only did it when he had to. So he took his old sythe and round sharpening stone and he and me headed down the field to the Lough to cut the sagans to repair the old thatched roof. My father picked a good place where the reeds were just the right length and thickness, and started to swing the sythe blade around six inches from the bottom of them. The reeds would fall over like soldiers taken by surprise in a deadly ambush, shocked and surprised by the sudden attack on their tranquillity and peace. I'd stand behind my father and gather the reeds into sheaf's and tie them together with long dry grass. It was hard work but we would keep going steadily in silence. After a few hours my mother would bring the tea and sandwiches. They tasted great. I don't think any food tasted as great as the food brought out of farmhouses to its workers, that food has something special. My father and mother would have a wee private chat. They always seemed to be having those little meetings just out of earshot of us children. I used to wonder why. When my mother had gone with the teapot, cups and spoons - she'd need them before we got home - my father sat on a sheaf to have a smoke. He smoked woodbines; he loved them, big long drags deep into his lungs, he enjoyed a smoke more then anybody I knew. The satisfaction and contentment just oozed out of him, it was nearly visible. I loved the smell. My father was a very deep, thoughtful man, could get angry sometimes, but I was never afraid of him. I think he got frustrated at times that he did not have more ready money, that his job wasn't better paid. We, as a family, were never ever hungry. The spuds grown in the fields, the vegetables, the hens' eggs, the cows' milk and my mothers baking skills meant we never saw a hungry day, but money would often be scarce. Any arguments my mother and father would have, would be about the scarcity of ready money; I don't think they disagreed about much else. My father was aware of that and I think he'd have loved to have been a tradesman. Serve your time he would say, your trade will serve you well all your life. I always missed having one; I had to take what was going, I had little choice. So get a trade, it's very easily carried and will give you a good living. He smoked his wild woodbine sitting on the sheaf of sagans, that would be used to repair the roof of the home for his wife, six boys and six girls.

He called me over to sit beside him. The sagans were about the thickness of a pencil and at the bottom they were dry and brittle. My father picked up a brittle piece about six inches long. "Break that" he said. I looked at him questionably but took the piece of reed out of his hand, put it into my two hands and tried to break it. It snapped easily with not too much effort. He continued to break off small pencil sized pieces of dry reed and put them together. I watched him puzzled. Then he handed me a bunch of pencil sized reeds and I took them. My father said "Break them" and I applied pressure on the bunch of reeds; but they didn't break. He told me to do my best to break them. I was a big strong lad with big shoulders and big strong hands, but I couldn't break that bunch of dried reeds, I just couldn't break them. He looked at me in that way a father has of looking at his son when he's trying to impart a good lesson on life. "You broke the single one, no problem, but you couldn't break the bunch. Well let that be a lesson to you Tommy. There are twelve in that bunch and there are twelve of yous, stick together in this life and you will never be broken by anybody or anything. Remember that I won't always be around, stay together, through thick and thin and you will always be very strong." He put out his woodbine butt and picked up his sythe and silently went back to work. I never forgot that lesson and little did I know how much we would need to stick together in the years ahead. We were not just a family, we were a clan. Once you joined our clan by birth or by marriage you were automatically one of us. My father would be proud. Rest easy my old man.

9

THE FARM

THE OLD FARM was small, even by the standards of a small farming county like that part of Tyrone. About fifteen acres of land that was, by and large, good arable black soil. It was divided into eight different shapes and sizes of fields by thick, high blackthorn hedges, hedges that just seemed to spring up naturally from the ground and did not seem to have any overall plan of division, as the fields were all different shapes and sizes. We had a pet name for each of the fields and it almost seemed as if each field had an entity all of its own. I can still remember the names of the fields to this day. Upper and lower Jane's were on the left, immediately after turning in. The lane or lonan as we called it at the time - lonan must have some Irish connection to it I think. Then, after the lane took its ninety degree bend to the right to face down to the old farmhouse, the Sheough field continued onto the left hand side. Then straight in front, down by the gable end of the house was the Lough field, where all the people drove in their cars on the summer days to sunbathe, picnic and have a swim in the Lough. By tradition, this field was never ploughed for crops; it was always the people's field, it was theirs as much as it was ours. Then there was the Back field behind the house and the Far field, both named for obvious reasons. The Meadow was the largest of them all with about three acres. The field on the right of the lane where the eldest son built a bungalow many years later is the only one which I can't recall the name of.

I can remember something different about each of these little pieces of earth; like where the hens and the turkeys were liable to have their nests, where the rabbits had their burrows, where the first spring primrose was likely to be, where it was easiest to get sticks to bring to light the fire for my mother, where the cows and calves were most likely to get out of the field they were supposed to be in, and where the half field of spuds and corn with the dozen or so drills of assorted vegetables were most likely to be planted. The fields with the thickest hedges were the best place to provide shelter for the cows and their calves from the cold north winds during the winter months. These hedges were never cut, maybe just tidied up but never cut down low. This would have been a mortal sin in the eyes of the small Tyrone farmers of those years. Good shelter for cattle was worth half fodder in winter.

My father always tried to have one of his cows calving during the month of October so that there was a good supply of milk through the winter months. My mother would regularly churn some of the milk with one of the old churns that had to be turned round and round for hours on end to make butter. We all took turns at this important job. The milk would be kept in earthenware crocks until thick enough to churn. So with the spuds in the pits in the field, the vegetables in their drills, the cow milking, the turf, coal and sticks in the shed at the side of the house, we never feared the winter months. The hay that had been made the old way was with pitch forks and wooden rakes and put into haystacks during the summer months. This would then be brought into the hayshed in the autumn, ready to be taken out in armfuls and fed to the cows and calves during the winter months. I used to love the comfort of the old byres in the cold snowy weather with the cows and calves munching on their hay contently. The warmth and peacefulness was soothing to the soul and the cares of the world seemed very far away. Many a time my brothers and sisters would play hide and seek in those old barns and sheds and there always seemed to be a new hiding place no matter how many times we played!

My mother always had a dozen or more turkeys for Christmas, hatched out by a couple of hen turkeys that she always kept out from the flock when the fowlman came to buy them a couple of weeks before Christmas. Little did we children know, that when we were sent out to put those turkeys into their shed at night in case anything happened to them, that we were insuring that Santa would come that Christmas, for that was how my mother would buy the toys that Santa brought us. The turkeys were always that extra few pounds at the end of the year. Some of the money would go on a few games like Snakes and Ladders, Ludo, Bagatelle and some books and sweets.

The rest would go to pay off the boot and shoe bill in the little shoe shop in nearby Dungannon. When any of us children needed a pair of boots or shoes during the year my mother would give us a piece of paper with a message on it for the wee small woman that owned the shoe shop. We would go into the shoe shop, three or four of us on the way home from school and the 'important one' of us that had the note would hand it to the old woman. She would read it and promptly put the important one of us up on a little old Victorian chair and proceed to fit him or her out with a pair of boots or shoes; there was always a lovely smell of leather. No money would be mentioned at this time; she would just ask us "how is your mammy" and then send us out on our way home. The one who got the new footwear would be the centre of attraction on the two and a half mile walk home. A road that would take us up the main road, and then out up the little narrow country lanes that we always called 'the short cut' and then home. We knew all the short cuts through the fields and glens around our location from an early age hunting with the dogs and going out with our father with his dogs and guns. We got to know every hedge and field around at very early ages. This would prove to be very important at a later stage in our lives.

10

SCHOOL DAYS

MY ABIDING MEMORY of school days was that we'd always have to walk to it. Down the little country lanes, onto the main road, on through the town and out on the far side was the Convent Sisters of Mercy school and the Christian Brother's school. The Convent came first, about a quarter of a mile before the Brother's. When one of us would start school, usually about five years old, two of the older ones would take a hand each of the little one who had just started, and look after him or her, especially for the first few weeks until he or she got used to the long enough walk. That was how we all started school, in the middle of the two older ones and away we'd go, on our often merry or rainy way, but we never minded. That was the way of it and we never questioned it. Little did we know that my mother had fought a continuous battle with the school authorities to get a bus, but it was to be years later that she would manage to achieve her objective, after many a bitter battle with the unhelpful and unfriendly N.I. education authorities.

We were second class citizens from a very young age. When my mother would write demanding that one of the state school buses that came down the road from Omagh, twenty five miles away, heading for the Royal school and Protestant Technical College Schools in Dungannon. The school bus then turned off our road, the main road, a half mile before they reached our home, and went on through a few little predominantly protestant villages before winding their way into the town, only half full of children. She would get the reply that there was a primary school within two miles of the statutory walking distance at Castlecaulfield, and to send her children to it, knowing well that it was a Protestant school and that we wouldn't be sent to it. So we walked three and a half miles to school, summer and winter with two state school buses turning off our road half a mile before it came to our home only half full of protestant children.

But then, didn't Lord Brookbourough of Fermanagh, who was Prime Minister of the North at the time, tell a Twelfth of July Orange Parade, that Northern Ireland was a Protestant State for Protestant people. So that was the way it was; they were bussed into the school of their choice while we walked. We never held ordinary protestant people responsible for this. It was the unfair system of local government.

Years later, when some of my older brother and sister were sent to St. Patrick's Academy Secondary School, my mother renewed her efforts, and pointed out that there was now no alternative secondary school within the two mile walking distance. The authorities reluctantly diverted one of the half-full school buses down our road to pick up the older children who were going to the secondary school, but insisted, that the younger ones, that were still going to primary school, were not allowed to get on the bus. So we watched our older brothers and sisters getting on a half full school bus for their ride into school, while we were forced to continue to walk. This was a bitter bone of contention in our family and the other families in the predominantly Nationalist area in which we lived. I never got a bus ride to school because I left school at fifteen years of age. That was when I got my first taste of the unfair nature of the six county state. But by and large our school days were happy enough, even though some of those Christian brothers were stern; and in one or two cases were downright brutal, but we took our slaps without complaining and got a good enough education. We were a bright enough bunch of children and took to education easily enough. We played sports like Gaelic football and hurling and I played on the school team and loved it. I kept my love of Gaelic sports all through my life and always got great enjoyment out of it.

I can still remember vividly the Christian Brother who taught us history lessons. When he would tell of the wrongs that the British did on our country, his face would go bright red and the veins on his neck would stick out like little pipes, and he'd hit the table so hard that he'd nearly scare you. He really hated the British for all the injustices that they did on our country. We'd sing 'faith of our fathers living still' with great fervour at the end of every history lesson and after roll call and morning prayers, he'd always remind us with great pride that we were the land of Saints and Scholars, and that we were a civilized and cultured people, while the British were still savages! He'd always tell us that we had no need for the interference from the British in our country and that the same interference brought upon us nothing but sorrow. We were taught that the Irishmen that opposed this interference with force of arms and died trying to break the connection with England were heroes, and were to be revered and respected for their gallant efforts. The Fenians, the United Irishmen, Father Murphy, Kelly the boy from Killane, the 1798 men, the 1916 men, were all the heroes of our proud land. I remember my heart fill with pride when he'd tell us how red Hugh O' Neill from Dungannon and the chiefs of Ulster were the ones that the English Queen could not buy nor beat. I recall the sadness I'd feel when he'd relate the story of some great defeat inflicted upon the Irish forces, the Flight of the Earls and the Plantation of proud Ulster. The joy when he'd relate to us of the great victory at the Battle of Benburb. One good fighting Irishman was worth ten British soldiers any day, because right was on our side and we could not be beaten. He'd preach about the Mass Rocks in the Glens, when the brave Priests would say Mass for the people; at the danger to his own freedom and his life. Faith of our Fathers living still, in spite of dungeon fire and sword. He told us that young Catholic Irishmen would stand up and be killed, rather than deny their faith to the British redcoats. That one day we would right all the wrongs inflicted on our proud nation; the final wrong being the division of our country that left the six counties cut off from the rest of our fellow countrymen. A Border that we didn't ask for, nor want, a Border that created a Protestant Parliament for Protestant people, an artificial state that we felt no allegiance to, never felt part of and never would. The injustices and suffering inflicted on our country was brought home to us in these lessons and I for one, never forgot.

11

TEN YEARS OLD TO EARLY TEENAGE YEARS

MY MEMORIES OF all these years are very normal. We just continued to grow up as a Catholic family in what could have been in many ways, any county in Ireland. We'd walk to school, walk home, get a big steamy hot dinner, then I would go outside and do the chores, like bring in the couple of cows to milk, feed the calves and in general the little bits and pieces of jobs that would need to be done on any small farm in the area. I had a great interest in farming and loved it. I worked for another big farmer round the road at every opportunity I got, evening, school holidays; Saturdays were spent working for the local big farmers of the district. I and my neighbour and best friend Ned McDonald had a reputation as hard workers who could be depended on to do the work without any fuss. The summers all seemed to be glorious, hot and sunny and very enjoyable.

The big family at the Lough got on with growing up and one by one we grew into young adults. Those growing years were very peaceful and quiet except for a border campaign by the I.R.A. in the late fifties when they blew up an army training camp hall in the town of Dungannon. It was a call for great glee among the Nationalist people at that time because it was heavily guarded by the Territorial Army and they thought that it was impenetrable. Somehow, it gave people a sense of pride and admiration for the 'boys' who could get in, blow it up and get away with it safely. There was a song written "Into our town one Friday night came men from God knows where, up the castle hill they went via the market square. Suddenly, a loud blast was heard, it shook our ancient town, the sirens blew, the B men flew but the T.A. camp was down". This hill is now a historical public amenity.

Our school, the Christian Brothers was situated near the Royal School, the local state Protestant school. I remember they wore a red uniform with a red beret. We would occasionally take their berets off and throw them to each other. We were quickly reprimanded by our own teachers and we stopped the practice. So the two schools existed within a few hundred yards of each other, but were really worlds apart. Somehow their school, was, in ways, on a different part of the planet! Really far away and kind of strange forbidden territory, almost alien!

One protestant boy who went to the Royal School lived on the short cut on our way home, down the stony lane and up the little boreens. This boy lived in a cottage beside the old stone quarry. He went to school on a bike and would get home before us and be waiting for us to pass by and throw stones at us as we walked down the lane. He seemed to think that it was his right to do this. Many a times he nearly seriously injured one of us. My father strictly forbid us to throw stones at anybody and that included this boy, who had us dodging his missiles and running the gauntlet up the stony lane to get home safely. I will never forget the day when our friends, the McDonalds, who normally went home a different road than us, they took the left fork of the road about a half a mile on this side of the town, we took the right, decided to come out our way and see if the stone thrower was at his dirty work. There was no such constraints of not throwing stones with them, and I was fervently praying to myself that our tormentor was in his usual ambush position. We walked down the lane with our two friends, and just as we came to the old quarry a big stone hit the ground right in front of us. Ned and Barney, our two friends, started to gather pockets full of stones and slipped up the side of the hedge into the field beside the quarry. We dodged the stones as usual, as our tormentor stood on his usual vantage point and fired away, knowing full well that we would not throw any back, even though the stony lane was full of good sized stones just right for throwing. Then suddenly, our two friends burst out of the hedge and started to throw stones very accurately at our attacker. Ned and Barney were two very good stone throwers, as they had often proved at the Lough behind our house when we would have contests to see who would throw stones the farthest out into it. The boy let out a frightened yell as Ned caught him with a good sized stone on the thigh. He started to roar and cry and belted across the open field in front of us towards his cottage roaring and shouting for his mammy! Ned and Barney were in hot pursuit yelling and shouting "get the cowardly bully". Suddenly, all the built up frustration came out of me and my two brothers Marty and Joe. We picked up a handful of stones each, abandoned our schoolbags, leapt the old iron gate into the field and gave Ned and Barney a hand to stone him all the way across the field as he made for his home as hard as he could run, still screaming at the top of his voice for help from his mammy. Me, Joe and Marty, Ned and Barney pursued him within sight of his house, still pelting the last of our ammo at him. Did that not feel good! At last we were getting to fight back at this boy who always seemed to get the better of us. He ran into his house and we turned and ran back onto the stony lane whooping for the joy of it all. I vowed after that that no-one would attack me or any of my brothers or sisters without expecting the same treatment back and more if I could give it. This boy never chanced to throw stones at us again after that, though we fought again when we were about fourteen years old with our fists and I beat him. It felt really good to teach him a lesson.

School continued on and I continued to play Gaelic football for the teacher who would later go on to become the Tyrone senior county football full back and still later its trainer. This man's burning ambition for his lifetime was to take the Tyrone Gaelic football county team to Croke Park and win the Sam Maguire Cup! In 1986 he almost achieved it! I got on well with this teacher and loved to play football for him, I was right good at it too. I played right half back and while I wasn't classed as a dirty player I had a reputation as being very tough and resilient. If an opposing forward got past me and scored, he was sure to have earned it. I went on the play for my parish team Donaghmore and won a minor club championship medal in 1967. There was one man in the parish that was responsible for any success that the team had, Vinnie the tailor. All of the Gaels of this part of Tyrone owe him a great debt of gratitude. He owned a men's tailor shop in Dungannon and only for his many hours of dedication and his Hillman hunter car, I for one would never have been able to get to training or games and would never have won anything or got the great love and enjoyment out of Gaelic games that I got for the rest of my life. This man was one of the greatest Gaels of Tyrone. Men like him were so important in keeping the Irish culture alive and well in the six counties right down along the years, when Nationalists had often very little else to cling to for their Irish identity, Gaelic football, Irish music etc., survived and flourished largely because of the dedication of men like this tailor from Dungannon.

Croke Park on a big match day is very special. It reflects all that is good about being Irish. I love every time I am in it to support County Tyrone, I feel so proud to be part of it all.

12

LATER TEENAGE YEARS

WHEN I LEFT school I worked for a local farmer for a short time, but my father persuaded me that there was no future in this work, so I went to serve my time as a bricklayer at a building site in Dungannon. I enjoyed the hard work and the good natured craic with the men on the building site. There were always some great characters on building sites then. All my brothers served their time in the building trade, brickies, carpenters and electricians. My father always said he missed having a trade in his life, "go and serve your time to a trade, it will serve you well". He was right. Work was going well and soon I was earning good enough money and was proud to be one of the men in the house who brought home the money for my mother. I was very proud to give my mother the money for the 'house' every Friday night; every one of us felt good about that. My eldest brother Shemie came home from England around that time, he was a brickie too. He brought my father home a little green minivan as a present. He loved that van and drove it for many years.

We set up a grip squad (take work on for a price, do it quickly as possible and for big money). There were six of us in this grip squad, myself and Shemie my brother, Ned from a neighbour's family and three from the nearby town of Coalisland. We stayed together for a few years travelling around to different counties for the best work. We also built bungalows and farm buildings in our spare time. We were making big money and doing well. We had a reputation for hard work and no messing. Work hard and get well paid was our motto, no-one messed about with the 'heavy gang' as we called ourselves. If anyone wanted a job done in a hurry, then call the heavy gang. We'd do it, but have our money for us as soon as we were finished. We enjoyed our hard work and our tough reputation. We went as far as West Cork for work, Whiddy Island, off Bantry Bay, we really enjoyed that job.

We carried our tough reputation to the local dancehalls, where we were involved in fist fights with nearby parish lads who wanted to teach us a lesson. Many of the fights were extensions of Gaelic football matches where some opposing club members felt they had gotten a raw deal on the football field and decided to settle the account at the local dancehall! We were always able to give a good account of ourselves. The fights were mostly fair fights, man to man, and nobody liked to see any man getting hit while he was down. There was sort of an oul pride giving a good account of yourself, but an unwritten law that when a man was down and beaten he was left like that. Bottles, glasses, chairs or knifes were unheard of. There was a lot of pride and honour in our fights, the biggest war wound would be a couple of black eyes or a broken nose. It was good to have a war wound; it proved that you had been in the heat of the battle!

It was all part of growing up in our corner of Ireland at the time. Hard work, tough football, Irish music, pop music, the Céilí bands, the Beatles, the old Ford vans, the mini cars, mini skirts, lovely girls, sunny summers by the Lough, swimming, hunting, fishing, courting; life taking shape for the future, which was good for us at that time. It was normal sixties living, there was fun in life. My eldest brother got married, the celebrations lasted a week. Mother and Father's twenty fifth wedding anniversary was held over a weekend in the house. The local newspaper was there, Mother and Father's photo was in the paper, the big family of Annie and Johnny were growing up, life was getting easier, money more plentiful, life seemed full of promise, and a good future in the building trade was there for the taking. The eldest of the six boys and the six girls of the Lough family were all working, the youngest were growing up well. The daddy was on early retirement with a lame leg, the mother looking much younger than she was. The toughest times were over, the old house had been renovated and extended, Shemie had a new bungalow built down the lane, a bright future seemed to beacon for this big decent hardworking Catholic Irish family, reared on a fifteen acre farm in County Tyrone. How wrong we all were. The toughest times were yet to come!

13

CROPPY LIE DOWN

AS THE TWELFTH of July approached the Protestant population changed, even the best of them changed a bit. The worst of them changed a lot! Growing up as a Catholic Nationalist Irish person in the wee Protestant north, with its Protestant Parliament for Protestant people wasn't easy. Some of the year you could live with it easier than other parts of the year, but not July. Oh no, this was the month Catholic Irish northerners were reminded who was boss. The Stormont Government was there, the Orange Order was there, the R.U.C. police force was there; but especially the Orange Order and the B. men. The B. men were the reserve police, an armed paramilitary Protestant force, made up of largely untrained members who kept their .303 rifles and sten sub machine guns at their homes and could set up local checkpoints at bridges and crossroads at will.

They were bullying and very intimidating at those checkpoints. They would ask their closest Catholic neighbours, people they would see everyday, their names and addresses at these checkpoints, in the dark of the night, as if they were strangers. The Catholic people were terrified of the B. men. This sectarian government force could shoot and kill Catholics and there would not even be an inquest. No investigation into the circumstances of their deaths whatsoever, if the B. men did it, then it was right. The Catholic people feared them, with very good reason. Another symbol of protestant domination was the lamb beg drum. This was a huge big drum strapped to the back of the drummer, so big it must have been hard to carry. The drummer would just beat it as hard as he could with no let-up! Just across the Lough was an Orange hall and beside it was an old mostly unused shooting range. This Orange hall and the shooting range would be opened up in the evening at the beginning of July. The Orange men would play the lamb beg drum very loudly and very consistently. It's sound came across the hill and up the Lough like something out of a jungle! It was tribal, very tribal. Its intimidating sound was a clear message to Catholics, we're here, it's July and we are your masters. Then the B. men would go out onto the old shooting range and 'practice' shooting their .303 Lee Enfield rifles. The sharp spat of the B. men's rifles mixed in with the sound of the lamb beg drums coming clearly over the hills and the Lough, in the still of a July summer's evening, held, just one message for us, it was 'Croppy lie down'; 'Croppy' being an insulting derogatory name for an Irish Catholic.

14

RUMBLINGS OF DISCONTENT
THE CIVIL RIGHTS ASSOCIATION

GUSTY SPENCE, a U.V.F.* man, shot a young Catholic man dead outside a bar in Belfast. It somehow seemed a far off event, somehow alien to us in the countryside, yet at the same time it touched us all inside, troubled us. It seemed so unjust and unfair that a good young man should be shot down just for being who he was and nothing else. Who and what were these men, who would do such a brutal act for no apparent reason? I remember the trial and sentencing of a man to life in prison. That seemed to draw the incident to a close and it went out of the mind. In the meantime, a lot of Catholic people were more aware of the discrimination that was being practiced against them, especially in the line of jobs and houses. The fact that a large portion of the population had no voting rights was a huge bone of contention. There were almost no Catholics in the civil service. When a Nationalist went to the interviews for these jobs they were asked, "Which school did you go to?" When it was stated 'the Christian Brothers' or 'the Convent', one's chance of a job was non existent. Lord Brookbouragh from Fermanagh, who was Prime Minister of Northern Ireland at the time, made his infamous speech at the twelfth of July Orange Parade when he stated "I have a lot of people employed at my estate, but I have no Catholics, as a matter of fact, I would not have one around the place, I do not trust them". This was from the Prime Minister of the six counties, and that statement hurt, and hurt deeply. A lot of the younger Catholic population, now better educated, were not prepared to accept this blatant second class citizenship and vowed to do something about it.

The same system of discrimination was practiced at local Government level. In our town Dungannon for instance, Catholics were 70% of the population yet there was a majority of Unionist Protestant councillors on the town council. They did this with a system of 'gerrymandering'.

---

*a protestant paramilitary group

Dungannon was divided into three wards or constituencies, each having the same number of councillors, say three. It did not matter how many of the town's population was in a particular ward, that ward could only elect three members. So the wards were drawn up in such a way that almost all the Catholic population were just in one ward, so that they could only elect three councillors. The Unionist Protestant 30% of the population elected six councillors for two wards, and so ruled the local council chambers and all decisions were made by them. The council had the power to award jobs, allocate houses etc. and generally keep everything for themselves which they did, with no regard whatsoever for the feelings or rights of the local Catholic people. Derry, Strabane and several other councils were 'gerrymandered' in a similar way and this caused a deep deep resentment in the Catholic Nationalist people, so much so that Dungannon Nationalists once elected the town idiot to the council as a form of protest!

Housing was a huge bone of contention. The council had the absolute right to decide where to build local authority houses, how many to build, and most controversial of all who to allocate them to! There was no points system; the council had the absolute right to give houses to whoever they liked at the stroke of a pen. Many Catholics were left to live in terrible conditions, while Protestants were housed at will. Big catholic families were left to live in rat infested one bed roomed houses. It was a terrible injustice and when a nineteen year old protestant girl who was not getting married till later on that year and had no children, was allocated a new three bed roomed council house in the village of Caledon, Co. Tyrone there was great unrest; as Catholic families, at this time, lived in terrible overcrowded conditions, and in some cases not unlike the slums of Calcutta or the South African black people. This terrible insult was the last straw and was the incident that in a lot of ways led to the Civil Rights Association being formed. Through this association, Catholics were demanding an end to gerrymandering, an end to second class citizenship, an end to discrimination on the basis of a religious head count, and a demand for 'one man, one vote'. Some big Protestant businessman had the right to vote several times in elections. In other words, Catholic people were demanding fair play within this Protestant state for a Protestant people. They were demands that would prove very hard to get. The house in Caledon was occupied by Catholic civil rights activists who barricaded themselves in the house and refused to leave. After several days the R.U.C and the council bailiffs went in and forcibly removed them; and dumped them and their belongings out on the lawn. The daughter of one of those women dumped out that day, would years later become the Sinn Féin M.P for Fermanagh South Tyrone, and a Minister in the Northern Assembly.

15

1968 THE CIVIL RIGHTS MOVEMENT

I WALKED THE first Civil Rights march from Coalisland to Dungannon in 1968. 'Walked' rather than 'marched' because a casual kind of walk by a scattered group of people was all that it was. It looked far removed from anything 'historical' or important as we walked in bunches of three, fours, or fives; just talking about everything and anything as we dandered jauntily along, good humoured and very unaware that we were doing anything significant or that the day would be marked in controversy. The distance was about three miles between the two towns, up a big hill as you left Coalisland, and up another big hill as you entered the old town of Dungannon. The march was destined for a rally and speeches in the town square but as it turned out we never got that far. The march was stopped by a line of R.U.C. police at what was known as Hospital Corner, just beside the South Tyrone hospital. The walkers with their placards calling for one man, one vote, no discrimination, an end to gerrymandering, and fair play in housing and jobs, walked right up to the police lines and demanded that the chief police officer allow them to walk the road into their own town and hold their lawful meeting in the town square. They were told by the police that they weren't allowed into town because it would cause trouble between the marchers and a group of Loyalists that had gathered illegally in the town centre.

So we were second class citizens again. The same old sinking feeling of being made little of in your own town. The marchers at the back of the crowd were by now pushing forward and causing pressure on the police lines. Suddenly, violence erupted and for the first time in my life I saw naked hatred in the eyes of another human being. The hatred was in the eyes of the R.U.C. and it was directed towards us. Big blackthorn sticks and batons came down on unsuspecting marchers heads with a suddenness and ferocity which was frightening in its intensity. It was pure hatred of

State Police against an unwanted section of its population. It was naked sectarian state hatred and I was angry, really angry for the first time in my life. We held our meeting at Hospital Corner. The speakers said that we would fight on, non violently, for our rights. Civil rights, rights to live as first class citizens in our own country. We would keep on the civil rights road until we got our rights and would not falter. I felt better after hearing that and we vowed to get involved in forms of civil disobedience and practical peaceful protests. A young woman, Bernadette Devlin, who marched with us that day, would later become an M.P for Mid Ulster. She famously walked across the floor of the House of Commmons, after Bloody Sunday and slapped the Secretary of State for Northern Ireland across the face and called him a 'damned liar'; as he had tried to say that the victims of Bloody Sunday were armed.

We sang what was to become the Civil Rights Movement anthem 'Deep in my heart I do believe we shall overcome some day'. It would be sung a lot of times in the future. We all went our separate ways home, after deciding to hold a meeting in St. Patrick's hall right away to plan our strategy. It was the beginning of what was to be a long hard fight, but at least we had made a start. Maybe if we could have seen all that was to happen in the future, we would have gone home and never came out again. Under our civil rights banner, we would march again and again and again, because we were people with a just cause, we were people who had taken enough. We were young, strong, and with right on our side, it was time to stand up and be counted, time to stand our ground. We were determined to get our rights; we would never lie down and accept all the injustices ever again. The resistance movement was born; things would never be the same again. Our generation would not accept the injustices that my mother and fathers generation had to live under. We would demand change and we would get change. My uncle told me years later, his father had told him that some generation of the Catholic Nationalist population of the North was going to have to stand up and fight for their rights. It fell to our generation to do it.

16

1969 – 1970

THE MEETINGS THAT followed that first march were intense. Strategies for future marches were discussed in detail. Heated debate and disagreements were the order of the day, but we were all in agreement that peaceful opposition were the way forward. Civil disobedience was high on the agenda. Don't pay rent on houses that were not fit to live in, don't pay rates, and withhold the payments that would be normally paid to a State that gave fair play to all its citizens. In other words we would withdraw the permission normally given to the Government by its people to be governed. We would refuse to participate in the unjust State.

Civil rights groups were set up in every town and city across the North. The peaceful withdrawal of authority from the State appealed to people right across the six counties and the Civil Rights Movement grew from strength to strength. But State oppression increased as well Marches were stopped by State Police, marchers were arrested in increasing numbers, brought before unjust courts, fined and sometimes jailed for up to six months under the Special Powers Act. This Act had very wide ranging powers to keep down the Nationalist population and it was being used more and more. The State Police were getting increasingly violent towards peaceful marches, aided by an ever growing number of Protestants extremists, who saw the Civil Rights Movement as a threat to their superiority. They saw the Civil Rights campaign as a threat to the Protestant State for Protestant people and wanted none of it. It never seemed to enter these people's heads that if they gave fair play to the Nationalist people, that if the State would grant Civil Rights for all, that if all the injustices were removed; that the State could be allowed to function normally. That the consent of the Nationalist people to be governed, may have been forthcoming, had they been made to feel part of the state in which they lived. But this did not happen and civil rights demands for fair play were met with more and more State violence and repression.

They viewed the Civil Rights Movement as a conspiracy to undermine the State of Northern Ireland. That was a huge mistake on their behalf, because the Civil Rights Movement was genuinely only interested in state reform, a fair system of government within Northern Ireland for all it's people. That was the true position of the Civil Rights Movement and it had no hidden agenda. But state violence and repression increased alarmingly, and Civil Rights marches were turning more and more confrontational; and were now ending up in violent clashes with the R.U.C. State Police and Protestant extremists. These would form up behind police lines; throw insults and stones at civil rights marchers, and always get a blind eye from the police, or even the open encouragement from them. Civil rights marchers were brutalised, arrested and jailed in ever increasing numbers. The whole situation was going from bad to worse very quickly indeed. It would soon reach a point of no return, where Nationalist people and the State with its sectarian police force and its unjust laws; with its never ending repression and violence towards its minority population, would end up in complete confrontation between the State and that section of its people.

17

1969 – 1970 THE RIOTS
FULL SCALE CIVIL UNREST

THE PEOPLE OF the Bogside and Creggan in Derry were in full scale war with the police. The Protestant apprentice boys had marched through the Nationalist part of the city, with the aid of the state police and Loyalist thugs. This led to the deaths of two Nationalist men, one in Dungiven, Co. Derry, and another in a Nationalist part of Derry city, both beaten to death by the state police after a civil right march, one of them in his own home, Fear was everywhere. People were afraid if they left their areas open to attack, they also would be beaten to death in their own homes. Derry people erected barricades at the entrances to their housing estates to stop the Loyalist thugs and the police from getting into their areas. Old cars, hi-jacked lorries and everything that came to hand was used to make the barricades effective. The scenes of the rioting were on the T.V., Nationalist people all over the North were concerned about the safety of the people of Derry. In solidarity with Derry, barricades went up in Belfast also and reports of rioting came in from other parts of the North; in Dungannon serious rioting broke out after a march in protest at the way people in Derry and Belfast were been treated.

The barricades went up in Dungannon as well. We broke into a farm machinery depot and used the tractors, trailers and farm implements to block the road leading into our part of the town and to keep the riot police and the Protestant mobs out. They tried to break the barricades several times that night but we managed to keep them out by throwing stones at them. The next day it was all over the news that the situation in Derry and Belfast was rapidly getting worse. The Loyalist mobs were gathering in ever greater numbers; police were getting even more vicious and there was rumour that the B. Specials were being called out. The B. Specials were the armed paramilitary force that the Stormont Government held in reserve. The Catholic people held this paramilitary force in great fear. The B. men, as they were known, had a terrible reputation for brutality since the foundation of the Northern State. Many stories were told down the years of the terrible actions of the B. men against the Catholic population. The very mention of the B. men was enough to send a shiver of fear down the spine of any Catholic man or woman. People felt that if they were called out it would be a terrible disaster for the whole situation in the North. Fear and tension was everywhere, one could just feel the effects of it in the air.

That night in Dungannon full scale rioting broke out. Townspeople made and threw petrol bombs for the first time at the State Police and Loyalist mobs. We took over a petrol station, and a yard that a local pub used to store its empty bottles. The women tore up sheets to make fuses for the petrol bombs, and we wheeled wheelbarrows full of stones and broken bricks up behind the barricades. We stored up petrol bombs and all the missiles we could get. We knew the big battle for the Nationalist streets of Dungannon, Derry, Belfast and other parts of the North was under way. The men behind the barricades in Derry were still under siege, but they held out. News was coming in that Belfast was under pressure. Loyalist mobs were on the streets in large numbers aided and abetted as usual by the State Police. It was rumoured now that the B. men were to be called out. It was a matter of when, not if. Civil unrest and full scale rioting had gone on now for three days and nights. People stocked up more stones and more petrol bombs behind the barricades and hoped for the best. Jack Lynch the Southern Prime Minister came on Irish T.V. and said he would not stand idly by while the Nationalist people of the North were being systematically attacked. We felt great hope in that statement. We were not alone after all! Help would soon come from the South! That felt good, really good.

That night in Dungannon I saw the first real war scenes in reality. The rioting was intense. The riot police would form up about fifty yards on their side of the barricades and begin to bang their steel shields with their batons. That sound was like nothing I had ever heard before. The riot police would batter the steel shields with their batons in an ever increasing crescendo, dim figures of hate in the night light; and then with blood curdling yells, run in a square formation at the barricades, intent on overrunning us. My stomach would tighten as they would come, ever closer all the time beating their shields and shouting hate at the top of their voices. We would let them come within stone throwing range and then let a barrage of bricks and stones down on them when they were about twenty five yards away. The stones and bricks would bounce off their steel helmets and shields, but every now and again we would hear the agonised yell of one of them as a stone or brick found its mark. When they would get to within ten to fifteen yards of the barricades we would light and lob the petrol bombs. The riot police really feared the petrol bombs. Stones and bricks they could take to a certain extent, but when the petrol bombs smashed on top of their helmets and set them alight, it was a different story! That was when they would retreat screaming and cursing and trying to put out the flames. It was the only effective weapon we had. Had it not had been for the petrol bombs we would have been routed out from behind the barricades in a very short period of time. As it was with the petrol station on our side of the barricades and a plentiful supply of bottles and fuses, we could defend our side of the town for days and nights on end. We were a match for the State Police and Loyalist mobs as long as we could man and defend the barricades. We were a community completely under siege fighting for the survival of our houses and our streets. It was an Irish town, our town, and it was time for courage and steadfastness in the face of state and state backed terror.

Derry was still holding out on the fourth day and night of continuous full scale rioting. Belfast was in flames, it was rumoured that whole streets were on fire but no-one knew for sure what was happening to other towns across the North. In Dungannon we were holding out, as we approached our fifth night behind the barricades. It was tough but we were surviving. That night I will never forget. The riot police were lining up in formation as was almost a ritual to bang their shields and roar their hate. One big attack by them got some of them up onto the barricades, but we had enough bombs, and one of the bombs set part of the barricade on fire just as the riot police were about to get over it. They retreated screaming and cursing, but it had been a close shave for us. We heaved a sigh of relief, made good the barricade and waited for the next attack. The next attack came alright, but it was much different than any that had come before. The riot police lined up cursing and screaming, making that terrible noise and made a run at us again, they were intent on getting at us tonight. We primed our bombs and got ready our missiles and got tensed up to repel yet another attempt to overrun us. Our men had shown great courage over the days and nights, as had our women who backed us up to the last, fed us and bandaged our wounds; for the Protestant mobs and police had taken to throwing some of our missiles back at us. We were not as protected with amour as they were, so we suffered a lot of wounds to our heads and faces, but we held out and still had plenty of petrol bombs and missiles. We were not afraid to fight.

They came at us again, ramming up the streets fifty yards, forty yards, thirty yards. Suddenly they stopped, and parted in the middle. Through the parting in the middle, I saw several shadowy figures carrying long objects in their hands, dark shadowy figures armed with rifles. Jesus – the B men! We all went deadly silent, stunned and frozen. The men in black got down on one knee. Suddenly the night was filled with gunfire. I thought the bastards were over our heads, and not at us; I was wrong. Some of our men took cover. Some got the women off the streets. One of our men threw a petrol bomb – a moment later his face was shot off. The .303 bullet caught him under his chin and took the whole side of his face off. Another lay groaning in pain beside me, the blood running out of his upper leg. Everything was happening in a haze. It was pure terror and disarray. Everyone had scattered; those who were able to. The man lying beside me was wounded too. Several of our men cornered two of the State Paramilitary thugs and, with great courage, moved in on them and knocked them out and took their guns off them! These State paramilitary thugs who had terrorised the Nationalist people of the North for more than fifty years, were nothing but craven cowards when confronted with our brave young men who were not afraid to fight!! It was said that the Nationalist people lost their fear of these State bullies after that incident. They realised that their own young men and women were well able to fight them, and win!!

Suddenly a rifle butt crashed down on the back of my head and I remember no more, until I woke in a cell in the local police station, black and blue and sore all over. The blood had run down my hair and face, and had matted. The cell was full of our men. All wounded and bloody. My younger brother was there when I looked around, and I told him to keep his mouth shut as they would let him out. He was only fifteen years old and lawfully a minor. He got out alright; I got hauled before the local court. A Protestant policeman gave evidence against me, a Protestant judge gave me three months in jail and a Protestant prison warden handcuffed me and took me off to jail. I was nineteen.

18

THE BRITISH ARMY COMES IN

IT WAS A Protestant state for Protestant people alright, and I knew for
sure from that day that I had no future in it, that it was rotten to the core
and I would do all in my power to dismantle that state, brick by brick, by
whatever means that it took. We got defeated in Dungannon that night,
but I vowed we would not always be defeated in Dungannon. I also vowed
that I would never again have to face 303 rifles with petrol bombs and
stones. Jack Lynch had stood idly by and let us down. Nationalist Belfast
had been burned street by street; men, women and children killed and
burned out of their homes fleeing to the Southern refugee camps. Derry
had fared as badly; the British army had moved in, bayonets on the end of
rifles. Some people welcomed them; but my father said "Don't welcome
any British soldiers into Ireland; for they had never done anything but
harm to Ireland all down the years". How right he was! The British army
was in effect sent into to prop up and support the sectarian Northern
state. It wouldn't take long to realise that fact. The state police and the
British Army would line up against the Irish Nationalist people of the
six counties, in what would turn out to be one of the most bloody and
protracted periods of terror and repression by the British establishment;
resisted by what was to turn out to be one of the most feared and
respected Guerrilla army's the world had ever seen. The Provisional I.R.A.
Backed by the Nationalist people, who had had enough of the sectarian
six county unjust state, that had been created by threat of force and would
only be demolished by force. We vowed that we would never again be
defenceless against the brute force of this evil little state. Let down and
abandoned by our own down South, and facing a state that hated us, I
swore that I would never again be in the position of having to face an
armed sectarian paramilitary force such as the B. men, shooting us down
while we had nothing but petrol bombs and stones to fight with. The civil

rights movements time was gone. Battered and beaten and terrorised of the streets. The fight would go on, but it would be different. For we would have our own army. "God helps those who helps themselves". So out of the ashes of the little streets of Belfast, Derry and Dungannon arose the I.R.A. Provisionals! The Northern Irish people's own army – the 'Provos'! We would never be let down again because from here on in, we would fight our own war!

19

1970 THE GUERRILLA WAR BEGINS

I JOINED THE I.R.A. Provisionals in the winter of 70-71, got training in the use of small arms and bomb making at a training camp on the border of County Monaghan. A southern I.R.A. training officer from Co. Cork showed us the basics of how to handle a .303 Lee Enfield rifle, a Thompson sub-machine gun and a .45 revolver; all guns left over from the I.R.A. campaign of the late fifties. The '56 men'*, as they were known, and the weaponry that was left from that campaign had formed the core of the new army. There were many willing recruits from the young men of Belfast and Derry and country areas as well. We were the first unit from the east Tyrone area and we were trained in that little farmhouse in North County Monaghan, by the Cork born I.R.A. training officer with the strange high lilting accent. The man who was our O.C. was a '56 man, and a totally dedicated I.R.A. man who would put his own life and liberty on the line countless times and always led by example. He had no time for frills, his motto being 'get on with the job that had to be done and to hell with the consequences'. He sometimes verged on the reckless but was held in high respect by all volunteers and he always could see humour in even the most dire of situations. A unit in Pomeroy was formed at this time as well.

Our unit consisted of my brother, three friends and neighbours, and the O.C's daughter whom we nicknamed 'Sofie' after Sofia Loren, because of her dark beautiful good looks. She took after her father and was as brave and as dedicated a volunteer as the 1st Batt east Tyrone had. We lads were very proud of her, and she was always willing to do her part in any operation no matter how dangerous or tough. Beautiful, brave and totally dedicated to the cause, she was an inspiration to us. We had another volunteer from a neighbouring village, who was known as 'the beardy man' because of his big bushy beard. Another volunteer was from

*I.R.A. men who fought in the 1950s

a family five miles away, near the village of Greystones. Several of them had been involved in the disarming of the State Paramilitary thugs during the "Fight for Dungannon". We knew then that we had good 'fighting men' in our unit.

We were all trained that winter and put on stand by for active service when we were needed. In the meantime we had dug arms dumps in different locations around our area and were staring to run guns and explosive across the border from Co. Monaghan to hide in our dumps for when they were needed for the destruction of the hated Northern state. We were trained to be wary, secretive and careful. We kept our unit and our dumps strictly to ourselves and got on with our ordinary lives as usual. It was like leading two lives. One outward, ordinary life and another hidden life far from ordinary; but it felt good because at last we were doing something positive and were getting prepared for the fight that lay ahead. We felt empowered; we were a trained unit of the I.R.A. We would never again feel that terrible sense of being alone and helpless, the way we felt that night the B. men opened fire on us in Dungannon, and when Jack Lynch had let us down so badly. No!! Next time we were shot at, we would shoot back and we were in a position to do so. At last we were doing something for ourselves that no-one could ever take away from us. The Nationalist community now had their own army forming and taking shape, and would never be defenceless and helpless ever again.

The aim of the Provional I.R.A. were set out by the leadership.

- The abolishment of The Stormont Regime
- Withdraw all British troops, RUC and B. specials to barracks
- Set a date for total British withdrawal; military and politically from the island of Ireland
- Release all the political prisoners immediately and amnesty for I.R.A. men 'on the run'
- Facilitate the reunification of Ireland in every way, including substantial monetary aid to the island as a whole.

20

1970 - 1971
THE BOMBING CAMPAIGN BEGINS

BOMBS WERE GOING off in Belfast regularly. Small bombs put into shops and businesses with warnings given to the people to get out. The bomb would then go off a half an hour later and blow the shop or business up. These economic targets were aimed at bringing the commercial life of the city to a standstill and therefore bankrupt the Northern state and bring it crashing down. It would be demolished, brick by brick if that was what was required. Every volunteer of the first Batt East Tyrone was deeply, deeply committed to the total destruction of this false, corrupt little state.

The country I.R.A. units were now active, as well as Belfast and Derry. Our unit was one of the first to move. We picked an electric power station as our first target. It supplied a factory that had never employed Nationalist people. Five pounds of commercial explosives with a black fuse timer and detonator were used. We pushed the explosive under one of the huge generators and pump house that supplied this factory with water from the Lough, which was vital to its operation. We placed the detonator in position and lit the fuse. We then drove to a nearby hill. As we stood watching, the night was lit up by a massive flash of red and white light. A few seconds later the noise of the explosion came, like a huge roll of loud thunder. It rose to a terrific crescendo and then seemed to roll away into the hills of County Tyrone, fading away like the sound of a fast speeding lorry into the distance. Following the explosion there was an eerie silence. We stood there looking at each other, a bit stunned at the enormity of what we had just done. Then big smiles broke out all round and we were delighted. Delighted, that after all the months of preparation we had finally stuck a blow at the hated northern state. We were elated. The high pitched sound of the siren in the R.U.C. army barracks at nearby Dungannon pierced the still night air. Our unit disappeared and we all went our separate ways home. We made our way home through the hills and fields that we had hunted with our dogs since we were young children. Their familiarity was comforting; these hills and fields were home. Even though we had just carried out a act of war, that could get us twenty years in prison, we felt safe in these familiar surroundings. The hedges and long grass closed in around us with the night sky, to form a safeness that I would often experience in the future, sometimes in the direst of circumstances. The hills and glens of my native Co. Tyrone would be our savers and protectors. We made our way home quietly, in silence and went to bed. The next morning we got up and got ready for work. It was important to keep our outward lives normal, so as to avert any kind of suspicion. I hadn't slept that well, and I don't think I ever had the sleep of an innocent at home again after that night. Life got like a cat and mouse game between us and the British security forces; always trying to keep a step ahead of them at all times. That first bomb attack in our area of East Tyrone caused a great stir. The Brits were like ants over the hills and fields for days afterwards. People were talking lowly about who in their midst had the capabilities to carry out such a successful attack. Was it a unit of the Southern I.R.A. brought up to do it or had the local I.R.A. been built up to such an extent that they were capable of doing it? The speculation continued for days, even at our own dinner table and at our jobs. We kept silent and got on with our lives.

After the first Batt East Tyrone Provisional I.R.A had carried out this successful operation against British rule in this part of our country. The O.C. was delighted "There are good men in Ireland yet", he said gleefully "and we will give them plenty more of the same. We'll lie low for a while and then we'll pick another target and strike again". I'd never seen The O.C. so happy. He was determined to make sure it was the first of many such attacks; he was right. The bombs continued to go off all over the North that winter and spring of '71. The Provos, as they were now known, were getting stronger and stronger and more efficient. They had spread across the North until there seemed to be units in every area. East Tyrone, West Tyrone, mid Ulster, South Derry, South West Antrim, South Armagh, Fermanagh, North Armagh etc. They seemed to be able to operate in most parts of the six counties. We felt we were getting to be a force to be reckoned with. We were no longer a defenceless people to be batonned off the streets at will. No; we were fast becoming a force to be taken very seriously indeed. We were inflicting very serious economic damage to the North's economy. Unionist and British politicians were calling more and more for security forces to be brought into the North. They were also calling for more and more harsh laws to deal with the worrying security situation. The O.C. said we had them worried. He said the more they squealed the more they were hurting. Keep up the pressure was his motto.

The fight was intensive that spring of '71. There was talk of worse security measures. Internment* was being mentioned. We were sent word down from G.H.Q. in Dublin to start sleeping away from home as much as possible. In their opinion, internment was a real threat and safe houses were to be used as much as possible. But it was difficult to do this without drawing any suspicions on ourselves. Myself and two of our unit had to abandon my car with explosives in it and we were now 'on the run' and could no longer live at home. The rest of the unit had come under more pressure since that happened and everyone was living on the edge. The unit O.C. had to make the decision to recruit more men in our absence. Three men from Dungannon were recruited. History would tell his choices were very good. They were to become my closest friends and comrades. The responsibility of re-organising and recruiting lay with him, and it was a very dangerous and treacherous time. It took a cool head and a very shrewd brain to re-organise and continue. He proved to be more than capable of this tough task. More and more bombs were going off and the whole situation in the North was becoming worse and worse. It was like a pressure cooker and the war continued unabated.

*imprisonment without trial

21

ON THE RUN SOUTH OF THE BORDER

WE RAN INTO serious trouble on Good Friday of '71. Myself and two of our unit had gone to Co. Monaghan to pick a load of explosives and bring them back down to our dumps for a couple of planned attacks in the Dungannon area. One of our men wasn't too happy about the day's run. He had a bad feeling about it. For a man who was usually delighted to be getting extra gear into the dumps, this was very unusual, so we put it down to tension. The Northern roads were getting increasingly dangerous to 'run in' gear needed for the war effort. So we pushed on up over the border at Aughnacloy and met our Southern contact in the car park of the local Four Seasons Hotel. The 'change over' of the explosives was done very quickly, and with a deep breath we headed back for the border and the six British occupied counties of Ireland. As we drove the no mans land stretch of the road between the Southern customs post and the Northern customs post everything seemed alright. We were waved on at both posts and drove slowly onto the main street of Aughnacloy where we met an R.U.C. mobile patrol. We carried on out the Dungannon road, tension in the car relaxed and we settled down for the ten mile drive to our safe house where we would put our new gear into the dump. Everything was going fine; we would all be back home in time for tea. It was Ned who was driving and noticed the car that was driving behind us first. "Don't like it" he said " it has been trailing us for the last five miles". Suddenly, we came into a series of bad bends on the road and we lost the car behind us for a short while. It reappeared and our driver said "there is something definitely wrong here". "Take the next left or right, "whichever comes first, and see if it follows us". As we turned the next corner, we could see that the R.U.C personal carriers had blocked the road ahead. Our man, who was a good driver, found a right hand turn up a little side road and sped up it. The car behind us was right on our tail and we could see the two men in it were armed R.U.C. Another mobile patrol was blocking our path up front. We were trapped! We leaped from the car and made a run for it but we were surrounded by armed police and army and were captured there in the fields.

Damn them, the bastards, they cornered us! Guns were stuck in our faces and we were roughly manhandled into enemy trucks and taken to Dungannon R.U.C. army base were we were interrogated for two days and nights. We held out and told them nothing of our other comrades or the whereabouts of our arms dumps or anything else they wanted to know. Damn them! They had us but they would get nothing else. We were remanded to Crumlin Road jail in Belfast, where we met some Belfast I.R.A. men who were already there for some time. They looked after us and filled us in as to the way it would be as a captured I.R.A. man in a British jail. Some of those Belfast men would become very famous in later years. We were remanded every week to Dungannon District Court. The Protestant Unionist judge said we had no stake in the community and could not be trusted to be given bail to await our trail. He was right on both accounts. We had no stake in the rotten little state. We were out to destroy it and we would not stand trail if we managed to get bail. We had talked it over in the jail and if we got bail, we'd jump it and go on the run across the border, join some of the Southern I.R.A. units and continue to fight along the border. That was our plan; but we were continuously remanded in custody 'they have no stake in this state'. The protestant judge and protestant policeman would nod their heads in agreement. No stake at all! Then, after about ten appearances in court it happened. The Protestant judge got sick and his place on the bench was temporarily filled by one of the token and very few Catholic judges. He said that people in front of him were innocent until proven guilty, and we found ourselves out on the street on a £1000 bail. Mine was put up by a neighbouring farmer, who assured me to go on the run. He would gladly lose his £1000 to see us continuing the fight against the British state. It would be his part in the struggle.

We met up with the O.C. that night. The rest of the unit were there as well. It was confirmed that we would go on the run south of the border but we could still join up in joint Northern – Southern operations. We were delighted with that and the unit was back in good spirits. The unit had a couple of operations planned for that weekend and we joined with them to carry them out. We only had a week out on bail so we had to move fast. That Sunday we bid farewell to our families and our homes and were spirited away across the border to a safe house in County Monaghan. My father and mother, eleven brothers and sisters were gutted and broken-hearted, but knew it was the only way. The Northern state would have made an example of us and would have given us twenty years in jail! Better to fight on, even if it meant leaving the county, the home and the big family at the Lough. Everything that we loved so dearly had to be left behind, but we vowed to be back some day as free men. It was to be many a long year. Though we would be back as active service I.R.A. men to carry on the fight in the occupied six counties of our country. At twenty years old, full of our own self confidence and ability to win our battle against our enemies, how could we be expected to see all the tragedies that lay ahead? And that we would be in our fifties and would still not be free men in our own county? That the homes we left that Sunday afternoon, so full of life and youth would be empty and overgrown. Mothers and fathers gone to their eternal rest, without the chance to be present at their last farewell. It would be a long, tough journey.

22

AN INQUIRY WAS SET UP

AN INQUIRY WAS set up by the I.R.A. as to how we got arrested. We would attend the inquiry. It was a slow process that dragged on the whole summer. We wanted our contact from the four seasons to be there as part of the inquiry as to how we were arrested. The three of us talked it over between us and we felt this man called Points should be a suspect, but the I.R.A.'s investigating team insisted on focusing on the northern side of the border. One of our men was a suspect. The R.U.C. had even mentioned this man's name in Dungannon barracks when we were been interrogated after our arrest. He was the O.C's right hand man and was known to the R.U.C. The finger of suspicion was being pointed in his direction, but we weren't convinced. We felt this man, was sound. We wanted Points in the frame too, but this was being resisted by the I.R.A. investigation team. Points was a '56 man, and an old republican, married into a very famous Belfast republican family. His credentials seemed impeccable from an I.R.A. point of view - above suspicion. He was a wee bit fond of the drink at times but the I.R.A. inquiry was focusing on the north and not Points, as we would have wished. We wanted to know who the second man was in his car at the Four Seasons hotel on Good Friday; he was to be on his own as far as we were concerned. Who was that second man? We knew at this stage that there was something wrong somewhere. The photos being taken in the street in Dungannon. The R.U.C. Brit checkpoint in the right place at the right time. Too many coincidences; something had gone wrong. Our position was, it could have been north or south, we wanted both sides investigated. The I.R.A. investigating team was only focusing on the north but we were going to insist that Points were in the final investigation. Then everything changed!

Internment came on Monday morning 9th August 1971. All hell broke loose! Hundreds came over the border on the run, and the whole struggle intensified. Our inquiry was lost in that different climate after internment. The I.R.A. was too busy; we were too busy to push it. It went way down the list and was eventually forgotten. Of the two suspects the man in the north went to the U.S.A., and Points was sidelined and not used. Our unit never trusted him, we always held our suspicion against him. If we ever saw him on the streets of Castleblaney we'd say 'There's that tout Points'. I had occasion to be in the same house as him in Castleblaney and when I walked in, he visibly flinched when I gave him a dirty stare. I stared him out and was more convinced than ever that he was a wrong one. Our new unit vowed we would keep him out in the cold as long as we operated along that stretch of border from Middletown to Castleblaney. He would know nothing from us; he would be treated like a leper! That was to save our lives! When we moved away from that border area back to Tyrone, we forgot about Points. An I.R.A. man from Lurgan, County Armagh, who escaped from Long Kesh internment camp dressed as a priest, took over that Castleblaney and north Armagh area. But he made one vital mistake that would cost him his young life and several more young I.R.A. and I.N.L.A. men. He took Points in from the cold and started to use him again! John, an I.R.A. man, escaped prisoner of war, and the O.C. of the north Armagh brigade I.R.A. was operating from a base in Castleblaney. On this occasion he was having a shave in a safe house; a farmhouse near the border in county Monaghan, when a British S.A.S. team, believed to be led by the executed S.A.S. spy, Robert Niaric, shot him twice in the head and left the two empty shells on his chest - an S.A.S. calling card. The man who led the S.A.S. team to John's safe house was none other than Points from Castleblaney - the tout and British mole who set us up at the Four Seasons hotel on the Good Friday evening in 1971; and who if we had been foolish enough to continue to use him would surely have given myself and the rest of my unit the same fate as he gave John and several other I.R.A. and I.N.L.A. men. His cover as a tout and British agent was finally blown when an R.U.C. man gave evidence at the inquest of three young Armagh men shot dead at a British army S.A.S., R.U.C. checkpoint, after leaving Castleblaney, and sent to their deaths by Points. When the R.U.C. man blew his cover, Points was seen being taken away from a pub in Castleblaney by his Brit handlers; never to be seen again in that area. A bad bastard whose cover would have been blown many years ago if we had been listened to, and the inquiry into our arrest had been brought to its conclusion. We knew it was Points. Points and his Brit handlers had done their best to set up a fellow I.R.A. man for execution as a tout. At least that didn't happen. If the inquiry had continued we would have blown Points cover at that time. Who was the man in the car with Points in the Four Season hotel on Good Friday? One of his Brit handlers? Why weren't we shot dead at the checkpoint set up for us? I'll never know. But we could have outed this Brit spy, if the enquiry had been completed, but because of the huge upsurge of activity after internment, a traitor had escaped his just reward.

23

INTERNMENT WITHOUT TRIAL

DURING SPRING AND early summer of '71 the war gathered momentum. It was now widespread over all six counties. We had joined a border unit made up of mostly Cork and Monaghan men. We had carried out some very successful operations, mostly economic targets, on towns just across the border. We were living all the time in safe houses in Monaghan. The Monaghan people were very good to us. We missed home, but were very much involved in the war effort so we did not get the time to brood. We were happy to have got the chance to fight on. There was a strong feeling among active service units that the British would spring internment on us in the north. They were stretched to the limit to keep control of the situation especially in Belfast. Belfast city centre was getting bombed repeatedly. Economic life was becoming seriously affected. On August 9th 1971 the Brits kicked in the doors of little terraced houses in Belfast and Derry. Internment had begun! They also raided the rural areas of the north and dragged out their helpless victims, kicking and beating them with their batons, their boots and the butts of their rifles, terrifying children, mothers, wives, little sisters and brothers. It had happened! The Brits had come like thieves in the night, only they weren't out to steal away our worldly possessions, no! They came to steal away our kith and kin! They came to take away our menfolk! Our fathers and brothers. With their English accents in the still summer morning air, they sounded so much out of place in the beautiful Irish countryside. Invading foreign storm troopers! Invading our country, our homes, our privacy and our dignity. They took away 500 men and young boys on that August morning in '71. They signed internment orders for them and put most of them into nissen tin huts in a makeshift prison on a plot of open ground not far from Belfast. This place became known as Long Kesh internment camp and later on the notorious H blocks! Some were put on a prison ship anchored in Belfast Lough.

Conditions in both places were terrible, living conditions atrocious! The north exploded in anger! Nationalist Ireland was incensed. The suddenness and the brutality of it stunned people at first, then they exploded in sheer anger; rioting erupted right across the north. The towns and cities were burning, gun battles broke out between the Brits and the I.R.A. men. The battles were sustained for days. Dozens of people were killed and injured. The first British soldier killed by an I.R.A. sniper, Gunner Robert Curtis was shot dead in Belfast. The first British soldier killed in Ireland since the tan war. He was to be the first of many.

They got our O.C. in Tyrone that morning, they burst his door down at six o'clock on the first morning and beat him down the stairs into a waiting army wagon and put him onto the prison ship in Belfast Lough. They got my younger brother, Martin. One of my other brothers got away and came on the run to Monaghan. He too joined the Monaghan unit and fought on. He was to get captured on an operation in County Fermanagh years later and spend almost ten years as a blanketman in the notorious H blocks. My comrade Ned's older brother were interned that morning as well. All over the north the word was coming in of who was interned and who had got away. A lot of men who had nothing to do with the I.R.A. were interned that morning. When the Brits couldn't get the man on their list, they often took another brother in his place, or they would take the eldest son if they couldn't get the father. It was purely indiscriminate. They took anyone out of the house if they couldn't get the one they wanted. The bastards, they'd pay a heavy price for this act of state terrorism. They would pay dearly; we'd make sure of that.

24

STATE TORTURE, THE HOODED MEN!

THE WAR INTENSIFIED after internment. Support was growing for our war effort. British soldiers were now getting shot dead on a regular basis. Huge bombs were been driven into town centres in cars and detonated, with devastating effect. The car bomb had been born. Terrible stories were starting to filter through from the internment camps that a selected number of men had been taken and systematically tortured for days on end before being taken dazed and disorientated to join their comrades in the camps. It wasn't enough to take our men and intern them without a jury or trial; they had to torture them and degrade them as well! They hooded our men, deprived them of sleep and food, kept them standing for long hours and played a high pitched noise constantly into their ears to try drive them insane. In some cases they succeeded in doing just that. Some hooded men never recovered. Some came into the camps like zombies and were never the same again. The people were stunned. They couldn't believe what was happening! Torture! This wasn't some farfetched war film about the Germans, Hilter or Jews. This was 1971 in Ireland - my brothers, my neighbours, my town land, my county, my country. God, I couldn't believe it! State sponsored torture! The Brits had gone too far! The whole country was aghast. In America and across the world, where large Irish populations existed, they took to the streets and protested at this British barbarity. Money and support was flowing in to the Provos from every direction. The British had made another huge mistake in Ireland and would pay a huge price for their cruelty to the Irish people. Would they ever learn? We, the Provos, the northern nationalist people's army would not be cowed or defeated by these kinds of tactics. We'd get stronger and more united and more determined to win this war, a war not of our wanting or our making, but a war we'd fight with every bit of tenacity, intelligence, cunning, courage and anything else that it took to win it!

Our O.C., Big Frank, was one of the tortured hooded men. He got a very hard time from the enemy as a P.O.W. but then he wouldn't have wanted it any other way. They got nothing out of him. I would have put my life on that. He went to the internment camp with all his secrets about his I.R.A. units in east Tyrone safely tucked away in that big heart of his, where no amount of British torture tactics could ever get at. They were wasting their time torturing him! They could have executed him and his big shoulders would have still heaved up and down at them with laughter right up to the last breath. It made every man and woman in the East Tyrone Brigade I.R.A. more bitter and more determined to get on with the job and win this war against an enemy that was getting more and more brutal and oppressive as time went on. We braced ourselves for this deadly conflict in the late part of '71 and into '72. The year of '72 was to be a watershed year for many unforgettable reasons.

25

1972
THE BORDER ROAD CAMPAIGN

IN A DESPERATE attempt to shore up the failing northern state the British started to blow up the border roads along the length of the 320 mile border. It could never have worked for them. I.R.A. units just took to the lanes and the fields and carried on as usual; switched cars on the southern side to a car on the northern side and continued on the journey north But this British tactic opened up a whole new front for the border I.R.A. units; instead of having to go into the north in search of the Brits they were now coming to us. The local population on both sides of the border were infuriated as their farms often straddled the border, and their cattle and sometimes their farmyards were split in half, leaving some of it in the north and some of it in the south. People often had to take a twenty mile detour to work and even in some cases the local church was cut of from its parishioners. So it was a very unpopular and stupid decision by the Brits. It became a running battle between the local population and the British army. The Brits would dig or blow up the local road on a weekday and the local people would promptly fill it in again by the weekend. Road committees and action groups were set up to co-ordinate the effort and it became a real battle of wills as to who would win. I.R.A. units became involved in all these action groups and became a real focus of resistance for the local people. Many more I.R.A. men were coming on the run out of the north because of the widespread continued use of internment without trial. So we border men had all the new recruits that we needed. Big Paddy and Red Joe were from my town of Dungannon in County Tyrone and had been active in that town for a couple of years, before their cover was blown and they had to go on the run. Very experienced I.R.A. men and two of the soundest men to ever put on a pair of boots. I was very happy to have them in the unit and they became the best comrades and friends I had throughout the long war against the Brits. Big 6ft men with big hearts to match - you could have never had better men on your side. But they also made very bad enemies, as the Brits would find out to their cost! Pearse and John Joseph were two more of these 'on the run' I.R.A. men to join the border unit. They were fishermen from the shores of Loch Neagh. Pearse was half blind! He wore real thick lens glasses at all times. He use to fix them on with a strong piece of elastic when going on an operation, in case he'd lose them. He was a brave man, he couldn't see his finger in front of him without them! A childless couple whose home was one of our safe houses treated these two men like their own sons. There would be a hot water bottle in their bed every night! The rest of us were jealous! They told us that if they didn't use this safe house for several weeks the hot water bottle would be still in the bed when they let themselves in! The woman of the house put the hot water bottle in every night, just incase they might come. They were spoiled to the world! These men and several local I.R.A. men made our border unit. It was allocated a stretch of the border between Monaghan and Armagh, running from Castleblaney to Middletown and we set up the unit in safe houses at Clontibret – Castleshane. We had good sound support in this area and were well looked after. People in this area showed great solidarity with the nationalist people of the six British occupied counties, and were great to be amongst. The Brits were blowing up the roads from late '71 into early '72 and gun battles and sniping were becoming common place. The people filled in the road craters at weekends. We would take up positions on Listinny Hill, wait until the Brits came to open them again, and then we would open fire. The gun battles were short but fierce, and the Brits superior fire power and their armoured helicopters would make it too lethal for us to shoot it out with them for too long. So we used the hit and run tactics to good effect. We made the cratering of those local roads very dangerous for them. Then we changed tactics. We got to know where the British units took up position on the northern side of the border to defend and protect their team working the roads. We went into the north and mined those positions, and when the Brits came to blow up the roads and take up those same vantage points, we hit them with sniper fire and then the landmines, with devastating effect. It was classic guerrilla army tactics. They were armed with much better guns than us, but that was no defence against our landmines! Time and again we caught them out and they suffered heavy losses for their stupidity in opening up a whole new front for us. We were so effective with those landmine ambushes that the roads were staying open much longer, before the Brits would attempt to re-crater them. One day we were within seconds of been shot to death by the British army, while patrolling our side of the cratered roads. As Kevin, Ned and myself drove down to one cratered road, I noticed a figure moving from one mound of clay to another. A British soldier!! It happened in a flash, but I observed it. We were only about fifty yards away from the mounds of clay. I tensed up and said to my two comrades, 'don't get out of the car, don't move'! Brits ahead! Kevin was a doubting Thomas. 'You're seeing things', he said. He had a .303 long rifle. If he stepped out with that in his hand we were all dead men! 'Stay where you are' I growled, as I carefully turned the car in a lane, 'don't get out'! Kevin did as he was told and I drove slowly up the top of the hill and parked the car. 'You don't believe me', I said to Kevin, 'I believe you' Ned said. I walked back to the brow of the hill, took up position and opened fire on the mounds of clay at the cratered road. Spat spat spat from the armalite rifle. Suddenly all hell broke loose, about fifty Brit's returned fire from the mounds of clay and surrounding hills. It had been a close one. We withdrew safely from the area, and lived to fight another day.

We were more popular than ever with the local people and our morale was sky high. We became a part of the community and attended all their weddings, christenings, local dances, pubs, football matches etc. Social events of all kinds. I remember being carried shoulder high at the local dance hall after a very effective hit against the enemy out at the border roads. We were treated like heroes. The British army got hit hard so many times during this border road campaign, that they actually refused to come down the small border roads. There was an outcry from Unionist leaders at the time. The British army was accused of handing over part of the north to the I.R.A. The British army replied, that to resume these patrols was continuing to give the I.R.A. a second front, and these patrols were not operationally good practice. We in the I.R.A. were Cock a Hoop, and claimed that we put the wind up the Brits, and had claimed part of Ireland back! A victory for the Ra! We have always been so very grateful to those people of Monaghan who cared for us, backed our fight, made us part of their own! Without such local support no guerrilla army could survive. They were also our eyes and ears, our intelligence gatherers, our safe houses, our transport supplies. I used one of their farm tractors to patrol the border. They gave us everything they had and often they couldn't even afford to, but they would have done without themselves to make sure we had a bed to sleep in and a change of clothes. They said 'your fight is our fight; it is as much as we can do to look after you'. They never begrudged us one thing they had. I made lifelong friends of those great people; without them we could not have operated. The local population is the life blood of the guerrilla army. Good Christian, God fearing people who would not harm a fly in ordinary circumstances, but who gathered shrapnel that we needed for our landmines. Old mowing machine blades, old farm implements cut up in the local forge and gathered into buckets for us to collect when we needed it. People who would go to mass every Sunday, but people who believed our fight against the Brits was a just fight and backed it accordingly. One of these good people was told by a protestant neighbour in the northern side of the border, that he wouldn't do to the animals in the fields, what the I.R.A. had done to a unit of British soldiers caught in one of the landmine attacks. When the story was related to the I.R.A. they told the supporter, 'the next time he was talking to the man, tell him they wouldn't do it to the animals either'! But as long as a British soldier insisted in being in our country, murdering and imprisoning and terrorising our people, we would hunt them down and kill them like rats in a ditch! If they wanted to be safe from the I.R.A. all they had to do is go home to Britain, For the family of a young British soldier, going to an early grave in some part of England was a personal tragedy for them too. But they were the invaders and the aggressors; they were the ones trying to cut our country in two. As long as they were here they would pay a high price. This was the same throughout the border counties and six northern occupied counties in early January 1972. It was a tough fight. We often lay in ambush in the cold and the rain away from our homes and families, our lives in danger continuously. A prison cell awaited us, or an early grave - whichever came first. We never complained, because this is how it was. We just got on with it.

26

BLOODY SUNDAY

THEN CAME BLOODY Sunday! The Brits opened fire on an anti interment civil rights march in Derry city and killed 14 unarmed civilians. Ruthlessly and deliberately shot them down one after the other. It was a massacre of the innocents! This massacre would change the lives of many people over the next 25 years. It marked a watershed in the lives of so many people; it was a turning point for the whole fight. It really was a fight to the bitter end now. No quarter asked, none given, I would have gladly put down every British soldier standing if I was given the chance. There were so many like me. I remember being in one of our safe houses when the woman of the house broke down and started to cry inconsolably when the coffins of those people were lined up for burial in the Cathedral in Derry city's Creggan Estate. She was one of the many many people in Ireland and all over the world who were shocked to the core of their being at this terrible crime against the Irish population of the six counties. Any pretence that the British army were in the north for any reason other than to protect British vested interests in Ireland were now dead in the water. 'Croppy lie down' was alive and well in the British establishment. But Croppy wasn't prepared to lie down, not this time! We would bury our dead with dignity and sorrow, we would take out some time to mourn our fellow countrymen, to stand shoulder to shoulder with the people of Derry at this terrible time and then we would renew our efforts to rid our country of the murderers in uniform, British uniforms. We'd send every one of them home in a box if thats what it took! We were angry young men, armed with a just cause, a fierce hatred of our enemy, armed to the teeth, and an unbending will to win. We were not interested in any more 'glorious Irish defeats' damn that! We were out for victory, nothing less would do! I wanted to do a 'Dunkirk' on them, to be sniping at the last of the bastards as they fled out across Belfast Lough on their way home to

Britain for good. I didn't ask for this fight, I never sent for it, I didn't even like it, I didn't glory in it, but I'd fight it, and I'd fight to win.

We were swamped with recruits after Bloody Sunday. We set up training camps all along the border and further into southern Ireland. Support was everywhere. The southern state turned a blind eye to us. The southern police and army ignored us; some of them openly encouraged us. 'I hope you have one set up for those bastards'. That remark came from a patrol car of Irish police who met us at the border shortly after Bloody Sunday. There was an understanding between us and the southern Irish security forces. They wouldn't bother us and we didn't bother them. We both honoured that understanding very well. In fact there was a standing order within the I.R.A. that under no circumstances were I.R.A. weapons to be used against the southern security forces. Even if that meant arrest and loss of these weapons, so be it! For any I.R.A. unit to have attacked members of the southern forces and killed or injured them would have been an absolute disaster. It would undermine our southern support base. It would turn the same security forces against us and would be a terrible own goal. So we were careful not to antagonize the southern state in any way and get on with our fight in the north. We didn't expect any help from politicians south of the border, nor did we want any of their help. They had let us down time after time after time! We'd do it our way. We'd fight them in every northern city, town, village, country road the only way the Brits really understood, with the bomb and the bullet, and we'd bring the fight to Britian as well, if we deemed that necessary to win.

So this is where we were in February of 1972, squaring up to the British for one hell of a fight. The campaign intensified against the northern state on·all fronts after Bloody Sunday. The training camps were full of new volunteers from all over the north, the border counties and down south as well. We had southerners; Cork, Kerry and Waterford men and found them to be great fighters. I realized why the black and tans couldn't live with them during the Tan War. Ruthless and dedicated, great men to have on your side. Several of them died on active service during those years. The raids on homes in the north continued unabated, internment was still being used, torture of men lifted was widespread. A few men broke under the interrogation methods by the Brits R.U.C. special branch, with the result that we had many more men coming on the run. Some of these men went on down south to live and work and some stayed along the border joining up with existing border units to fight. The border units were very important because they were the connection between the southern units and the northern units. All war materials coming into the country from the U.S.A. and other places were stored by the southern units and then brought up to the border to be distributed into the northern units as was required. All training camps were jointly run by the southern units and the border units. Mini-bus loads of young men and women came from all over the north disguised as football teams to stay a week at the camps. Normally a disused farmhouse owned by a sympathizer was kitted out with sleeping bags and bedclothes. The training officers or T.O.'s as they were known, were mostly from the southern units. Experts in their own field, there could be five or six of them all training groups of ten or twelve in their own specialist way. Bombs, booby traps, landmines, weapons and field craft; all aspects of guerrilla warfare were covered. Then there was a talk by a high ranking I.R.A. man on the history of the resistance against the Brits for over 800 years. This man always referred to the British as the never ending source of all Ireland's political ills! We must get rid of them before we can get the best out of our country. Padraig Pearse's statement at the grave of the Fenian O'Donovan Rossa 'Ireland unfree would never be at peace' was often quoted at the camps. When we looked at the state of our country in 1972 we believed he was right. When the formal training was over these young people would walk the fields and hills, the city ones always said how beautiful Ireland was, and how much it was worth fighting for. I would think sadly to myself, how many of them would go to an early grave, how many would end up in prison, how many would be on the run, and how many would be lucky enough to escape these fates. They, like us, believed there was no other way, politics and politicians had failed us and the only way left was to fight. We'll finish 800 years this time, so at least future generations of young Irish men and women, and indeed whole families, would be spared the same kind of hardship as our generation was suffering. One family in east Tyrone lost three sons to the conflict. When we achieved permanent peace on the island of Ireland, the sacrifices of my generation would be worth it all. We had to make sure this fight was the last fight. It was always the families who suffered. The price some families paid, was very very high.

The war in the north intensified even more. British soldiers were getting killed all over the north on a daily basis. Huge car bombs were ripping out the commercial heart of the economy, landmines were making it very difficult for the Brits to move on country roads. There were whispers of a campaign starting in Britain. Britain was still reeling from the bad press all over the world for the way they were trying to defend the corrupt, the unjust and the failed little statelet they had set up against the will of the vast majority of the Irish people. They set this state up on the threat from Lloyd George of 'immediate and terrible war'; well they were now getting their fill of war. Their soldiers were dying every day now, trying to defend it. Its whole infrastructure was being blown apart; their reputation across the world was in tatters, so they were paying a big price for their military and political stupidity in Ireland. At a rally outside the British embassy in Dublin protestors burnt it to the ground. So they, the British Establishment, were being made to pay north and south of the border, in the U.S.A. and all over the world - wherever there was an Irish population there were protests outside all British Embassies. The British were under pressure from all sides. Our morale was sky high, we felt we were winning. The I.R.A. was popular, vitally important to all guerrilla armies. Our support base was very strong. A group of men from my home area were brought into the interrogation centre in Armagh. One of these was a good friend. While this man was very active, he was also very shrewd and had managed to avoid suspicion from the Brits. But they told him that they knew that I was very active on the southern side of the border. They put the blame on me for a lot of hits they had taken at the border roads campaign. They told him before they released him, that they would get me eventually and there would be no arrest or trial! They would execute me on the spot. At least they didn't like me, I must have been doing something right!! This man told me to be very careful about my personal security, especially out along the border roads at night. "Keep your safe houses a very tight secret", he said. "If they get to you, it would be deadly dangerous".

27

EXTRADITION

SHORTLY AFTER THAT I was walking down the street in Monaghan town. I often stayed in safe houses in this town as it was very close to our border area. It was also a good town for support and for socializing and good craic. It had several good hotels with functions almost every night. When we weren't out in the country we would stay in the town, have a drink and chase women. We were young and very popular with the local girls. There were certain quodo's to being an I.R.A. man! A lot of I.R.A. men married local girls and settled in the Monaghan area. I was very well in with a group of student nurses from the local hospital and they often kept me in their dormitories! There was one I was particularly close to and if things had have gone differently I might have married her. At that time I would have been bad marriage material! No home, no job, no money and a war to fight. She had good sense, and married someone else! Many a good nights craic I had with them. So I was walking down the street in Monaghan town and I was suddenly stopped and arrested by two special branch plain clothes Gardaí. They had a warrant for my arrest on the foot of an extradition warrant from the British! They wanted me to stand trial for possession of arms and explosives in Co. Tyrone, the charge I jumped bail on. The bastards! If they couldn't get me one way they would get me another. I was taken to a local court and remanded to the high court in Dublin for extradition proceedings.

This was the first time I was in jail in the south, but it wouldn't be the last. D Wing in Mountjoy jail was the I.R.A. wing in that jail at the time. There were about thirty men in there, mostly southern I.R.A. men who ran into Garda checkpoints when moving war material north. There was also some border men mostly caught coming back into the south after attacks on the Brits in the north. It was very frustrating and annoying for I.R.A. men to be arrested in this way, but the army order number 8 had to be strictly obeyed, no action against southern security forces under any circumstances. So you had the spectacle of tough I.R.A. units after engaging the Brits in huge gun battles, been arrested and disarmed by a handful of unarmed Garda. But this policy gave us a lot of freedom in the south. The Gardaí at that time often turned a blind eye to us. You'd have the small number of Gardaí trying to make a name for themselves by arresting armed I.R.A. men, but the vast majority of them knew that if these I.R.A. men turned on them, they wouldn't stand a chance. No I.R.A. man ever did because of the very serious effect it would have on our capacity to wage war in the north. The Gardaí were like a little terrier dog, always snapping at our heels but doing very little harm, more annoying than anything else. The Rottweiler was in the north, that's the one we wanted! So I had some good company when I arrived in Mountjoy jail D Wing in that early spring of 1972. When I went through the formalities with the governor of the jail and was shown onto D Wing the O.C. of the I.R.A. men in the jail took over and made me feel welcome. I.R.A. prisoners in jail, any jail, are classed as a unit of the I.R.A. When you reached the jail you were automatically a member of that unit. So I reported to him the circumstances of my arrest, what I was arrested for and what legal representation I would need etc. Also, if there were any urgent messages I needed to send out to my outside unit, that would be done right away. I looked around the cell and thought to myself how similar it was to the Crumlin road jail in Belfast. This should have come as no surprise, as the Brits had built them both! We wore our own clothes in jail. We tore up the card with the prison number on it from the slot in the cell door, and insisted that we be called and addressed by our own names. The prison authorities agreed to this request. We weren't ordinary prisoners; we were political prisoners fighting for a cause we believed in. This status always made us feel good about ourselves. We were shown a lot of respect by the prison authorities and in return we didn't give them any trouble.

The I.R.A. O.C. in the jail was a Dublin man in his fifties. He was active in the 50's campaign along the border. This campaign was run by mostly southern volunteers and some northern men as well. These men made up some of the leadership of the I.R.A. in 1972. They were much more aware of the political history of the south, or the 'free state' as they always referred to it. A lot of them had very bitter memories of the civil war against the 'staters' as they called them. These men didn't recognize any of the two states created by the partition of Ireland and hated both of them with equal measure. Their allegiance was to the First Dáil in 1918 when Sinn Féin won a big majority of the seats and formed a government for all of Ireland. The fact that a lot of the men who won the seats were in jail or on the run didn't matter. They maintained that the 1918 Dáil was the legitimate government of Ireland and was torn apart illegally, and therefore was still the only parliament that they owed any allegiance to. Both states in their eyes were illegal and therefore they did not recognize the right of either to exist. This was all new to me but it did explain why there was a policy of not recognizing the courts in either state when arrested. This policy was adhered to for a time but it was soon abolished. Too many good men ended up in jail. These older southern I.R.A. men were accused of trying to re-fight the civil war. To me it seemed that there was a certain amount of truth in that. I myself believed that the southern state was now accepted by the vast majority of the Irish people and republicans; old and new would have to accept that fact. I believed that if a man was up in court he should fight his case. The main thing was to get out and rejoin the fight. I learned a huge amount about how politics worked in the southern state from these men. Jail was a great place to get politically educated. Some of them would say to me at that time, 'You young I.R.A. men will beat the Brits, but watch your back, because if you become any kind of a political threat to the southern establishment they will come down on you with a vengeance and a ruthlessness worse than the northern state'. 'You might not like to hear this' he said 'you think this is "God's own country down south". Well it's not, there is more corruption south of the border than there is in the north, and if you live long enough, and I hope you do, you will find out that I am right' 'The southern political powers don't want a united Ireland now, they pay lip service to it alright, but they don't want the politics of this island to go into the melting pot, because they wouldn't be sure that they would come back out of that pot again. So you watch your political back, young man, because they will stick a knife in it to preserve their own little corrupt state and their privileged positions within it. I believe we should have cleaned up the southern state first, there is as much political corruption in the south as in the north, it's just that it's not as easy to see down here'. It was a shock to hear all that from this old republican from the south, and while I had more important things on my mind at that time, like beating an extradition attempt against me, I still remembered all the political lessons I learnt in the jails. My case was heard in the High Court in the Four Courts in Dublin and I beat it. I was awarded political asylum. I had the best legal barrister available in Ireland to fight for me. The I.R.A. top brass got the best for me because if one I.R.A. man was extradited north, it would open the floodgates for many many more. My barristers McEntee and Sorochan told me to tell the judges the truth; that I had the guns and bombs in the car I was driving into the north to help to bring down the irreformable, corrupt, evil Stormont government, a government that treated its minority worse than the Black people of South Africa got treated. I told them I was a member of the civil rights movement in the late sixties, but I got battoned and put off the streets, and had done the only thing a young man could do in those circumstances - fight back. I said I did not apologize to anybody for doing that. The northern nationalist catholic people in the north were on their knees and defenceless, and we had a right to fight for our survival. You could have heard a pin drop in that courtroom. The judges put their heads together for some time, before the chief judge addressed me. He said 'your case is definitely a part of the political unrest in the northern part of Ireland and therefore we grant you political asylum under the relevant legal act'. My barristers and legal team were delighted and so was I, not just for myself but for all the I.R.A. men and women who would not be extradited either. Women were not exempt from this process either; the next person up for extradition was a Belfast women, accused of ambushing three British soldiers. She was safe now too. A legal precedent had been set that was to hold for many years to come. My barristers said they couldn't have gotten a better case than mine for a test case. They said I deserved an Oscar for my performance in the witness box! They also said the political climate at the time suited too. Bloody Sunday, Internment, torture of internees, the Irish Governments case against Britian pending in the human rights courts in Strasbourg, all helped our case. But he said I was the right young man in the right place at the right time. I laughed and said I was not so sure about that. It was chancy enough in there for a while. But I was free again and it felt great. I would re-join my I.R.A. unit now and get on with the fight. They hadn't heard the last of me yet, not by a long way.

When I was in Mountjoy, the I.R.A. in Dublin sent into the jail that famous tailor from Copelands of Capel Street in Dublin to fit me out with a suit for my big day in court. So I was measured up for a three piece suit by the most famous tailor in Dublin, in Mountjoy jail! I had a brother getting married. The reception was in The Hillgrove Hotel in Monaghan town. So I was free, dressed to kill, had been given a bit of money by the finance officer of the Dublin Brigade I.R.A. and I was looking forward to meeting all my family, friends and comrades for one hell of a party in Monaghan town. A good looking woman wouldn't go amiss either!

Tyrone Man will not be extradited

A 25-year old Co. Tyrone man, who is at present, serving a prison term at Portlaoise for being a member of the I.R.A., won an appeal in the Dublin High Court against an order extraditing him to the North to answer an explosives charge.

Thomas Anthony McNulty a native of Dungannon with an address at Park Street, Monaghan, was granted an order revoking the extradition by the President of the High Court, Mr. Justice O'Keeffe. He was also awarded the cost of the application.

At Monaghan District Court, in June last year he was ordered by District Justice Shaw to be handed over to the RUC at Moybridge, Co. Monaghan, on foot of a warrant charging him that on April 9, 1971 at Drumshalogue, Co. Tyrone, he had 124 sticks of explosive substances in his possession or under his control in such circumstances as to give rise to a reasonable suspicion that he did not have them for a lawful object.

In his action against the Attorney General, McNulty claimed in his statement that the offence in the warrant was a political offence or an offence connected with a political offence and there were substantial grounds for believing that if removed from the State he would be charged with a political offence or an offence connected with a political offence.

In evidence he said that he joined the Civil Rights Association in the North in 1968 and had been a member of the I.R.A. for the past four years. He joined the I.R.A. to overthrow the Stormont Government which, he believed at the time and still believes, to be "rotten to the core". He hoped it would lead to the withdrawal of British troops from Ireland.

In April, 1971 he had explosives in his possession or under his control to help in the campaign to overthrow the Stormont Government. He was at the Civil Rights movement march which ended with a confrontation with the RUC. He was arrested and fined £15 and given a suspended sentence of three months imprisonment. He was arrested twice in the South and charged with membership of the I.R.A. and is, at present, in Portlaoise prison.

The President said that in the evidence the plaintiff was entitled to an order under section 50 of the Act. Mr. T.K. Liston, S.C. for the Attorney General agreed that he was.

McNulty is due to be released from Portlaoise next month on the expiration of his sentence.

Irish Independent circa 1973

My legal team said my win had now set a legal precedent, and that all the extradition cases coming up would be entitled to the same judgement!

McEntee and Sorochan were my legal team. The best Barristers in Ireland.

28

THE FALL OF STORMENT
I.R.A. – BRITISH TRUCE

THE FIGHT WENT on into late spring and early summer with even more intensity, British casualties were getting higher and they were losing the propaganda war as well. They felt they had been badly advised by Brian Faulkner's Stormont Government as to the impact internment would have on the I.R.A's capacity to continue the war against them. Instead of weakening them it had the opposite effect. They were a far more formidable force now than there were before internment. The intelligence the Brits had been given, as to who should be interned was very bad indeed. The Brits got very few active I.R.A. men on internment morning 9th August 1971. They got names and addresses to go to, but they often arrested the wrong brother, they even went to the wrong houses altogether. Even worse, it alerted all the I.R.A. to stay away from their homes, so they had even less chance of getting their hands on them.

All these failures could be laid at the door of the Stormont government. Failure to grant civil rights to the nationalist minority before civil unrest took hold and the failure of internment. The north's economy was getting blown apart and the cost to the British taxpayer to prop up this puppet government was crippling. The terrible disaster of Bloody Sunday and the loss of face worldwide was too much for the Brits to stomach so in the early summer of 1972 Brian Faulkner was summoned to London and told that his corrupt, protestant parliament for a protestant people was no longer sustainable. Stormont was being abolished by the British Houses of Parliament! This hated instrument of oppression that had been used against the Irish nationalist population, trapped in that artificial state, that had been created against the will of the vast majority of the Irish people, no longer existed! Their private paramilitary wings, the B. men and the armed R.U.C. would both have to go. We'd fight on and make sure they went. We had five demands to the Brits for peace - one down and four to go. No-one, only the people who lived under its wrath could really appreciate the significance of the fall of Stormont. It was a victory in itself. My mother and father's generation, who bore the brunt of Stormont injustices, just couldn't believe their sons and daughters had managed to bring it down. That generation cried with the joy of it, and well they should. To be rid of something that seemed so permanent, was for them a beginning of a new era. To them it was a great victory. To us in the I.R.A. it was but a start in the right direction, we wanted our country back. We wanted Brits out, partition to end, the prisoners released, the right of the Irish people to determine their own political future; without British political or military interference and a definite time scale for all this to happen. This is where we stood, and would fight on to achieve just that. In the summer of 1972 the I.R.A. and the British army called a truce. The I.R.A. would suspend all military operations; the British army would do the same. Negotiations would take place soon as possible. We I.R.A. men were told to maintain their own personal security at all times during the truce, as there was no guarantee negotiations would be a success. We may have to go back to war, so it was very important to keep the war machine of the I.R.A. well oiled up. The I.R.A. kept a low profile and waited. An I.R.A. delegation went from Ireland to London that summer to meet with the British government. Our men were very blunt and to the point. Concede to the principle of British disengagement, politically and military within a certain time frame and we could do business. The British were stunned with the direct no nonsense approach of the I.R.A. delegation. They, the British, wanted to play politics and have long drawn out negotiations. Our men were military men, black was black and white was white. We wanted a time frame set out to outline when exactly they would leave this country. That was it with us, everything else could be worked out after that principal had been accepted. The meeting broke up without agreement and our men came back to Ireland. Shortly after they came back the truce broke down in Lenadoon Belfast, over nationalist families having to leave their homes because of loyalist violence. The Brits sided with the loyalist paramilitaries and there was a gun battle between the Brits and the local I.R.A. units.

The truce was over. It was back to war.

29

TRUCE OVER, BLOODY FRIDAY IN BELFAST

THE I.R.A. IN Belfast went out and planted 20 bombs all over the city. Many civilians were killed and injured. The Brits said they were too stretched security wise to cope with all the bomb warnings at one time. The Belfast I.R.A. said the Brits deliberately didn't act on their warnings, but wherever the truth lay, we in the I.R.A. were shocked and dismayed, as was the wider population of the north, south, U.S.A. and Britain. All over the world in all the countries in which we had backing people were horrified. People who were never for us were having a field day. They were already calling it Bloody Friday. It was a bad blow to our popularity as a guerrilla army. The I.R.A. had always done its very best to avoid civilians causalities and up to this time we had succeeded to a large extent. I didn't like what had happened in Belfast. I didn't like it for the harm it was doing to our cause and I didn't like it from a personal point either. To see people's remains swept up into plastic bags on T.V. is not something anybody wants to see. I didn't know where the truth lay – whether the Brits did it deliberately or the Belfast I.R.A. overstretched them. I was disgusted and felt 'a plague on both your houses'. A lot of harm was done that day and it would take time to recover from it. I disliked it immensely. But the truce was well and truly over, the war was back on and the fight still had to be won. Our support base survived Bloody Friday. New rules were brought into place for commercial bombings. A warning would be phoned into the Brits. But a second warning would also be phoned into the local priest, the local radio station, the Samaritans or any second source, so as to leave the Brits they couldn't do the same on us again and deny that they got warnings in the first place. We found this worked well. The war continued on as before. There were no more negotiations planned between the Brits and the I.R.A. But at least we had face to face negotiations with them and no doubt would have again in the future. We had got rid of Stormont and it was London we were eyeballing now, in more ways than one. There was serious consideration about taking the war to the English capital and other English cities. We fought on that year with grim determination. Our desire to win this fight was as strong as ever. There was no ceasefire that Christmas. The I.R.A. had decided that there would be no more ceasefires until the Brits got real. The next truce would be the last one. Fighting on was the mood within the I.R.A. For the I.R.A. men on the run, the visit from family at Christmas was very special. We knew that our homes were watched very closely at this time of year for any fleeting visits that I.R.A. men might decide to make. There was an understanding that there would be no sentimental visits home, especially at Christmas time. Feeling sentimental in our situation could cost you your life and sometimes it did cost lives. An I.R.A. man getting married to a girl from his own town land in Co. Armagh, made a trip to his fiancée's house just before the wedding. The S.A.S. had his girlfriend's house under constant surveillance because they wanted this I.R.A. man very badly; they also knew he was brave enough to defy them. He was a big, strong 6ft black haired man. But his visit cost him his life. The S.A.S. squad arrested him in the house at gun point, took him outside, put him up against the wall of the shed and shot him in the head. A helicopter landed in the front garden and as the S.A.S. squad were racing to get into it. A family member stood out in front of them and said 'shoot me too' but they pushed him out of the way and said 'we got who we came for, our mission has been carried out'. They climbed in the helicopter and swooped low over the south Armagh hills and away. The S.A.S. prided themselves that they carried out their orders to the letter. If their orders were to arrest that man and they shot him dead instead, they would count that mission as a failure, so their orders for that I.R.A. man was to shoot him dead. I remembered what my friend had been told about me at the interrogation centre in Co. Armagh and I knew that if they ever got me they would do the same. The S.A.S. were a very formidable enemy and we gave them due respect. Never underestimate your enemy, one of the first rules of war. So Christmas time, weddings, funerals and important family occasions were fraught with danger for wanted I.R.A. men on the run. Weddings and any other family functions that could be moved to the southern side of the border were moved, so that I.R.A. men on the run could attend. I even remember one man's mother was taken in her coffin across the border so her son could say goodbye to her. That Christmas of 1972 we had a family get together in the Four Seasons Hotel, Monaghan town. We had a great night's craic. My mother, father, brothers, sisters, old neighbours and friends, comrades and Monaghan people turned out for the drink, food and music. My brother Marty was interned so he wasn't there. My father had arthritis for many years and always used a stick to walk. I was used to this as I couldn't remember him any other way. He also had the worst smoker's cough that I ever heard in anybody. He would go outside in the mornings when he got up and you could hear him coughing and wheezing to try to get his system cleared. He was like a child with a bad whooping cough, sometimes you would think he was going to collapse, but he'd get his system cleared and come into the old living room sit at the fire and light up a willy woodbine, or a coffin stick, as they were commonly known, and then he'd be right for the day. So when he limped into the Four Seasons just after Christmas of '72, he didn't look a lot different to me. At 68 years he was still young enough. He made several attempts to speak seriously to me that night, but sure the craic was ninety and I was hard to pin down. He told me he had changed his will. He had always told me that the old house was mine. I had a love for farming growing up and had always done the farm work around the house ever since I was a very young lad. But I knew it wasn't a good idea to have me on the will. I didn't know what was going to happen to me from day to day. I said I understood and that it was alright, not to let it worry him. He said' when you can come home, we will look at it again'. He was a bit sentimental that evening, talked about old times a lot. He said he was worried about me, I said 'don't be worrying, this whole war thing will soon be over and everything will return to normal'. He kept shaking his head sadly and saying 'I don't know, I worry about you and your safety' I told him not to worry that I would be alright, but he wasn't convinced. He still looked really worried and a bit upset. I put it down to the fact that him and me always got on really well and that he was missing me being at home, but I told him things could change quickly and I could be home in no time at all. The craic went on till all hours of the morning, we loved a good party, we all knew how to enjoy ourselves. My father got tired and went home halfway through it with one of my brothers. That wasn't unusual as he wasn't a drinker. He was a teetotaller, a pioneer all his life, he didn't like drink. So I said goodbye to him and went back in to join the party, which was still in full swing. Early that January I was involved in an ambush against the Brits out near the border at Middletown. Myself and another member in my unit was driving to the weapons dump when we ran into two Gardaí in a patrol car. It was a narrow road and my comrade pulled the car into a gap in the field, and I jumped out of the car with two rifles and made down the field. The two Gardaí made to run after me but my comrade banged the door of the car really loudly and shouted at the Gardaí 'I.R.A., get down'. The two guards - they were only young fellas - dropped like two stones in the middle of the field and I got away with the two rifles. My comrade got arrested there and then and as I was walking in towards Monaghan town later that day I was arrested as well. We were both charged with possession of weapons, and remanded into custody at Monaghan district court. I found myself back on D Wing in Mountjoy jail to await trial. Mountjoy was a very old prison. The wing I was on was the hanging wing! Kevin Barry, the young I.R.A man from Dublin, arrested in 1918 was held on D wing and hanged in the hanging house at the end of the wing. We made a request to the Governor to be allowed into the death cell, and the hanging quarters, and he said o.k! It was a very dismal place even then. The death cell was on the right hand side, the hanging quarters on the left. I felt a great sense of history standing in the death cell and the hanging quarters. I knew that Kevin Barry was no different than me. Same fight, different time. I was here for fighting the Brits in my part of the country and he was hanged for fighting the same army in his part of the country. I pictured him at 18 years of age being led out to the hanging house. A brave young man. I sang his song often when I was a boy. It was one of my favourite rebel songs.

"Early on a Monday morning, high upon the gallowstree,
Kevin Barry gave his young life, for the cause of liberty."

Now here I was, in the very place where they had executed him. We paid our respects to him and walked back out of the hanging house. I also read Brendan Behan's book, called "The Quare Fella", a book about a condemned prisoner, the weeks and months leading up to his execution. It was full of Dublin black wit! It was very funny, and very tragic, all at the same time. I got a great sense of presence that I was reading his very famous book on the very landing where the whole book was set. I also read his other book 'The Borstal Boy'. He was a remarkable writer. I used my time in prison to do a lot of reading, especially Walter Macken's books, Frank O'Connor's short stories and the Leon Uris' trilogy of famous works.

Meanwhile in County Tyrone the raids by the British security forces continued. I don't know whether my arrest in the south had any bearing on it, but a really bad raid took place on the old home place just outside Dungannon. It was a very dangerous situation. They bogged down one of their very big armoured cars in the front field and they had to bring an even bigger one to get it out. They were there for two days. They carried on very badly. I heard about the raid in Mountjoy and I was fit to be tied. I sat down that night and wrote a letter to my father. I normally wrote letters home to my mother, but this time for some reason I wrote to my father. He used to have an old joke about the cheapest hotel in Dublin City when we were small - it was Mountjoy jail! I reminded him about it and said he'd never expect me to be in it. I laughed at that, put the letter in an envelope and left it on the table to get it posted the next day, and went to bed. Early next morning the warden and the I.R.A. O.C. opened my cell door and accompanied me down the stairs to the visiting area. My mother and brother Malachy were there and when they saw me they came over to me and said 'Tommy, your father died last night'. I was stunned. The visit was like a blur. I remember giving my mother a big hug, shaking hands with my brother and then I was back in my cell. God, my father was dead! I sat down on the chair by the little table and looked at my father's name on the envelope and I just couldn't believe it. I took it out of the envelope and read it, with the tears streaming down my face. My old man, dead, but I had a letter for him here in my hand. I read it till the end, tore it up and put it in the waste paper bin. I felt it was too personal to let anyone else ever read it. That letter was between me and my father and nobody else. If I had kept it, and my cell was searched, and it was taken and read by anyone else I would have been very annoyed. So I tore it up into small pieces and put it in the bin, but I kept the contents of it in my heart. I was glad I wrote it. I just somehow knew that he knew that that letter was for him. I applied for bail to the court in Dublin but I didn't get it. So I spent the time of my father's death, wake and funeral in Mountjoy jail. I wrote another letter, this one was for my mother, brothers and sisters; telling them I would be alright and to look after themselves and to keep their spirits up. I was young and strong. I would survive. Some of my other brothers and sisters came down and told me that my father knew he was going to die after Christmas and he prayed that I would be lifted and put in jail and wouldn't get out. For he knew that if I was out and free I would have had to be at his funeral, come what may; and that I would be in deadly danger. So my sister said 'Tommy, his prayers were answered and mother is glad as well'. She said I would be represented by the rest of them at his funeral, 'for us' she said 'it will be the same as if you are there'. I felt better about that and went back to my cell a happier man. The O.C. and the governor asked me if there was anything that I wanted. I said no and that I just wanted to be left in peace, so that's what they did. They gave me their condolences and they left me mourn in peace. My father's funeral was like a British army military camp. The Brits were everywhere, and that was only the ones you could see. My father got the traditional Irish wake and funeral. He played the fiddle in a Céilí band in his young day; he'd take the old fiddle down at night and play all the old Irish airs. The Cúlin, The Lark In The Clear Air, Danny Boy, Carolon's Concerto, The Mason's Apron and countless more traditional airs. He used to call me "Danny boy" as it was my favourite tune. So they played all these old airs at his funeral. Some of the best fiddlers in Ireland turned up to give him this tribute, he would have loved that. It was one of the biggest funerals in that area of Tyrone for a long time. My father got the funeral he'd have wanted. He even got his last wish for me granted. He knew I would have been honour bound to be at his funeral, so he wanted me out of danger. I said my prayers for him in Mountjoy jail in Dublin City and vowed to fight on when I got out.

30

THE BATTLE ON THE BUS

WE WENT FROM the I.R.A. wing of Mountjoy jail for a court appearance in John Joe's country of Balinamore, Co. Leitrim. It was before the special court in Green St. was established and not long after Bloody Sunday, when the support for the provisional I.R.A. was at its height. At that time the fight in the north was a popular uprising, spearheaded by the provisional I.R.A. The arrests made on the I.R.A. men along the border were token arrests to show the British government that the Fianna Fáil government led by Jack Lynch was doing something. Provisional I.R.A. men at that particular time were very popular. So when this group of I.R.A. men were taken from Mountjoy jail on this lovely spring morning it was a C.I.E. coach that pulled up at the gates of the prison! Everyone was in high spirits, I.R.A. men, our Garda escorts and the bus driver. As we pulled out of the North Circular Road in Dublin City for the long drive up to Balinamore in Co. Leitrim, John Joe's Country, it was like a bus tour to the North West. There was about 15 or 16 I.R.A. men on board and about 20 Gardaí, mostly young fellas with a couple of senior ranking Gardaí who were in charge. They were a friendly bunch of Gardaí and we all got on well. The I.R.A. men were mostly from Tyrone and Armagh. Ned, my best mate and comrade, Coalisland Kevin, Tommy from Lurgan, T.C. from Dungannon, same as me, Seamus from Armagh City, and a couple of his comrades. All in all we made up a tough but friendly enough group of I.R.A. men. We had all been arrested at different times along the border, but were now all on the way to a court appearance in Balinamore Co. Leitrim. No-one was worried about today's court; it would just be a five minute appearance. None of the district justices were handing out jail sentences to I.R.A. men anyway so there wasn't much to worry about. Today was just an appearance, the next day we would probably get off on some technicality or get a caution and let go. We were needed in the fight.

In the meantime the C.I.E. bus rolled along the country roads as we made our way up to lovely Leitrim. We had set off early, about 7 o'clock in the morning and we pulled into Balinamore at about 10 o'clock. As we all filed of the bus a big crowd of supporters were there to cheer us. We were like a G.A.A. football team just after winning the county final! They clapped us on the back as we made our way into the small country courtroom and took up most of the seats in it. The local justice came in very solemnly! This was his domain, he was boss! We all stood and he sat down and surveyed the scene. I'm sure he was thinking, there's a crowd today. The first case called was a local middle aged bachelor farmer, who was found drunk driving his tractor home from the local cattle mart, the Gardaí had to lift him out of the cab and let him sober up in the local Garda station cell. The judge evidently knew the offending farmer well. He asked him did he get a good price for his cattle and was that why he was celebrating? The farmer mumbled in a very trite voice, 'they did well justice, they did well'. The court burst out laughing and the justice looked suitably stern at everyone until silence prevailed again. The justice looked kindly enough down on the unfortunate farmer, like he was some kind of delinquent but favourite child. I will apply the probation act this time, don't do it again and put some money in the court poor box. The middle aged bachelor farmer looked a bit shocked and surprised. Someone whispered the shock was because he would have to part with some money!! The whole scene was very funny. There were a few more cases for the justice, which mirrored Irish rural life at that time.

The inspector of the Gardaí and the sergeant went forward to the justice and whispered a few words in his ear. The justice cleared his throat and said importantly 'I'll take the I.R.A. men's cases next'. Our cases were called one after the other. All were put back to another court day. The whole hearing took about ten minutes. We filed out of the courtroom into another room in the courthouse, where all our main supporters including John Joe, the Sinn Féin T.D. in the Leitrim area, a very popular man who owned a pub on the main street in Balinamore. There were a group of women, young and old, who had home cooked food in containers and bags for us, it smelled great! We started to eat and gave the Gardaí something to eat too. It was lovely food and there was loads of it. Then John Joe came in with a bottle of whiskey and some beers and we were having a good drink as well as good food! The Gardaí looked a bit uneasy at the start but we gave them a shot of whiskey and a few beers as well and they were happy to join the party. John Joe went back to the pub for more beers and spirits, drinks to order this time, drinks to order for the Gardaí as well. It was a real relaxed atmosphere in the side room in the old courthouse. It could only happen in Ireland! After about an hour or so we all said goodbye to our cooks and supporters and filed out into the bright sunshine and back onto the bus.

Everyone took their seats and the bus pulled out of Balinamore on its way back to Mountjoy jail in Dublin City. We had a few spare bottles of beer and a small amount of spirits left and we drank it as we went along the road. We made sure the Gardaí handcuffed to us got a wee drink as well. It was all good craic. After sometime into the journey Coalisland Kevin asked the chief of the Gardaí to stop the bus as he needed a piss. The Garda Chief obliged and the bus pulled up along the roadside and we all got out. It must have been an odd looking sight for the few passing motorists! Garda with prisoners handcuffed to them standing along the roadside, side by side on the roadside, pissing away, not a care in the world. We all got back on board to continue our journey south to Dublin. The spare drink ran out and we would have loved to have more. An I.R.A. man had started to sing Sean South from Gerryowen. Some of the Gardaí joined in as they knew the words too. Coalisland Kevin and T.C. from Dungannon were up talking to the Chief Garda trying to persuade him to stop at the next village pub to stock up on drink to keep the party going. The chief Garda, who was a good sport, agreed to stop, provided that Coalisland Kevin guaranteed that no I.R.A. man would try an escape. Kevin gave his word and then announced that the bus was stopping at the next village pub so that we could buy some drinks; no-one will attempt to escape he ordered, I've given my word to the chief Garda. No escapes, we agreed. We made a collection of money to pay for the drinks - some of the Gardaí gave money too. We pulled into the next village and parked up alongside the local pub and filed out of the bus. We went to the toilets two at a time, a Garda and his prisoner handcuffed to him. Then we made our way back to the public bar. Kevin was at the counter buying the drinks to take away. Suddenly he said to the barman, who couldn't believe his eyes, 'give everybody a drink before we go'. The barman looked at the Chief Garda who was standing guard at the pub door, he nodded his head, 'give them one drink'. The barman did as he was told and set up a halfun and a bottle for everybody. We all drank up and then the Gardaí, not to be bested by the I.R.A. men, ordered a round of drink for everybody as well. At this stage there was an I.R.A. man walking around with his handcuff dangling down with no Garda on the end of it. His Garda had let him go to the toilet on his own! The I.R.A. man obeyed orders and didn't try to escape; anyway the craic was too good to want to escape!

The Chief Garda called time and everybody, went back onto the C.I.E. bus for the rest of the journey. T.C. from Dungannon had talked the Chief Garda into letting him do barman on the bus. He was now free from his handcuffs and handing out the drinks for everybody. Several I.R.A. men were singing rebel songs and so were the Gardaí. It was like something out of a film. Suddenly I noticed Kevin in an argument with the Chief Garda. Kevin was getting annoyed. He couldn't hold his drink anyway at the best of times! He was like a hand grenade with the pin pulled when he had drink taken. He was totally unpredictable. Suddenly, Kevin turned around to us and said 'I want the bus stopped for another piss, this man (the Chief Garda) has said no, I've told him either he stops the bus, or he gets a fight, and I have the men to do it'. The Chief Garda had said he had wasted too much time already and couldn't and wouldn't stop the bus again. Suddenly Kevin hit the Chief Garda. The Chief Garda hit back, Kevin hit him again shouting 'attack, attack, ATTACK!' All hell broke loose! Prisoners and Gardaí were fighting each other up and down the bus. The Sergeant of the Gardaí was on the radio to his superiors, he was shouting into the radio mic 'We're under attack, WE'RE UNDER ATTACK, the commander of the I.R.A. on the bus has ordered an attack, we're under attack, we're under attack'. It was mayhem! I saw a Garda hit my best mate Ned and I reached over and hit the Garda who hit Ned. I hit him under the chin. The Garda who was handcuffed to me hit me, a dig on the side of the head with his fist. I hit him back on the nose and it spurted blood like a fountain. I got punched several times in the face by different Gardaí. My eyes, my nose, mouth and forehead were all bleeding. I was giving as good as I got, but it was a tough battle in such a confined space. The bus was rocking from side to side like a boat in a storm. It was in danger of turning over. Suddenly half a dozen squad cars overtook us. The bus driver pulled over to the grass verge, and all the drink was thrown out and Garda reinforcements boarded the bus and got control of it again. Every bone in my body was sore. I couldn't see out of my eyes they were that swollen. My face, hands and jumper were soaked in blood. Both my hands were cuffed to the seat rail. A Garda had his knee right in my groin, if I had tried to move he dug his knee into my belly. It was agonizing. I had to stay still.

The bus had quieted down again. It arrived in Dublin Mountjoy Jail hours late. The governor of the jail refused to accept me, Kevin, Ned, T.C., Tommy and several of the worst injured. He said he'd have a riot on his hands if the rest of the I.R.A. men in the jail saw the state of us. The glasshouse in the Curragh Irish army camp in Co. Kildare had also been opened for I.R.A. men. 'You may take them to the Curragh military camp'; the governor said 'I'm not having them here'. We were put back on the bus and drove down to the Curragh of Kildare and put into the glasshouse, a military detention jail with a glass roof; hence the name 'the glasshouse'. The I.R.A. men already in the jail were locked in their cells before we were let in. We got supper in our new cells before we went to bed to sleep it off. It had been an eventful day, one hell of a day! I enjoyed every bit of it! I was a bit sore all over, but hey, where would you get a day like that! The next morning we were the centre of attention in the jail. Everyone wanted to hear what had happened. They couldn't believe their ears. We never got C.I.E. buses ever again to court! It was black prison vans the next day, but I'll never forget that spin on the C.I.E. bus up to Balinamore Co.Leitrim. That was a one off day in life, it could never happen again! This incident was officially forgotten about by the Gardai, we never heard about it again.

31

1973
A TOUGH YEAR: THE FIGHT TAKES ITS TOLL

IRONICALLY THE CHARGES were dropped against me when it came to court. The Gardaí never found the two rifles I hid, so without the guns their case against me fell apart. Ned got a two year sentence. I went back to Monaghan town and lived in a wee terrace house in Park Street. This house was the home of Fergal O'Hanlon, who was killed in an ambush during the '56 campaign, the song 'The Patriot Game' was written about him. I lived at this house on and off for the next few years and it would feature a lot in my life. When I got out of jail after my father's death I was told to take a while off as I had gone through a hard few years and with all that had happened me I deserved a good break. I stayed in the wee house in Park Street; Fergal's father and brother lived there. It was a busy little house, comings and goings all the time. J.B. a '56 man from Lurgan was the top I.R.A. man in that area. A more honest decent straight up front man no-one could ever meet. He was a dedicated republican fighter, very calm, cool headed; there was no bullshit with J.B. I respected J.B. as much as I had ever respected any man, I got on well with him. He was the quartermaster and he made me his right hand man, with responsibility for moving war materials up from the southern units and distributing them into the mid Ulster area, East Tyrone, south Derry, south west Antrim and parts of Fermanagh. I loved working with J.B. When he was away on I.R.A. business down the country I filled in for him. I got to know a lot about the running of the war against the Brits in that area. My loyalty and respect for J.B. was unlimited. We also still co-ordinated with the training camps. Men would be coming all the time on the run, those who decided to stay and fight had to be accommodated locally, the rest went on down the country or emigrated on to America. There was no pressure on any man to stay on and fight; it was always a personal decision. I had another safe house out the country that I loved to stay in. Mick was an old man who lived on his own, he'd been married and all his family lived in England. He still did a bit of part time work on his old farm. It reminded me of home and Mick was a real character, loved the drink and the craic. He knew everything about the whole border area and loved to sit by the fire at night into the early hours of the morning telling stories about the times he lived through. He was a real local historian and loved to have us in his house. He used to send me to milk the cows and get the milk out for collection when he'd be too sick to do it himself! I'd often get the word from some of the lads 'Come and milk the cows'. I'd always do it, if I could at all. Myself, Red Joe and Big Paddy were his main men, he loved Big Paddy like a son, and they were very close. The three of us often stayed in there. It was one of those long old farm houses with byres and out houses at each end with a very long lane that took you up the side of a mountain overlooking the border. You could see for miles around and it was a very safe place. Myself, Red and Big Paddy often stayed in there together, we'd all have our own I.R.A. duties to carry out, so we could be in different places at different times, on active service for the I.R.A. But every now and again we'd meet up at old Mick's and sit talking and swopping stories into the early hours. While we were not as much together anymore we were still closer than brothers. We had a great laugh about a holiday we went on in Bundoran, Co. Donegal that summer. There had been a fundraiser in Dungannon, Co. Tyrone that week, Big Paddy and Red were on that job. It was a success by our finance team, and so we met up at old Mick's afterwards. We were allocated a bit of money by the finance officer and told to take a break. The finance officer controlled all I.R.A. money, proceeds of the I.R.A. fundraisers were handed over to his control and he gave it out to units as it was needed. I.R.A. finance officers were very tight fisted. It was like getting blood out of a stone. So we got some money and headed to Bundoran, Co. Donegal. We went the long way around the border in an old wreck of a car and it got a flat wheel on the mountains near the Shannon Pot at Blacklion. We spent the night on the mountain singing rebel songs; we were young and didn't give a damn! Big Paddy had escaped out of the Curragh detention camp, I had beaten an extradition order and Red had just got out of the North in the nick of time. So we had all reason to be happy up on that mountain. We also had a young neighbour of mine from home who was in Fianna Éireann and had escaped out of a borstal school in Belfast. We kind of had him 'under our wings' and were looking after him. He'd real long hair and looked like the lead singer in the rock band Thin Lizzy. He was mad into T-Rex. Mad as a hatter and full of life! He would get captured in co Tyrone and do many years in jail. So we sang and acted the bollix until the next morning. We paid a farmer to fix our wheel for us and headed on into Bundoran. We bought some new clothes, booked into the hotel of a supporter in main street Bundoran, lived it up for ten glorious women-chasing carefree days and then headed back to Monaghan and old Mick's high up on the mountain!! Mick welcomed us in with his usual hospitality but I thought he was a bit worried looking. Later on that night he came out and told us that he had been raided by the special branch Gardaí when we had been away; but it was alright, there was nothing found. Our dump was away down the back of the mountain and was safe. Big Paddy was worried, he was wanted for escaping from the Curragh detention camp and wanted to stay free. He said to me later on that night that there was no back door in the old farm house and that was bad - even if he could see the special branch coming up the mountain lane he wouldn't be able to get out. The next morning at breakfast we looked at the little kitchen window at the back of the house. It was just a little stationary window about 2.6 x 2.6 and it didn't open. The bedroom ones were the same. We asked old Mick would he mind if we did a job on the little window and made it an opening window. Mick laughed and said 'not at all, work away'. Me and Big Paddy got some tools out of old Mick's tool shed and set about doing a job on the window. We prized the inner frame with the glass in it until we separated it from the outer frame and lifted it out. We looked at the opening that it left and I looked at big Paddy's 6ft frame and said 'you're never going to get out of that, you idiot'. But he did! It was by going head first and falling into the ditch at the back of the house, up the bank and away down the mountain. Me and Red laughed our heads off at the antics of Big Paddy. But he was satisfied that he now had an escape route. We asked old Mick to get us a couple of small hinges for the window frame to open it, and a small latch to secure it, and he said he would. Just then a car with three men in it pulled up outside the old farmyard. I recognised the two passengers. One was a young Cork man who came up as a training officer for the camps but joined the East Tyrone Brigade and classed himself an honouree Tyrone man. Dermot from Cork he was known as. The other man was a real character, he was from Dungannon. He had been active in the '56 campaign and when it fizzled out in early sixties he went to work in England. He'd got married over there but when the fight broke out again in the early seventy's he came home to join the struggle again. A little black haired, swarthy skinned fella, he was known as 'The Crow' a real joker with a great sense of humour. He was great company. Big Paddy went out to them and a few minutes later came back in for his coat and said to me and Red 'I'm away; I'll see you in a few days'. Me and Joe said goodbye to him and he jumped into the car and drove off down the mountain lane. We knew that Big Paddy was going north on an operation and we both silently wished him good luck. We never saw Big Paddy alive again after that. The bomb they were transporting to a commercial target in Co. Tyrone went off prematurely in the car. Big Paddy, The Crow and Dermot the Cork man died instantly. Me, Joe and the young lad T-Rex that came to Bundoran with us were hard hit. Big Paddy was dead. We couldn't believe it. The man who was so full of life in Bundoran, the comrade who was as brave as they came, the sound man you could have trusted with your life with as we often did, was gone. Old Mick was broken hearted. He looked upon Big Paddy as a son. He sat at the fire in the old farmhouse, tears streaming down his old wrinkly face; he made no sound, just sat by the fire with his head bowed and silently cried tears of bitterness and sorrow. I went for a walk up the mountain just too think quietly to myself, I couldn't shed tears, I was too hard and tough for that, but the sorrow and pain and loss was so painful. It was right into the very core of my being. We had already lost so many volunteers from the East Tyrone Brigade, but none as close as these three men. This was a hard hard blow, but we knew that any of us could die in this fight at any time. This was war and people die in a war; that is the brutal fact of it all. They weren't the first of our comrades from east Tyrone to die, and unfortunately they wouldn't be the last. Not by a long way. Joe decided to go north for Big Paddy and The Crows funeral, or at least as close as he could get to it. Dermot had left word with his family in Cork that if anything ever happened to him in the fight he wanted four comrades from the East Tyrone Brigade to do the honours for him and carry him into his grave. Myself and Ned, Sig from Coalisland and Dan from Eglish, Co. Tyrone, who was also on the run, went down to Cork to carry the coffin of our fallen comrade. Dermot the Cork man came from a big working class housing estate known as Mayfield, in the north of Cork city. The cemetery was in the countryside just outside the city. We met his family who thanked us for coming down as they knew how much it meant to Dermot. We'd have gone to the end of the earth for him, and it was an honour for us to do it. Myself, Ned, Dan and Sig carried our dead comrade 'Dermot' from the hearse to his grave and then got in our car and drove back to Monaghan to fight on. Big Paddy and The Crow were laid to rest just outside Dungannon on the same day. Old Mick went to Big Paddy's funeral, I went back out to his old farmhouse after coming back from Cork and milked his cows and did the usual farm chores because he was drinking heavily and wasn't able to do it himself. When I was there he said that he was sorry to have to ask me to do it, but would I finish off doing the window as it wasn't secure and he was afraid of it falling out. I told him not to worry that I would do it before I left. I put the hinges and latch on the window the next day and it was then that the tears ran down my face for Big Paddy. I was glad I was alone. I gathered up the tools when I was finished and put them back into old Mick's shed where me and big Paddy had got them out of just a short time ago. Old Mick told me years after that, he never opened that window and neither did I. I still used old Mick's as a safe house for years after, but it was never the same, there was always sadness there. But I still loved that old farmhouse way up on the mountain as a quiet place to go when things got rough and to rest up. I'd need it again sooner than expected; life was tough and cruel in the year of 1973.

32

THE CONFLICT GOES ON

I WENT BACK into the wee house in Park Street Monaghan after that. J.B. had organized a big old house in Mill Street opposite the Post Office for men on the run. A lot of men had come over the border in previous months so the big house that was laid out in flats was very useful. Dan lived there in one of the flats with his wife Bertha. They made a lovely, quiet couple. Bertha had got work in a shop in Monaghan town. Dan was one of the men that decided to fight on after he came on the run. Tyrone I.R.A. men used these flats as their home when they came to Monaghan town. Patsy escaped out of a young people's prison in Belfast. He and his mates were sent down the country as they were considered too young to fight. Patsy wouldn't settle down there, and came back into Monaghan. Dan took him under his wing and was like a father to him. Ned H. joined Fermanagh I.R.A. and spent most of his years as a very active volunteer in that area. He was a brave and dedicated I.R.A. fighter. All these men and more were available for active service with the East Tyrone Brigade I.R.A. along with volunteers who still lived in east Tyrone. We had a very well organized fighting unit. The Fox was an older man, also stayed in Mill Street. His house in Tyrone was a safe house. The I.R.A. were organising an operation there when the Brits came up the lane, The Fox shouted 'run for it lads' and he along with others got away. The Brits carried out a "controlled explosion" on the fox's car and it promptly set his house on fire! Controlled explosion how do! He was our driver, and was supplied with an old but sound Morris 1800, a big, old, white car. The fox called it the I.R.A. staff car. He looked after the flats - got in grub, washed the clothes and so forth. He loved keeping things in order for his 'cubs' as he called us! He was a very shrewd, smart, street wise man; he watched out for us in every way. The fox was nobody's fool. I.R.A. men were given an allowance of £8 a week for socialising, at that time a fiver would have got you a good night out. When we went into the north on active service, for weeks at a time, the fox would have the money for us when we got back into town. He loved to go with us for a good party. He loved having the craic with the 'cubs'!

When I.R.A. men went into the north on active service there was a lot of organising to be done. On the run men would join up with the home based men to carry out operations. The on the run I.R.A. men would carry out the barefaced parts of the op. and so save the home based men from the danger of being recognized and pulled in by the Brits and R.U.C. The R.U.C. were the eyes and ears of the British army. They were the ones who knew the locals and the local roads etc. A bigoted bad shower of bastards they also colluded with loyalist murder gangs. They were gangs made up of protestant extremists whose sole purpose was to murder innocent catholic nationalist people at random, so as to intimidate the people from giving their support to the local I.R.A. units. It said a lot for the steadfast courage of the catholic people as they never allowed themselves to be intimidated. A lot of them were shot and killed by those murderous gangs made up of the R.U.C., U.D.A., U.V.F., S.A.S. etc. These gangs made a very determined effort over the years to terrorize our support base within the nationalist catholic population and cut the I.R.A. units off from the people, but they never succeeded. Our support base held firm for over 25 years of Guerrilla warfare. We hit the R.U.C., U.D.A., U.V.F. and S.A.S. murder gangs as often as we could, but we never allowed ourselves to be drawn into 'tit for tat' shootings of innocent Protestants, just because it would have been easy to do so. While we had a duty to defend the catholic nationalist population, and we were always acutely aware of this, we could not allow ourselves to be drawn into the shooting of innocent protestant people. But the I.R.A. did take action every time it could, to reach those that were carrying out these cowardly murders of defenceless innocent catholic people. It was always a thorn in our side that we could not get to these murder squads as often as we would have liked to; but we hit the R.U.C., U.D.R., as these ones were as guilty and were easier to identify. The fox used to say to us 'you cubs will beat the Brits but you still have another enemy to contend with when you have that done' He meant the U.D.R., R.U.C. and Loyalist paramilitaries that would have to be confronted and defeated. It turned out he was right. We had no problem with our ordinary protestant neighbours, we truly believed in a post Brit

Ireland where Protestant, Catholic and dissenter could live in Ireland in peace and religious freedom. The only requirement that we had on that was that you would put your shoulder in behind the 'wheel of Ireland' and push. If you could do that we didn't care what religion you were or if you had none. But if you insisted that you were British, after a British withdrawal from Ireland, it wouldn't matter to us if you were protestant pro British or catholic pro British (they did exist) or just pro British - if you loved them that much, then we believed those people should just go live with them. Simple as that. But we would cross that bridge when we came to it. That bridge was still some way off, we had to get rid of the British army and British establishment first.

33

THE ATTACK ON POMEROY BARRACKS

A BIG ATTACK was being planned by the East Tyrone Brigade I.R.A. on a British army barracks in Pomeroy in the mountainous area of Tyrone. This mountainous area of Tyrone was known as God's Own Country. It was a 95% catholic nationalist area and we used it a lot for the safe keeping of I.R.A. men and war materials. This old barracks had been taken over by the British army. The R.U.C., U.D.R. would have been unable to man this isolated barracks on their own. A barracks in the middle of this stronghold of ours, was not acceptable and would have to go. The southern units had perfected homemade mortar launchers and mortars capable of being fired from the hills near this barracks. We would use them and heavily arm units with R.P.G. Russian made rocket launchers, A.K.47 machine guns etc. We would throw everything we had at them. The I.R.A. was out on the Brogan Mountains near the Fermanagh Tyrone border, training on these weapons. The mortar launchers had come from the southern units. Some of their experts were on the training site to help out. Dan was on the mortar launcher, a very intelligent man, he soon had it mastered. Young Patsy was handing him the mortars. These training mortars had no explosives in them yet but they weighed the same as an armed one, so as to give the men the ability to work out the distance from which to fire them; the height, the length etc. They had a map of the barracks, the hills, and the position they were going to use as a launching pad for the mortar lorry. The launcher was to be welded onto the back of a lorry and loaded up with 25 live mortars and launched down on top of the Brits barracks. The machine gun unit would open up to deny the Brits access to their armoured cars and helicopters. The plan was to keep them in the barracks until the mortars brought it tumbling down around their heads. Dan was launching the mortars from the launching lorry, young Patsy and a home based I.R.A. man would prime them and then hand them to Dan. Young Patsy was reluctantly allowed to join this operation. Dan was looking after him. A home based I.R.A. man drove the lorry. Two of the men on the run were leaders of the machine gun units. A number of home based I.R.A. men made up the rest, about 10 I.R.A. men in each unit. Overall, we had men driving the teams to the site of the operation, scouts to check the roads, safe houses to come from near the barracks for the attack, safe houses a good distance away from the barracks to go to after the attack, and safe places to dump the weapons. A lot of effort and organizing went into an operation like this, we hoped it would go well and was worth all the trouble and danger to I.R.A. men and women and all the backup teams involved. As long as everyone returned safely to base, that was the main thing. But we hoped to really hit them hard at this barracks in the heart of republican Tyrone, and drive them out of the barracks and the area.

I volunteered to go on the operation. But Dan and Ned said to me that J.B. wasn't in town and someone like me who knew how things worked in Monaghan was needed to be there. Anyway, they said, the last position had been filled and no-one else was needed. Ned looked at me and said really seriously, 'Wish us luck, this is going to be a tough one, a very tough one, there might be men not coming back'. I knew the I.R.A. men were moving into Tyrone over the next few days, into safe houses near the barracks. I wished my good friend and comrade good luck and hoped I would see him when he came back into town when the attack was over. To move men into and through the north was an operation in itself. Especially men whose photos were at permanent check points and road blocks. A safe car would meet them at a pre-arranged safe house on the southern side of the border. This car would always be driven by someone very respectable. A business man or woman in a good car, taxed, insured. This person would always carry their license, insurance cert, wallet, cheque books, credit cards, membership cards of the unionist party or alliance party! This person would also have a wallet for the I.R.A. man, full of identification of their brother or make believe brother so the I.R.A. man would assume that identification for the journey. The I.R.A. man would also be dressed very well. A set of golf clubs or a couple of fishing rods would complete the identification necessities. It would also help if the I.R.A. man knew as much as possible about the driver's family in case they would be questioned separately at checkpoints. There were numerous times these respectable people got us through these checkpoints with a parting 'have a good game mate' or 'good luck fishing, hope you catch a few mate' or if it was a woman 'have a nice meal'. They were looking for straggly dressed I.R.A. men in combat jackets and big boots, not these very well dressed golfers, fishermen, middle class couples or smart business men who were members of the unionist party, or the ultra respectable alliance party. We always had a good laugh at that! Moving war material was different as we had to use the scout system, as we did for I.R.A. men as well. It worked like this: two cars would go ahead of the vehicle with the war material and I.R.A. men in it, these drivers were under strict instructions, not to use an indicator for any left or right turn under any circumstances, the only time an indicator was to be used was when there was immediate danger. So the three vehicles would drive in convoy. If the first car drove into an army checkpoint it would put on its indicator. The second car would see its indicator and immediately put its indicator on as well. The I.R.A. men in the third car would read the danger signal and immediately take action. This system worked well for moving many I.R.A. men and war materials through the six occupied counties of the north and in the south as well. The mobile phone didn't exist then. How handy it would have been, but we made our own ways of out smarting the enemy and it worked. Local people who worked with us always scouted the roads on an ongoing basis, they were our eyes and our ears. Without local help the I.R.A. unit could not survive, they were an unending source of information, intelligence and support. We also used what we fondly called the 'Ho Chi Minh Trail'. This was a trail over the fields from the border bridge at Aughnacloy. A dozen or so I.R.A men and local helpers would each take a large bag of war materials on their backs, and complete the half hour trek over the fields to a pre-arranged spot where a van, also driven by I.R.A volunteers, would be waiting. We'd silently dump all of our gear into the van. The van would take off into county Tyrone and we would return over the 'Ho Chi Minh Trail' back into Co. Monaghan. This route was used very often and was only a very short distance from a huge, permanent British army base at Aughnacloy. We used the 'Ho Chi Minh Trail' to bypass this huge British base right under their noses! This system was made possible by the vigilance and intelligence of two old republican sympathisers who lived beside this famous trail. Through these two old men we knew every move of the Brits in this area! We owed these two old men a huge debt for our continued safety in this very dangerous area.

So this movement of I.R.A. men and war materials went on for the next week. Soon the job of moving large number of I.R.A. men and war materials near to the Brits barracks in the republican area of county Tyrone was completed. It was all systems go. I was sitting in the wee house in Park Street the night the attack was to take place, when the door opened and Bertha, Dan's wife came in. The house of flats in Mill Street is too quiet she said with nobody there. She sat down and I made her a cup of tea. We were sitting there chatting when the Radio Éireann news came on at a quarter to midnight. It said that a British army barracks in the Pomery area of county Tyrone had come under heavy I.R.A. attack and that no casualties had been reported. Bertha said to me, 'they wont be too pleased with that' but she was happy enough that no casualties had been reported on either side. She got up to leave and I could see the relief in her face for she knew that it had been a dangerous operation. I asked her would I walk her around to the Mill Street house and she kindly refused and said she was happy now, and that the fresh air would do her good. I bid her goodnight and she left.

No casualties, I thought. But then the attack might have just ended, and the Brits always hid their battle losses and defeats if they possibly could. The morning light would tell a truer story I thought, and went to bed. The old man of the house and his son were already in bed so I put off the light and went to sleep. The next thing I knew there was a small stone being thrown at the bedroom window, which was situated at the back of the little house, as you could walk up an entry from the footpath. I looked out the window and saw an I.R.A. man from the north that I knew as Pat the Bard. I told him to open the window beside the door and let himself in, and I'd be down in a minute. I dressed and went down the steep stairs of the little house; the kitchen door was on the right at the bottom of the stairs. I opened it and walked in. I said, 'Well Pat?' He looked at me and said 'Dan and young Pasty died last night'. I was hit with shock, I was not expecting what he was after saying, I was not expecting it at all. 'Yea', he said, 'they both died on the attack at the barracks and we have a badly injured I.R.A. man as well, we got him as far as the hospital. He was very badly injured'. The attack turned into a nightmare, one of the mortars went off in the launcher prematurely and killed Dan and Patsy instantly.

The injured I.R.A. man was also on the back of the lorry. 'I have to go', he said, 'we are all still sorting out the bodies, we are going to have to get them into Dungannon hospital morgue so they can be sorted out. They have terrible injuries'. I took him by the hand and caught him by the shoulder and said, 'Jesus, I'm sorry Pat' and the next thing I knew he was gone. Bertha, I thought, God almighty poor Bertha, how am I going to tell her? It was 7 o' clock, she'd be getting ready for work in an hour, I have to go around to her before that. Jesus, how was I going to do it? The old man and his son had got up. They were both very annoyed and shocked. The priest's house and the chapel were just across the street. Father Cassidy was his name. I'd better get him I thought, and he will come around with me. 'There are two nurses that live around the next street' the son said 'in a flat, I'll go around for them, they're sound' he said. I went over to the priest's house and knocked him up, he came over to the little house and then the son arrived with the two nurses. I said 'We'd better go around there it's a quarter to eight' So the four of us walked around to the Mill Street house and I let myself in. We went up the stairs and into the big living room with the old Aga cooker in it. Bertha heard me from the rooms below and shouted to me 'Is that you Tommy?' I called back and said, 'Yes it's me. I'll be up in a minute'. She called back, 'Just ready for work'. She sounded light hearted and happy. I winced with pain. What am I about to do to this wee girl's life? Just then the door from the rooms opened and Bertha took about two steps in and halted in her tracks. She looked at the priest, looked at me, back at the priest and the colour just drained from her face, the white started from just below her hairline and drained down her face and disappeared down her neckline. White as a sheet. I never knew what that old saying meant until that day. She said to me, 'It's Dan isn't it?' I nodded. 'How bad?' she asked. Just at that the priest stepped forward and said 'Bertha, Dan is dead. He died last night'. The two nurses caught her before she could fall and eased her into a chair, they gave her a glass of water and held it to her lips. Just then Dan's sister and family came in and took her into their arms and hugged her, they were all crying uncontrollably in that terrible place of complete grief that I think only women can truly reach. The devastated mother, and the inconsolable widow: these two suffer the most in war and conflict.

I quietly left the flat and made my way up to the hospital. I sought out a worker, who was one of our supporters. I asked him about the injured

I.R.A. man. He went away for a while, then came back and said to me 'He has really bad injuries, very bad, but he is going to live. It will be a long road of recovery for him, but he will make it'. Thank God for that I thought. I went back down to the flat in Mill Street, there was nobody there. I closed over the door and made my way back down to Park Street, the little house was fairly crowded with people. I got the keys of my car and went out to Rossmore Park; full of trees and rocks and rivers and little walkways. I walked about aimlessly just trying to get my head together. Jesus, Dan and Patsy. Patsy was only sixteen, Dan was only in his mid twenties; I wasn't much over twenty myself. We were all so young. We should have been off in Spain on a holiday with our girlfriends, playing G.A.A., working and making a life for ourselves, instead of been stuck in the middle of this conflict, a conflict we didn't send for, or want. I was really angry and bitter about all the suffering I'd seen this year; my father, my comrades, one after the other. I was sick of it, damn partition! Damn the Brits! I thought of my other comrades up in east Tyrone, the terrible night they had had, lying low in safe houses in Brit occupied Tyrone, while their enemies searched everywhere for them. I hoped they would all make it back to Monaghan safely, over the next week or two. It wasn't an easy time for them. I vowed to fight on. If only to save another generation from our kind of suffering. The whole northern nationalist republican catholic community was suffering terribly. I don't like your war mother Ireland, I don't like it one little bit, but I'll fight it, and I'll fight to win! I'll give it everything I have to give! I got back into my car and drove slowly into Monaghan town.

34

THE FUNERALS

THE FUNERALS TOOK place in Tyrone over the next week. The injured I.R.A. man was still in intensive care in hospital. He was a tough hardy fella. He would survive. It would take him a long time to recover, but not only did he recover he joined the border I.R.A. men and began active service again. A big, quiet fella, but as tough as they came and very resilient. He and I became lifelong good friends. Rossmore park had trees of all kind in it including laurel trees. The laurel wreath is the soldier's wreath, made from the flat oval shaped evergreen leaf of the laurel tree. Moss and twigs are used as well. It is woven into a circular shape and is about 30 inches across from side to side. It is a wreath with a special significance to the fallen solider. The son at the little house in Park Street was an artist, a gifted man. He was like a monk in appearance, the Jesus sandals, no socks in summer or winter, the little goatee beard and always dressed really casual. He drew plans for houses and extensions, for payment. Money meant nothing to him. He could have made a fortune drawing portraits of sons and daughters of wealthy people. His ability to do perfect likeness of his subjects was uncanny. You'd think you were looking at a photograph of the person. But he'd turn wealthy customers away, with a little shrug of the shoulders, 'Ah I don't like those people, I won't paint anything for them'. Yet he spent days perfecting a portrait of my younger sister for no payment at all. He was about as eccentric as artists come; a real character. It was him who made the laurel wreaths for the dead I.R.A. men of East Tyrone Brigade. Whichever I.R.A. men happened to be in Monaghan town at the time of their comrades death would go out to Rossmore Park and pick the laurel leaves, moss and twigs that were used to make the wreaths and bring them up to the little loft workhouse, and help him make the wreaths; one for each dead I.R.A. man. These would be taken to the I.R.A. man's family and would get pride of place at the funeral. They were always the first wreath to be laid on the grave. The artist would often go on the drink after making the laurel wreaths, sometimes for days 'to drown his sorrows' he'd say. He had a special concoction of a drink he used to drink. I think he thought he was mixing paints, so many different drinks went into it, but while he could get very drunk sometimes, none of the pubs ever barred him. He was a bit of a character all the time, but especially when he had a few drinks. He had a sister who was married to a Wexford man and they lived in Wexford. A great couple, Matt & Padraigín, they had several children and always loved coming up to Monaghan to the old family home and spend weekends there. They used to love to meet the men and made very good friends with a lot of them, including me. They took me down to Wexford that autumn of '73 for a break. They took me to meet a lot of republican supporters in that famous county of 1798. Vinegar Hill, Father Murphy, All the great names of men and places I had learnt about and sang about since early schooldays. It was amazing to be at all these famous historical places in reality. We went out to Kilmore Quay and the J.F.K. memorial park and the old ancestral home of J.F.K. We got photos taken in that famous park and they still have them to this very day. They moved back up to Monaghan after Padraigín's father's death and still live there in the wee Park Street house, an Irish speaking family, one of the few families that use the Irish language as their everyday language. It's very special. They became very involved in the local and national politics in Sinn Féin and Padraigín represents that party at town and county level. A very hard working and popular family in Monaghan, they're still great old friends of mine, and I still call to visit them in the wee Park Street house. I can remember that short holiday I had in Wexford as one of the happiest times I had during my time in Monaghan as an active service I.R.A. man.

35

STRANGER THAN FICTION

SOMETIME TOWARDS THE end of that year the north Armagh brigade arrested a man believed to have connections to loyalist paramilitaries in mid-Ulster. Mid-Ulster loyalist murder gangs were very active through all these years. It was a constant effort to try and stop them from murdering innocent catholic civilians. They interrogated the man with the loyalist paramilitary connections and passed on the contents of his interrogation to Monaghan border I.R.A. There had been some loyalist paramilitary activity on the southern side of the border in recent times and the I.R.A.'s Fermanagh brigade was concerned about it. Loyalist paramilitaries were also very active in Fermanagh. I.R.A. intelligence studied this information in the report. It mentioned a name of a farmhouse on the southern side of the border that according to this report was being used in the south by loyalist paramilitaries. The report was sent on to the Fermanagh I.R.A. based in Clones, Co. Monaghan. The I.R.A. in east Tyrone were preparing another big attack on a U.D.R., R.U.C. British army base, The same I.R.A. unit that hit the barracks in Pomeroy with such tragic consequences were to hit this one also. They were moving men and war materials into the area for the operation. A lot of material was being moved through the Clones area of Co. Monaghan. Me and Bill were very much involved in this part of the operation.

When we finished moving supplies down to the border, me and Bill went back to Monaghan town. Bill went to his safe house and I went to bed in the wee house in Park Street. The next morning all hell broke loose in Co. Monaghan. There were Gardaí, Irish army and special branch everywhere. A man had been shot dead at a farmhouse near Clones. I was arrested in the little house on Park Street and taken to the barracks. The man shot dead at the burning farmhouse was a prominent politician from Co. Monaghan. Holy God! How did that happen? I was completely puzzled, and in the dark about it all. Talk about stranger than fiction, but this wasn't fiction! It was all too true. The politician was dead; I.R.A. men from Clones were charged with his murder and put in jail for life. I was charged with I.R.A. membership and given a year in jail! Portlaoise jail was the I.R.A. jail now and the court was the Greenstreet courthouse in Dublin, called the special court for I.R.A. men. Hell, how quickly did that all that happen? The attack on the barracks was successful. East Tyrone were a tough hard unit of I.R.A. men, afraid of nothing. I was proud to be their comrade. Some of them would arrive into this jail before my term would be even half served. The southern security forces and a new right wing 'law and order' Dublin government; pro Brit in their outlook would mean a lot more I.R.A. men getting arrested and jailed in the no jury, three judge special court in Green Street, Dublin. Things on the ground in the south were changing. This government was very anti-I.R.A. and collaborated with the British security forces in a bid to defeat and put down the fight for the north. They didn't succeed. Tom was in the jail too. He was great craic, he was always telling humours stories. Here is one of them.

It occurred when north Armagh I.R.A. ambushed a mobile patrol of Brits on the Keady border and they opened fire on them with rifles and machine guns. When coming away from the ambush they were arrested by Gardaí, they weren't armed at this time so it wasn't serious. They were taken to Monaghan Garda station. On arrival at the barracks that day, the sergeant took their personal things from them, which was normal when arrested. The sergeant being a friendly kind of fella would bring the I.R.A. mens' cigarettes to the hatch on the cell door and give them a smoke. Tom was in one of the cells, with his caustic, dry sense of humour. After an ambush he'd be known to lift his shirt and ask someone to check his back for holes! Tom was smoking Embassy cigarettes, and the sergeant, got to know, that this was Tom's brand. Meanwhile out at the ambush site on the Keady border Brit reinforcements arrived for the customary post-ambush search. A British army Major kicked opened the door of an old cowshed in a field and the shed blew up and killed him instantly. He was one of the highest ranking officer killed in the northern conflict. Meanwhile, back in the barracks in Monaghan the I.R.A. men had a visitor, a local supporter, who promptly told them about the Brit major caught up in their I.R.A. brigade booby trapped farm shed. When the visitor had left, Tom called the sergeant for a smoke and the sergeant brought Tom's Embassy smokes to the cell door. Tom looked the old sergeant in the eyes and said 'I don't want Embassy this time', the sergeant looked at Tom puzzled and said 'That's what you smoke'. Tom looked at him real seriously and said 'I know you're right, but this time I want to change my brand, this time I want a Major*, I love burning up Majors, give me a Major this time!' The sergeant crinkled up his face into a big grin, shook his head and walked away to tell his mates in the day room. Tom the Joker and his comrades fell about laughing in the cell! Tom and his I.R.A. comrades were promptly charged with I.R.A. membership and ended up in Portlaoise prison with us doing a year. He was always the practical joker in jail and you would never know what he would get up to. If you were going through the big D, a low period in jail which every prisoner gets once in a while, he was a great fella to snap you out of it. He could see the funny side of anything. He and I became great friends there.

*an Irish brand of cigarettes

36

PORTLAOISE JAIL,
CHRISTMAS 1973 – SEPTEMBER 1974

THE JAIL WAS filling up. I.R.A. men were being charged with membership every week. If a Garda superintendant got up in front of the three judge, no jury court in Green Street and said he believed you were a member of the I.R.A. then that was it. No further evidence was needed; his word was taken. No argument! So most of the I.R.A. men in jail were doing 12 months; some six months for membership. There was a handful doing 2 to 5 years for possession of war material, guns or explosives. There were a few from the fund raising department. There were mostly southern I.R.A. men, commandeering funds for the war. It was a thankless task, especially if you get caught. There were also a few lifers; the lifer in jail was a man apart. He was just someone you didn't annoy, leave the man alone, let him do his time; his burden was already heavy enough. I was doing a year; so with remission I would be out the following September.

I found time in jail hard enough to do, I wasn't one of these prisoners who were happy and sailed through their time no bother, these fellas did exist but they annoyed my head. To meet a man whistling down the jail early in the morning, irritated the hell out of me. I would be grumpy. Time dragged for me in jail, I always had my eye on the release date, I wasn't a whinger but I hated the place. I got on with it. Jail when you were a political prisoner wasn't too bad. The cell door was opened at 7 o'clock in the morning but the warden never called you. The same rules and regulations weren't forced on the political prisoners. Any message they would have for us would come through the 'officer in command', the O.C., of the I.R.A., in the jail. I.R.A. prisoners in jail are an I.R.A. unit, and the jail governor always worked through the O.C. for the smooth running of the jail. Most wardens were ok, except for a few who seemed set on getting a hard man reputation for themselves. There was a few of them that were just psychos. We never took any bullshit from any of them. However, mostly it was a case of 'live and let live' between I.R.A. men and prison wardens, they were mostly just doing a job for a week's pay, though we believe that every prison that had I.R.A. men in it had at least one or two government agents planted amongst the prison wardens, keeping their eyes and ears open for any loose talk or any kind of information they could get. I.R.A. men were ordered to be security conscious at all times in jail. These I.R.A. prisoners knew a lot about what was going on outside and any loose prison talk could have serious consequences for the I.R.A. at the front line. Joking and swopping stories about what happened when you were on active service outside was alright, and many a good story was told in those cells and exercise yards, it was for which brigade area could tell the biggest story! South Armagh and east Tyrone were great friends, but also great rivals. When it would come onto the radio news about a successful attack on the Brits in Crossmaglen or Cullyhanna, the south Armagh I.R.A. men would come running out of their cells, cheering and shouting, beating their chests and jumping in the air and celebrating. 'We got more of the bastards', they'd shout, delighted with themselves. Then, when news came that crown forces were killed in an ambush near Omagh or Dungannon, east Tyrone would do the same. 'Where the hell is south Armagh now?' we'd shout. 'Up east Tyrone, we'll beat the bloody Brits on our own'. It was great craic, it was great for morale! There were several brothers from south Armagh in Portlaoise at the time, hard hard tough men, the wardens were shit scared of them. Medium sized, broad bodies, broad faces with thick black beards and piercing hard eyes, they had a fierce reputation as guerrilla fighters. I said, 'you are tough bastards'. He said, 'you think we're tough, we have six brothers and they're tougher than us'. I found out they had six other brothers! He wasn't joking when he said they were tougher! He completely wrecked his cell on several occasions because something annoyed him! It was comical when the wardens came around to the cell doors with the food trolleys in the evening, every prisoner was allocated tea, bread, cheese or an egg. There was so much for each prisoner, but this man had a fierce appetite, he was always starving. The warden with the grub trolley could only look in amazement as he took enough food off the trolley for 10 men! The warden never stopped him, he knew better! We use to watch and get a good laugh! The south Armagh I.R.A. men and me became great friends and comrades. There was great mutual respect there. Respect from those type of tough guerrilla fighters didn't come easy! But east Tyrone and south Armagh had that type of respect for each other. After all, we were the best fighters in the north, he was right about that. He reckoned I was the only man in the jail who would give him a good fight, but we agreed that we would never fight for real, because one of us would end up badly hurt. We knew neither of us would give in, we were like blood brothers.

Derry city men were great fella's too. Not as tough physically as south Armagh or east Tyrone but good men all the same! South Derry men were sound too. Martin from the Bogside was on the same landing as me. He was well respected by all. He would be a peace negotiator, a household name in the future. A tough, quiet, very sincere intelligent man not to be messed with. A different type of toughness than the man from south Armagh had but very tough all the same. I used my ability for playing chess that I got from my father, to pass the time in jail, I even ran a class for beginners. Another Tyrone comrade called Kevin was in there at that time too. A Tyrone man who spent time in the tough mine fields out foreign. He was doing well out there when the conflict in the north broke out. He came home to fight. A very tough uncompromising man. The loss of his best friend and comrade Dan, who was killed during the attack in the British barracks in the mountains of Tyrone hit him hard. He said that after that he'd never give up, he'd fight for the rest of his life if need be. He went on to be part of the struggle for many years. You could easily dislike this man and many a person did, friend and foe. But he drew grudging respect from even those that did not see eye to eye with him! There was another Tyrone man in there at that time too, Kevin from Coalisland. He escaped from Mountjoy jail in Dublin by Helicopter. A '56 man who was famous for doing a life sentence for an alleged execution of a member of the crown forces in Coalisland in county Tyrone during that campaign. A brilliant man in many ways, but unpredictable and easily angered. Him and me never got on well, there was no love lost between us at all, but we tolerated each other, that was about it. He had a very good military mind and often put it to good use. A man who could get great loyalty from people. Kevin was a formidable organiser, was very politically aware and very well read. He did a lot of good in his time but was not easy put up with. Brendan and Mickey and Hensey from South Derry I.R.A. brigade were there as well. Very sound men too, that I had the honour to soldier with on the border. Ian from South Derry who would get captured in the north with Francie Hughes - the second man to die on the Hunger Strike of '81 after Bobby Sands. Hughes was a legendary I.R.A fighter in the South Derry area. The Belfast men were a breed of their own. They had that cockiness that every city man has. As the Derry man said to me, 'No matter what I tell the Belfast man that I have, he'll say, sure we have a big one of them in Belfast'! Aggravating, very self opinionated, they counted themselves the elite within the I.R.A. and the prison. Belfast men were the best as far as they were concerned. If the fight in Belfast was going well then the fight was being won, nowhere else mattered. The most famous Belfast man in that prison at that time was Joe Cahill. Joe was a fifties man and even a thirties and forties man. A legend in Belfast for defending the catholic areas from armed rampaging loyalists during the burning out of the whole catholic areas in Belfast in the late sixties. Only for him and a few I.R.A. men from the fifties fighting back, the burnings would have been much, much worse. He got life for shooting an R.U.C. man in the forties. He was originally sentenced to death for this shooting but while his comrade I.R.A. volunteer, Tom Williams, was hanged in Crumlin road jail, Joe's death sentence was commuted to life imprisonment. When Joe would apply for an American visa during the run up to the I.R.A. truce in 1994, they said that they were appalled at his C.V! but they did let him into America because he had a huge influence on how the peace talks were going at that time. A very gruff man, a man of few words, but his words carried a lot of weight, he was well respected. He had bad health for years, a serious heart problem. He spent a lot of time in his cell in bed; he had a panic bell in his cell in case of a heart attack. He got out early because of his health. The Dublin government were afraid he'd die suddenly in his cell and cause a riot inside and outside the prison. But then he'd live to be eighty or more! I often wondered if he put some of it on just to get out early, and to bluff the government at the time. 'Did you bluff them Joe?', I asked him years later but he just laughed, 'I wouldn't do the like of that', he said.

The Sinn Féin president and vice president were in there as well, Dathaí, a Corkman, and Ruaraí from Rosscommon, two leaders of the republican movement at that time. Two teachers by profession, they formulated Sinn Féin policy for an all Ireland solution based on the four historical provinces of Ireland; Ulster, Munster, Leinster and Connaught. Each province would have its own parliament to rule its area on a regional basis and an all Ireland government would be drawn from the four provisional parliaments and based in Athlone, the centre of Ireland. It was a well thought out policy called Eire-Nua, the new Ireland. Based on a federal model, but it never got very much support and faded away over the years. The both of them often gave political lectures on all aspects of Irish politics and history and also Irish language lessons. They were very well educated men and very well spoken. Dathaí was a very political and smart man but I could beat him every time on the chessboard and he disliked that very much! He felt he should be able to beat me! He could blame my father for that, he had tutored me from an early age. There were some very good chess players from Dublin and Cork in that jail, college educated men. We got a trophy in from outside, a lovely trophy and ran a chess competition. I won it after a fierce final with a Dublin player. He was good, but I was better! Me, a country lad from county Tyrone that left school at fifteen years of age, beating all the city boys, Sinn Féin presidents, teachers and college educated graduates, at the brainiest, hardest board game of them all! My father would have been really proud of me. I still have that trophy. It was at this time I taught others, including Martin McGuiness, how to play the game. He was a very good chess player, we had many a good game. I hope it was helpful to him in later years.

We also ran a seven-a-side G.A.A. football competition for trophies sent in by Derry county board of the G.A.A. It was played on the league basis with a knock out stage at the end. I was on the winning team of that competition as well. It was very hard fought for and many a lump and bruise was gotten before that trophy was finally won! I had won a club county championship medal for my parish of Donaghmore when I was a minor, so I was good at playing G.A.A. football. That medal and the trophies for G.A.A. Portlaoise jail are prized possessions of mine, as is the chess trophy. All very hard earned indeed.

Time in jail was rolling on and it would soon be Christmas. Christmas in jail is a tough oul time. You think a lot of family and what Christmas was like while growing up. I loved Christmas at home. It was a very special family time with great memories. My mother would take us to midnight mass in Dungannon, it was a lovely mass. All the Christmas carols would be sang by the choir, the big old church would be packed to the outside doors. Everybody who was anybody would be there. All the neighbours, family, friends and relations. We'd stand chatting and talking in the cold night air after mass, the frost in the air showing our breath in white puffs as we talked. Then we would make our way home and my mother would make tea with Christmas pudding for us and some of the neighbours too, even at that time of the morning! The next morning my mother would be up early, she'd light the big black coal stove, stoke it up really well, then fry the sausages, bacon, eggs and fried bread. The smell of that coming up into the room, you'd just have to get up to eat it. The smell of that big fry on Sunday mornings and Christmas is something I can still smell to this day. It was an absolutely beautiful smell! The heat from the big black stove, my mother fussing around it getting everything ready for breakfast and the big dinner later on that day was lovely. It was so homely! After my breakfast I'd go out and feed the cows and calves and take the milk from the cow for my mother. There was something really cosy and warm about animals in a byre on a cold winter's morning, the chewing of the animals on the hay, the heat from their bodies, the frost and cold outside, it was very peaceful. Maybe it was something got to do with the similarity with the child in the manger in Bethlehem, yea I think that was it. I'd bring the fresh milk into my mother and strain it from the milking bucket, to a better bucket, a house bucket, and leave it to the one side for my mother to use it later on that day. I'd go back out then and do any more farm chores that needed to be done. By this time my mother would have the turkey and goose in the oven of the big black stove. I'd get my dog and my father's shot gun and head out across the fields to hunt for game birds, pheasant, wild ducks, grouse, partridge etc. There was game in the field and ducks in the lough, game aplenty for the game hunter. The cold air and the walk would give me a huge appetite. I'd be well ready for my Christmas dinner when I'd get back to the old farmhouse by the lough in rural county Tyrone. I'd be really ravenous after a few hours trekking through the fields and around the edge of the lough. I'd always go in a circle from the house and end up walking down the old lane to the front of the house. The smell of my mother's cooking would meet me half way up the lane, then I'd go into the old kitchen where the big country table would be loaded with the most beautiful hot, home-cooked food, and sit down with my Dad, brothers and sisters for the most wonderful Christmas dinner. It was all very special.

This year I would get my dinner in a prison cell way down in the middle of southern Ireland and I'd be on my own, my father was dead, and the old farmhouse was empty. My three oldest brothers had married and were gone, my eldest sister was teaching in Belfast, my next sister just a bit older than me, was in England, Joe was on the run in Monaghan and Martin my youngest brother was interned in Long Kesh internment camp just outside Belfast. My mother had to flee the old country farmhouse with her four youngest children, the twin girls and two other girls for their own safety from the Brits raids. So the old farmhouse was empty, there was no-one there that Christmas day. Even the old byres were empty as there was no-one to look after the animals. So much change, in so short a time. The grub warden came in my cell door with my Christmas dinner. I took it off him, ate a bit of it and got into my bed pulled the bedclothes up over my head and tried to go to sleep. I wished Christmas day was over. The New Year came and went too and on into the spring time. I love the springtime.

Everything is new and gets a new lease of life, it's a wonderful time of year, I was glad to see it. I had to stand up on the end of my bed to see out as there was a prison wall twenty five foot high. Over the wall was big, green fields. A farmer was ploughing a field. The day I went into Monaghan for the load of war materials, when we ran into the checkpoints, I was ploughing a field that day on the little farm at home. I never got back to finish that field. But I watched this farmer out of my prison cell window. I wondered what he was ploughing for? Grain or spuds? I looked at the depth of his furrow and opted for grain, his furrow wasn't deep enough for spuds. There was an old saying in county Tyrone, never plough for spuds when you're only sowing corn! In other words don't be stupid! So I knew that this farmer was sowing grain in his ploughed field. I could smell the new turned soil in my nose. The crows and gulls came down on his new furrows for their feast of food. Ploughing and springtime was a great time for them - all that free food after the winter months! I thought to myself as I watched him, I'd just about see this field of grain harvested as I was out of here the end of September. The day I see that field of grain harvested I'll be almost a free man, roll on the harvest! I called it my field of barley after that. I told my comrades I had a field of crop being sowed, my field, and they laughed and said 'you're a mad Tyrone man'! The routine of prison days went on. Up early, get breakfast, clean and tidy cell, get washed, get dressed, and visit other cells for chat, out into the exercise for a jail walk. The morning yard was a small yard, just good enough for walking around having a yarn. The afternoon yard was a big yard, good enough for playing G.A.A. and sports. The armed soldiers from the Irish army or the Staters as the old I.R.A. men called them, kept a wary eye on us all the time. We never bothered them, they never bothered us. Back inside for dinner time, dinner was taken in the cell, listening to the news. So, so important. It was like war bulletins to us! How the fight was going outside was the most important thing, it was vital the war was going well, but the news could be good and bad. We'd hear on the news that I.R.A. men had died on an operation. Whatever area they were from they'd have close comrades and friends in here. We always carried out a memorial service for dead comrades. We'd all line up in the morning yard in military formation, the front man had a tricolour. The O.C. would call us to attention. An I.R.A. man from the same area would step forward and read out the dead comrade's name or names. He'd give a short oration, written by himself about the dead I.R.A. man or men. Then another I.R.A. man would step forward and read the proclamation. The flag would be lowered in respect; two minutes silence would be called and honoured. The flag would be risen again and the I.R.A. parade dismissed by the O.C. The wardens and the soldiers on the roof would always keep the silence and respect for the dead I.R.A. men. These memorial services for dead I.R.A. men were never interfered with by the prison authorities. During those early years of the seventies when the war in the north was being fiercely fought, we were in that little yard very often indeed, doing those commemorations. East Tyrone today, south Armagh tomorrow and Belfast the day after that and so on. There wasn't an I.R.A. brigade in the north that wasn't suffering casualties, but we honoured them all with great dignity in that little prison yard. After we'd had our dinner and listened to the news we'd have a rest for a while or do some craft work in the cell or read. Celtic wooden crosses were very popular as were crafts done out of matchsticks stuck together. Some of those crafts were real works of art. We could go to the workshop or laundry at that time too or have a shower. We had free association all day, our cell doors were never locked during the day. So we had a good amount of freedom within the jail, this made time easier to do. Then in the afternoon we'd go out to the football yard and play matches. These were tough matches! Some men would do running. There were some great athletes in there then, some good Gaelic football players too, including myself. This is where the competitions for the G.A.A. trophies were played. It was a tough, hard, no holds barred competition that everyone wanted to win. There were 3 or 4 hundred I.R.A. men in there at that stage, so there was plenty to choose from. My team, the winning team, was made up of a mixture of men. I was from Tyrone, a Dublin man and a Derry man and me were the three backs, another older Derry man was in the goal, a young Dublin fella was our scorer, from Cabra, he almost became a T.D. in later years for north Dublin City. A very good Gaelic footballer. He did become a Dublin City Councillor in the years to follow. Nicky was his name. A Belfast man with big, thick glasses, he paired up with the Dub. Another Derry man and a southern man made up the midfield and forward line. My strategy was, we had a very strong backline, me, Peter, the Derry man and the Dub. It was up to us to deny the other team any scores. If we could do that then our scores would come, young Nicky from Cabra in Dublin would look after that, and it worked!

There was a really good runner from Dublin who was always practicing running around the yard. Brian from south Armagh reckoned he could beat him in a marathon. Brian wasn't built like a runner, but pure pig iron could win it for him. The Dublin runner accepted his challenge and Brian went into training. It was the talk of the jail, who would win, the athlete or the hard man? I backed Brian, he was a south Armagh man, I couldn't let him down. The day of the big race came, the yard was marked out. So many circles of the yard were so many miles. It started off with roars of support from their prospective backers, the athlete and the hardman were neck and neck for a long time. The athlete running loose and with ability, the hardman oozing pure determination, grit and raw courage. The hardman should have been beaten three quarters way through the race but he wasn't! Towards the end of the race they were still running alongside each other. The face of Brian the south Armagh man would have scared you to look at it. The long black hair, the big Dubliner black beard, the fierce, piercing eyes, the mouth shut tight in pure determination. A truly fearsome sight and the sweat was lashing off him. Coming up near the end, running shoulder to shoulder, they stared at one another eyeball to eyeball. Suddenly Brian, the hardman pulled ahead and won the race. The yard erupted with cheering. It was said afterwards that the Dublin athlete should have never have locked eyes with that man. It was reckoned that the look into them fierce eyes in the last lap was what beat him! We believed that the Dublin athlete decided in the last lap, that second place was the safest place to be!! So Brian from south Armagh I.R.A. brigade one of the fiercest fighters they had, won the race! Who could blame the Dublin athlete? But it was all good craic. The football, the sports, the craft making, playing cards in the recreation room in the evening, the chess, draughts, the T.V., the politic lectures. The debates in the cells between I.R.A. groups was sometimes loud and fierce.

I realised while we were all I.R.A. men, our political views were often very different. From real lefties, to men who would have had very middle of the road views, and some right wingers, took these debates in the cells sometimes nearly to blows! I'm talking about real anger, real differences of views. It was an eye opener to listen to all the different views about how Ireland should be run politically when the war was over against the Brits. I learned a lot at those angry debates. Some of the main players in the Good Friday Agreement were in those cells and in those debates. The political division came in mainly two ways; the left-right division and the north-south division. The political left was all about perfectionism, the doctor and the dustbin man, the barrister and the brickie, the politician and the pauper, the men of property, and the men of no property, were all worth the very same in the world of left perfectionism! I argued against this because I believed that it couldn't be made to work! I felt that it was a pie in the sky unattainable dream. The two Sinn Féin leaders would almost always quote James Connolly, Padriag Pearse, Jim Larkin and Wolfe Tone and took a lot of their political view points from the 1916 rising and the first Dial of 1918. Even though James Connolly and Padraig Pearse were miles apart when it came to social and political backgrounds, nearly all the southern men's politics, especially older men, stuck to the Sinn Féin victory in the 1918 general election which was an all Ireland vote. They counted that election as sacred. It was the only legitimate government of the Irish people. Torn apart by a British government act of parliament that enforced partition and backed by the free state government which resulted in the Civil War. Old comrade against old comrade, brother against brother, as is well depicted in the film 'The Wind that Shakes the Barley'. The 'Free Staters' won that Civil War and went on to establish the Irish free state Dáil. The majority of Irish people accepted this, a twenty six county Irish republic, with the other six counties to come later. Most of the southern people believed Michael Collins when he stated that some freedom was better than no freedom, and that limited freedom was a stepping stone to the full freedom of Ireland. I believe that the people on the ground of the twenty six counties believed it was only a matter of time until the other six counties were won back again. They saw partition as only a temporary short term solution, and always backed a thirty two county Irish republic; this was evident when the troubles erupted in the north in 1969. There was a huge support for the northern nationalist people from their fellow Irishmen and women south of the border. The first safe house I stayed in, in county Monaghan, out along the Armagh border was not a Sinn Féiner's because Sinn Féin did not have a political presence among the twenty six county people of that time. The people of Monaghan who kept me in their houses in the early 70's were a mixture of all political persuasions, just ordinary Irish people who believed in our fight and saw the Border and the loss of the six counties as unfinished business, and were backing the provisional Irish republican army to complete that business. In the meantime they saw the Dublin government as the legitimate government of the Irish people and accepted them as such. But these older southern republicans in the jail saw the two governments, north and south as wrong and accepted neither of them. They would quote the 1918 general election and its victory for Sinn Féin as the only legitimate expression of the whole Irish people, and would give allegiance to the first Dáil and the first Dáil only. I found that they were very bitter over the civil war, very, very bitter. They had a little book called 'The Tragedies of Kerry' and when I read it in my cell in Portlaoise jail, I could understand why the old republicans were so bitter, they hated the free staters with a vengeance. The execution of I.R.A. men during the civil war by 'staters' as they called them, still hurt badly. I was learning about southern politics every day, this jail to me was like a college. I found that northern republicans were much more pragmatic about politics. The way we looked at it, was, as long as we didn't get too much hassle from the southern security forces, and the Dublin government didn't bring in internment without trial in the south, and we could still carry on our fight in the north, we'd be happy enough, let sleeping dogs lie. We didn't need an old civil war to fight, we already had a war in the north. I pointed to the wide range of support that I.R.A. units had in the south. Sinn Féin in

1973 opposed the south's entry into the E.E.C. or E.U. as it is now called. The people who were keeping us in safe houses along the border were mainly small farmers. These small farmers voted yes for entry into the E.U.; they deemed that it would be good for Irish farmers and therefore good for their families. I was eating breakfast in one of these safe houses with three more members of my unit when the farmer and his wife dressed up to go into Monaghan to vote yes for entry into the E.U. They saw nothing wrong with this, they supported our fight for the six counties one hundred percent, but they also had the responsibility to do what was best for themselves and their families and their futures. I had no problem with this, I wasn't fighting for any political parties point of view on the E.U.; I was fighting for a cause I believed in, I was fighting for Ireland, I was fighting for the rights of an Irish population left north of the border after partition, a minority who were treated as bad as the black people of apartheid south Africa. I was fighting for their rights to be Irish in their own country, without having to pay for that right with their freedom, and often their lives. I was fighting to right the wrong of partitioned Ireland, this fight for me was bigger than any political party. There was a small, Dublin man in one of the cells, he was an oldish man, a lifelong republican. He was also an accomplished journalist and writer, a historian. He was a historical authority on Dublin city and all its history in every aspect. Eamon McThomas was his name. A lot of the heated political debates took place in his cell. Kevin and he used to clash regularly. Helicopter Kevin used to get very hot headed, a man of six foot plus, he could be a very imposing figure. Eamon was a very small, slightly built little man with a beard. One evening when the political debate got very heated and Eamon won his point, Kevin lost the head and said to Eamon 'What the hell would you know about it, you're like a little leprechaun in that bed'. Eamon jumped up from the bed, stood up beside Helicopter Kevin's big six foot plus frame; all five foot of him and roared 'So here is the big preacher for the far lefties, everybody the very same as everybody else, no-one gets anymore kudus than anybody else, and you insulting me, just because you were lucky enough to grow up to six foot and I stopped at five foot. So much for your bloody sense of equality and fair play! You're claiming kudus over me just because you grew bigger than me! I suppose that entitles you to a bigger wage packet than me, you left wing capitalist bollocks!' Everyone fell about the place laughing at Eamon's razor sharp

Dublin wit. It was precious. Kevin looked stunned for a moment then started to laugh too, gave Eamon a big bear hug, lifted him up on his feet and sat him back on his bed, 'You win this one, you smart Dublin jackeen, I'll get you next time'. I wrote a couple of short stories for Eamon, he said they were very good, that I had a gift for storytelling. He asked me to write a story for 'An Phoblacht' but I refused. He advised me to do it in the future sometime because he thought the talent I had was too good to waste. For a long time, when I was thinking of writing this book and did not know if I could or not, I'd think of Eamon's encouragement. He went on to write very successfully, his book 'Me Jewel and Darling Dublin' was a best seller . He wrote another about 'Gurcake and Coal' or something like that. He also presented his own R.T.E. show about old historical Dublin. Years later I'd watch him on the T.V. show and be proud that I knew him well. Time was going along well, I was keeping an eye on my field of barley, for that's what it turned out to be, I'd watch the farmer tend to it and think about what a good job he was doing for me. Roll on harvest time!

37

THE ESCAPE

THERE WAS AN escape committee in every I.R.A. jail. We looked upon escape as a duty for long term I.R.A. prisoners. We were prisoners of war, so escapes were always being planned. There were a lot of long term I.R.A. prisoners in the jail in 1974. Helicopter Kevin was the chief escape planner and co-ordinator, he was very good at it. Tom the Joker was his main spy, spying on the warden's times and habits - when they would change over from one shift to another etc. I wasn't on the escape committee but I helped Tom on his spying duties on occasions. He was very exact about times and habits of wardens duties. He was a joker but also very, very shrewd. Not one detail of their habits escaped his prying eyes. I knew there was an escape in the pipelines and was being planned for months. Quietly and secretly, the escape committee were planning the escape of 20 longtime I.R.A. prisoners, many of them experts in their own fields of guerrilla warfare; men who would be a real asset to the war effort in the north. The plan was a very daring plan indeed. It would need split second timing and serious co-ordination if it were to be successful. The whole plan was very cunning. They were going to take over the wardens as they changed afternoon shifts on a rooftop. A one storey flat roof, where a warden stood all day overlooking a little yard. He came off it beside the laundry room, that was where they were going to take him and his relief warden. The lookout warden in a security cage on the same landing would be taken over as well. A warden at each side of the landing would have to be taken at the same time. The 20 men would then gain access to the flat roof, jump down into the little yard, make their way quickly over to a door in the high perimeter wall and blow it open with a small readymade bomb! There was a field between the perimeter wall and the public road, where an outside team would be waiting with transport to take the I.R.A. men away. The soldiers on the roof were a problem, but the escape committee came up with a ingenious idea to overcome that! They planned to have ten of the I.R.A. men dressed as wardens. The ten 'wardens' would then chase the ten escaping prisoners. The ten warders would keep close to the ten prisoners all the way up the field to the road. The soldiers on the roof would think the ten prisoners were been re-arrested by the prison wardens and were so close to the escaping prisoners that it wouldn't be safe to open fire, even if they wanted to! It was a daring, dangerous and brilliant escape plan.

Everything would need to go right, all the preparation needed on the run up to the escape day and on the escape day itself. There would be at least one 'gung-ho' hardman warden trying to make a name for himself. This warden could be dangerous and needed to be taken care of! We would see on the day just how tough he was! All 20 of the I.R.A. escapees were selected, now we would have to have ten looking like wardens. Slowly I could see I.R.A. men appearing in the exercise yard with short back and sides haircuts, one every now and again so not to raise suspicions from the warders. Black shoes and dark trousers were gradually brought in from visitors. Black shoes, dark trousers and blue shirts were suddenly the fashion trend! Everything had to be done very low key and over a period of time. Low key and water tight planning was vital! I.R.A. men who always did crafts in the cells were given dark pieces of fabric by the O.C. and were told how to cut and design warden's caps. They were to be kept in cells in separate pieces until the night before the escape and then glued together last minute. Once the warden's hats were glued together along with the dark trousers, black shoes and blue shirts, we would have our ten I.R.A. prison wardens for escape day! Timber for wood crafts was brought to the jail by I.R.A. prisoner's families; lumps of mahogany, oak and pine etc. They were stored under the beds of prisoners until needed, then taken to the work shop and cut up for Celtic crosses, Celtic harps etc. and given to family and friends. Some were used as prizes at fund raisers for the I.R.A. One day, when new timber was brought in for crafts, two big pieces were taken to one side and carefully put under a prisoner's bed. This prisoner was a member of the escape committee. Inside these two pieces of mahogany was the makings of the bomb that was needed to blow open the gate in the perimeter wall. Now we had everything! A small gun was also in there. An I.R.A. escapee who would be a lifer would have this small gun.

Escape day was now very close at hand; everything was in place! Helicopter Kevin, who was escaping again, sent the word around - 'Friday is D-Day'. It was now Wednesday. I didn't know everyone that was going to escape but I knew some. All the lifers except one who wasn't well enough to go, several of the south Armagh brigade, several East Tyrone Brigade, including Kevin, and Brendan the fund raiser from Coalisland, Co. Tyrone. This man was an expert, very good at raising badly needed funds for the I.R.A., a man as cool as a cucumber and a wry sense of humour. A few Derry I.R.A. men and a few from Belfast brigade and finally some southerners who were expert homemade weapon makers, made up this group of escapees. They were a very tough experienced unit of I.R.A. men hell bent on gaining their freedom. They would be hard to stop. Brian the south Armagh man was going too. I wished him luck - God help the prison warden who would stand in front of him! The evening before the escape the two big pieces of timber were taken out from underneath the bed and a saw was smuggled down from the workshop by a member of Monaghan brigade I.R.A. The man's name was Peader from Monaghan, he would die tragically in a car accident some years later. Kevin and Tom were also there. The timber was sawn through very carefully, at marks put on the timber by the I.R.A. men on the outside who had made them up. Very carefully, the two ends came off the timber to reveal hollowed out compartments with all the components for a small bomb - gelignite, detonator etc. and a small handgun with ammo. One of the men joked wryly 'There is enough in this cell to get us all an extra fifteen years! There had better be no search raids by prison wardens tomorrow morning, or we are all in serious trouble'. The warden's hats were assembled and glued together, everything was ready! Friday morning was kept normal. Breakfast, walk in the yard, lunch. I watched several escapees that morning, they were the same as any other morning. Three o'clock approached, Tom the Joker watched until the changeover of the prison wardens was just taking place. Then it happened. A lifer with the gun, took the two prison wardens as they changed on the small flat roof. 'I'm doing life anyway' he told the wardens, 'it will make no difference to me, don't be a fool, you have a family'. All prison wardens did as they were told, including the gung-ho hardman. When Brian confronted him, he wasn't hard at all, he just did as he was told, meekly enough. The bomb team blew out the door, the rest of the escapees had run down the landing, out onto the flat roof, jumped into the small yard, out through the bombed door and up the green field towards the road. Me and Tom watched them run up the field from a cell window. The ten I.R.A. escapees, the ten I.R.A. "prison wardens" in hot pursuit and the soldiers on the roof totally mesmerised by the suddenness of the whole thing, they could only stand and do nothing. They watched the escaping prisoners and the pursuing prison warders all get into the I.R.A. getaway vans and go off down the road together at high speed. Later, when they found out that all twenty men were I.R.A escapees, I'm sure they just couldn't believe their eyes or their ears! It was the very definition of man bites dog! 19 I.R.A. men escaped, one I.R.A. escapee, an older man Jimmy from Newry, Co. Down I.R.A. brigade broke his ankle jumping off the flat roof and had to be carried back into the wing like a wounded soldier of war, but the daring escape was a complete success! Me and Tom the Joker danced a jig in the prison cell. The whole landing was in chaos! It was like something you would see in a war film, but this was for real. It felt just great. We hid in different cells for the rest of the day, so the prison wardens couldn't establish who had escaped and who hadn't. Eventually the O.C. called us to line up on the landing, and let the prison warden's count who was present and who wasn't. "Nineteen men a missing and they didn't use the door; they just blew a little hole where there wasn't one before!" This song which became famous was penned in a cell by a Tyrone I.R.A. man from Strabane within an hour of the escape happening! We went into our cell that night and listened to the radio news, oh the blessed radio; it was such a lifeline in jail!

We followed everything that was happening in the search for the escapees, for days on end - none of them got caught! As each day went by we knew our I.R.A. comrades were safely away. We had to put up with cell searches and a bit of inconvenience from the prison wardens etc. but it was a very small price to pay for a victory like that! The days and weeks seemed to pass quicker after the escape. My field of barley was doing very well; I was keeping a good eye on it. It was midsummer and it was just starting to open and colour slightly. Outside, the constitutional parties put together a political solution involving only the middle of the road 'respectable political parties' backed by the British government, Irish government, the catholic church etc. But because it excluded and marginalised the working class people on both sides of the political divide, it was doomed for failure. When would the so called establishment in Dublin and London realise that a solution wouldn't work without those mostly involved in it, the ordinary people, especially those people on the nationalist republican side, who were marginalised and kept out of the running of the six county state for over fifty years. To attempt a solution without bringing those people in from the cold would be doomed to failure. So the Sunningdale solution of 1974 fell apart because of the failure of it to be inclusive! It would take a long time and a lot more suffering on both sides before a political leader with enough courage and foresight to break that mould would emerge from an Irish political leadership. A man who would put aside personal, political gain and ambition, and act for the good of the country. I was walking down the landing one day in the jail when Tom shouted to me 'McNulty, there's a great big yellow combine harvester in your field of barley', I ran up the stairs and into my cell, jumped up on the end of my bed and there it was, a great big beautiful yellow combine harvester in my field of barley. I watched it go round and round the field, like a child would watch Santa on his sleigh at Christmas. It was beautiful! I'd soon be out of this jail, I'd soon be free. I felt great. That year the Monaghan Dublin bombings came. A man who lived next door to the wee house in Park Street, Monaghan, was killed. He was a great fella and a good friend.

The night before a prisoner is released is always good craic. The I.R.A. man who was getting out would be drenched with water, this turned into water fights between all the prisoners. It was kind of like a jail ritual and a letting off of tension. It was always taken in good sport by the I.R.A. man getting released. What was a bit of ducking when you knew you were getting out the next morning? Bring it on. The prisoner who was getting out would say his goodbyes to all his comrades in jail before lock up the evening before his release, because he would be gone out of the prison before the rest of the I.R.A. men would be up. Releases were always about six o'clock in the morning. I said goodbye. Tom would soon be released too, so it wouldn't be long until I'd see him again. It was harder to say goodbye to long termers, but at least there were nineteen long termers I didn't have to say goodbye to! They had gone out through a hole in the wall. I walked into my cell for the last time with a chorus of good luck ringing in my ears. I listened to the radio for a while, every prisoner's lifeline, then I went to bed, thought about all that had happened to me that year, and how I'd gotten through it all with my morale still high. I was ready for the fight again. I got out the next morning, got picked up at the gate, drove up to Monaghan town and rejoined my comrades in the East Tyrone Brigade I.R.A.

38

1974
SURVIVAL

I WAS BACK at the front line again. Red Joe was the brigade O.C. We were set for another stage of the fight in the north. The war went on as before, with landmines and gun attacks on the crown forces, commercial bombings were still crippling the north's economy and costing the British exchequer a huge amount of resources. There was also a bombing campaign in England. The Brits had their hands full, the I.R.A. were still very strong. The fight was being brought to the Brits strong as ever. Coming up towards Christmas of 1974 there was whispering of an approach by the Brits for another ceasefire. The I.R.A. chiefs were back negotiating with the enemy. I had come down to this safe house on the Armagh Tyrone border to plan an operation. Noel had picked me up in Monaghan. I travelled as Noel's brother, I had I.D. to suit. We got to his house no problem, no checkpoints. I often stayed with Noel, his house was at a little country crossroads, his house actually formed the crossroads. I loved staying with him, as did other I.R.A. men, it was a good safe house.

Noel seemed a bit preoccupied the evening I arrived, not his usual self. I had a good few I.R.A. men calling to the house, making plans - maybe that was it. Noel's mother was an old woman, but a very interesting person to talk to; I used to sit and talk to her for long periods of the day. She asked if I was married, I said no. She looked at me real earnestly and said 'Son, you should be married, a man without a women in his life is similar to a donkey, not much different' she said. I laughed. She advised me as soon as I stopped being an I.R.A. man to get myself a nice young woman, marry and settle down. A man is only a half a person without a wife she said. She told me about her childhood growing up, she loved county Armagh, she loved her locality, she loved Ireland. She also said she loved her husband who was dead years. She said he was always good to her and the children, provided for them well, and always felt cared for when she was with him. Care comes first she said, love comes second. You cannot love someone if you don't first care for them. Care and kindness from a man to a woman is always first, love will then follow automatically. My husband was a good, kind, caring man she told me, it wasn't hard to love him. I still miss him, even though he is long years dead. But you'll find that nice young woman, she said with a smile, you are a fine young fella and you will need a wife and children in your life. I enjoyed listening to her, she had a wealth of knowledge and loved to part with it. Noel worked late and then he'd come home for his supper. His brother lived in the farmhouse next door and he had a big family of sons and daughters. He used to come in for a chat now and again. Noel's house was a big house, so some of his brother's children slept in his house. The I.R.A. room, as my room was called, was upstairs, the window of the room was in the gable end, looking down onto the road. To the right when I looked out was round to the front of the house, to the left was the road past the farmhouse and on into the countryside. The hedges were high with access through a little garden gate into the farmyard. It was a lovely, quiet, safe place. We all sat beside the open fire that evening; Noel, his mother, his brother and his sister who lived there too. Noel's mother went to bed and the brother went out, and into his own house. Me and Noel chatted for a while, and I left him making safe the fire, and tiding up, and then went to bed myself. I always said a prayer at night, no matter where I was, I was not a great Catholic. The Catholic hierarchy was against us, and were very verbal. Lots of ordinary priests were for us, but they had to keep quiet for obvious reasons. A priest could hardly preach from the altar that he supported the I.R.A., but I said a prayer anyway every night because I had a good belief in God. Then I went to sleep.

The next thing I knew Noel was in the bedroom ashen faced and acting like a man demented. 'They're already in the house Tommy, the Brits are searching downstairs, I only got up to here to waken the children, you're gone, you're gone God help you, but you're gone' and then away out the door again. I was wide awake in an instant. I remembered a discussion I had with a comrade, Louis, from Dungannon, an I.R.A. man I often soldiered with and a very smart resourceful one at that. If there is a slimmest chance I can escape he had said, I'll take it, no matter how slim a chance, I'll be gone. This came into my head in a flash. I got up, made the bed, got dressed and put on my shoes, leather ones my brothers had bought for me. I did all this in seconds. The wardrobe was no good, under the bed was no good, I couldn't get out the door. The window! The steel window opened out, one half of it. I thought of what the Brits had said in Gough Barracks; they would kill me on the spot. It flashed through my mind, the terrible danger I would be in if I was captured. I opened the bedroom window and looked out into the summer morning. A British soldier was standing underneath the window, a little to the right hand side. I could also see the back half of a British army jeep protruding out from the front of the house. Suddenly the British soldier moved around to the front of the house. I ducked in, took my shoes off and jumped out the window in stocking soles onto the road. I stood up immediately and turned left past the little garden gate. I glanced into the farmyard, it was alive with Brits, like ants, removing hay from barns etc. I walked by briskly and on up the little country road with thick hedges. I wondered what it would to be like to get shot in the back. If the Brit came back around the gable end of the house and called halt, I was going to make a run for it. But the halt never came. I walked a couple of hundred yards up the road and around a bend and out of sight. I'd made it so far! I took to the fields. There was a little wood down in the glen but I stayed clear of that, first place they'd search I thought. I got a place in a hedge in the middle of a big field, same as any other place on the face of the hills, made a den for myself and waited. I had my watch with me, I was grateful for that. At least I'd know what time it was. I heard helicopters in the distance towards Dungannon. They'll soon be a lot closer than that I thought to myself. I hated helicopters, I still do. I pictured myself getting caught out in the open with a British helicopter, the gunship one! It playing with me, the way a cat plays with a mouse, knowing it has the mouse under full control and can kill it any time it likes. My worst nightmare! The hair on the back of my neck stood up. I waited patiently all day long, a lovely summer's day.

This part of the north was a mixed area, Protestants and Catholics. That meant there were R.U.C. and U.D.R. personnel living in the vicinity. If I called to the wrong house in my stocking soles, all dishevelled, I was in trouble. These members of the crown forces took their guns home with them. Calling to a strange house was out. I knew another safe house in the area, other than Noel's. I decided when it became dusk I'd make for it. I had a good idea where it was. The search for me hadn't intensified as much as I thought it would, there were no helicopters in the immediate vicinity, no Brit personnel carriers on the little country roads. But then I thought of the open window with my shoes right below it and wondered if they had copped anything. I had made the bed; that was a big help. I'd have to treat it like they were onto me for now. I noted the place I was in before I moved out at dusk. We were always told to have a starting place, to come back to if needed. I stuffed the bottom of my socks with dry grass to save my feet and moved out. I got to the top of a hill, I couldn't see my other safe house. I got to the top of the next hill, nothing. A dog had started to bark. I'm going to get lost I thought, then I'll be in trouble. I turned and made my way back to the place in the hedge I had some from and settled down for the night. I slept a bit on and off, morning came; no big stir.

They didn't know that I had been in Noels, I thought, it was a routine search. I decided then I would sit the day out and return to Noel's that night. Better the devil you know than the devil you don't. That night on the edge of darkness I set out for Noels. I darkened my hands and face with mud, hid the light coloured clothing and started out. My socks were in flitters at this stage, I was starving. I was drinking water out of the ditches to stop the thirst. What I wouldn't give for a pint of water and a big mixed grill, a clean bed and a good night's sleep. But I was a free man. Against all the odds I was still free! I crawled down the backs of the hedges towards Noel's. I was close to it now. I hoped the Brits had gone, my biggest concern was that they would have left a few of their men lying around the hedges watching. Apart from the obvious danger in that, there was also the danger of crawling into one of the bastards in the dark. Talk about putting your hand on a rat; but there was no-one there. I watched the young lads going back and forth across the farmyard giving a hand at the farm chores. After a while I called softly to the eldest fella. He initially thought I was a Brit. Then he looked again and said excitably 'Wait till I get Uncle Noel'. He ran away over to Noel's house and disappeared. A minute later Noel came running over, he had tears in his eyes and he gave me a big bear hug. 'God Tommy I don't know how you got out of the room. I took the Brit search party all over the house, past that room several times until one of the Brits said 'What's in here? Open that door'. When I opened the door and saw that you weren't there I was a new man'. The tears running down his face. I laughed. 'You weren't half the new man I was' I said. 'No, I suppose not, but it was a miracle to get out of that room' he said 'nothing short of it. I have been praying with thanks ever since'. Noel's mother gave me a huge hug and kiss and wished me luck with my life as I left. I was never back there again.

Years later I was in San Francisco visiting some friends of mine. My friend said 'There is a man that wants to see you before you leave town, he works here in California'. He took me down town to a big office and introduced me. It was the young twelve year old lad I had whispered to in the farmyard that night! He made a big fuss of me to all his office staff, and laughed his head off. Don't know which of us was more pleased!

That night I left Noel's as quickly as I had arrived. I moved on over into a different part of Tyrone. Me, Bill and Barry were meeting up to plan a commercial bomb attack. We met up in the Cappagh part of the country. We had chosen our next operation and Bill went on into that part of Tyrone to forward plan. Me and Barry stayed in a safe house together that night. The next morning the area was a hive of activity. We turned on the news on the radio. Several men were arrested with explosive materials in a quarry. It was Bill and several other I.R.A. men from East Tyrone Brigade. Bill got 20 years, all the rest got long term jail sentences too. It was a big blow and a big loss. The safe house we were in was surrounded by a Brit search party. Barry looked at me and said, 'we're surrounded Tommy'. I knew by the look on his face he wasn't joking. We heard their boots on the gravel driveway, we were waiting for the door to be bust open. It didn't happen, they moved on, another 'life' lost. How many had we left? I wondered as I heaved a sigh of relief.

39

TAKING THE FIGHT
TO THE ENEMY

THE LOCAL O.C. was raging at the time. 'It's the bloody R.U.C.' he said, 'without their eyes and ears the Brits wouldn't know what to do'. We needed a strike against the Brits and the R.U.C. But he was finding it hard to get the enemy into the right place. He couldn't fool them into the traps he had set for them. He decided to blow up huge oil storage tanks in a depot to lure them out. There was a crossroads just a quarter of a mile down the road towards Dungannon. We were on the main Ballygawley to Dungannon road. The burning oil tanks would make the roads dangerous. They would have to divert traffic at the crossroads and we'd ambush them there! We gathered up heavy weaponry from all over the brigade area. Myself, Barry, Brian, the O.C. and six other local I.R.A. men were the ambush team. We had heavy machine guns, Bren's, A.K.47's, R.P.G.s, a Russian rocket launcher. We had a good hill position overlooking the crossroads. If we could get the Brits and the R.U.C. into ambush position we'd give them hell. They had been very brutal to arrested I.R.A. men. If we could get them here, we would give them what they deserved! We set up our ambush. Me, Brian, the O.C. and Barry placed the bomb under the oil tanks. We set the timer to give us time to get back to ambush position. A ten minute walk, it was a mixed area and care was needed. We made it back no problem, took up our position and waited. 15 minutes later the bomb at the oil depot went off. Flames went up into the night sky hundreds of feet. They would have to close the road. The British army siren went off in Dungannon, they soon would be on their way. Sometime later we could hear the R.U.C. and fire brigade trucks. The heavier whine of British personnel carriers could be heard as well. They were coming! Every muscle tensed up ready for action! When suddenly, all the sirens stopped. There was no other cross roads near, that would do for diversion, it had to be this one, but all the sounds had stopped. Then we heard helicopters going up. They were coming our way. Something was wrong. Suddenly the helicopter search lights came on, huge lights sweeping the fields. They were on to us! Time to make an orderly withdrawal. We gathered the men, and told them I was well used to helicopters on the border road campaign. They can't see you unless you move I advised them. When the searchlight was in the field, you have to lie in the ditch and stay still. Don't move, until it passes! 'That's an order' the O.C. said. We set out to go back to our base safe houses with the two helicopters searching for us, the ground Brits would soon be searching too. We kept going at a brisk pace with all our heavy gear. Every now and again we'd be forced to take the ditches and stay still until the searchlights had passed. Sore on the nerves, but the only way to safety. Suddenly, the searchlight hit our field, we jumped into the ditch! The huge light kept going up and down the field in swathes, a very, very powerful light. All of a sudden one of the men lost his nerve and broke cover! The light was coming across the field, I jumped out of the ditch and pulled the man back into safety. Barry gave me a hand and we held him down until the helicopter search light passed by. I didn't blame the man, he just lost his nerve. We made it back to base and safe houses. The helicopter and mobile Brit and R.U.C. patrols were on the road all night. We found out after that a protestant loyalist household had seen us going from blowing up the tanks, to the ambush position and rang the Barracks in Dungannon. We almost had them in our ambush position. The warning came to them, just before they came to us. They were very lucky. The crown forces had managed to escape us again! Not long after, several very successful attacks were carried out by east Tyrone I.R.A. against crown forces in this area.

The East Tyrone Brigade had sent a clear message to the hated crown forces. Torture our men at your own peril; if you do you will pay a big price. The I.R.A. won't stand for its men being tortured by anybody. Several British army personnel were blown up in a landmine ambush and also killed. This area of mountainous east Tyrone was almost 100% republican and a very strong support base for the East Tyrone Brigade I.R.A. The local population didn't need or want a British army presence in their area. There was no pretence of so called 'peacekeeping' role in this area, because in this part of Tyrone everybody lived in peace with each other anyway, except for the odd war breaking out on the Gaelic football pitch or at the local dancehall!

So the British army in this area was nothing but a purely occupational force. There to keep the local population down, harass them and often shoot and murder them. It was in this part of Tyrone where the infamous incident of murder happened, where they brutally killed a local farmer. He was a harmless man, who farmed his hill farm to keep himself and his elderly mother. A patrol of Brits came to his farmhouse, took him out of his kitchen where he was having his evening tea with his frail old mother, marched him down to one of his fields beside the house, forced him to walk across the field and then shot him dead. They shot him in the back as he walked away from them. His poor elderly mother heard the shots that killed her innocent son; the one person in the word she depended on for everything. Paddy McElhone was that man's name, it's etched on my brain even to this day. This act of murder was carried out purely to intimidate the local population. It sent out a clear message – no one was safe. Not one British army murderer was ever charged or did a day in jail for that infamous murder. So the I.R.A.s summary justice at the landmine ambush was the only justice that was available. This was the justice meted out by the East Tyrone Brigade I.R.A. as often as it could, and it made no apologies to anyone for doing just that. The Brits were an army of occupation here, and the I.R.A. would wipe out as many of the black and tan murderers as they could. This was our country, Tyrone was our county, and if the Brits insisted they would occupy it by force, then they would pay as high a price as the East Tyrone Brigade could exact! I was in a local safe house in this area, on a Sunday morning, myself and Barry, when the old woman of the house came home from mass and was very annoyed. The local priest at mass had condemned the I.R.A. men who hit the plunger on the landmine that killed the Brits. He condemned them to hell. Big deal! The I.R.A. were used to pro established clergy condemning them and using the captive audiences at a mass to do it. While at the same time the parish priest's house in another parish, was a safe house, and helped the I.R.A. on many, many occasions. But he couldn't use the pulpit to expose his personal political views, for obvious reasons. The poor priest would be arrested or shot. But this priest didn't stop at condemning us, he condemned his own parishioners who supported us, to hell as well. That would be most of his flock! I said to Barry that we would call up to the priest's house that evening and have a word with him, to see if he could explain himself. So that evening we made our way up the fields and the little country roads to the big imposing house, the biggest house in the parish by far, built and paid for by the very people whom he had the brass neck to condemn to hell! We walked up the gravel driveway, where the big new car was parked, us in our khaki green jackets and big boots. We knocked the big brass knocker on the front door. Far from what I was reared with, I thought to myself. The priest's housekeeper opened the door. I asked her politely if could I speak to the parish priest. She was a cheerful friendly person, 'Come in and wait' she said with no hesitation at all. Me and Barry stepped into the plush hallway. I felt my feet sink into about six inches of carpet. He'll not like this I thought. Barry grinned at me as we were led into this large room with dark expensive furniture, big wall mirrors, wall paintings, more plush carpets and a big mahogany table - a huge one, situated in the centre of the room, and a big white marble fireplace as well. A much, much better parish house than the one that was a safe house for us. Maybe he got perks for being pro establishment, I thought! The housekeeper pulled out two chairs from the end of the table and motioned for us to sit down. I was at the end of the table next to the door coming from the hallway. Barry was to my left. 'He is just finishing his tea' the housekeeper said of the priest, 'he'll be with you shortly'. Barry whispered to me through the side of his mouth 'He'll be having the best of steak and onions' he said. I laughed quietly. As we gazed around the luxury room, the door opened and the parish priest came in. He stopped for a moment, a bald headed man about fifty and looked at us and said 'What can I do for you?' he said as he pulled out a chair and sat opposite me and Barry. I looked at him in the eye and said 'I'm an I.R.A. man and I am here on behalf of quite a few of your parishioners. Who are you to condemn people to hell? I thought your job was to save people from going there?' He was taken aback a bit and looked at me more closely, 'I'm also here on behalf of East Tyrone Brigade I.R.A., I want to tell you on their behalf we have no apology to make to you or anybody else for the execution of British crown forces in this area. They are armed, aggressive, occupational forces. Armed and dangerous, and they have already murdered in this area. They are a threat to the lives of every person in your parish. The ones executed in the landmines are no longer a threat to these good people, and if the I.R.A. could render all the rest of these crown forces to a position of 'no longer any danger' to your parishioners, then they would, and will do it. If you don't agree with us, for whatever reason, that's your personal choice, you're entitled to that. But what you did this morning wasn't fair, because you forced your personal political views down the throats of a captive audience, a lot of whom don't agree with your choice of political view, and to condemn people to hell for holding a different view to you is wrong'. 'I am a man of God. I don't agree with your point of view' he said. I said, 'I can accept that, but you have to remember that there are people in your profession who do agree with us'. Down south, during the Tan War, in west Cork, Tom Barry's I.R.A. flying column was excommunicated from the Catholic Church by the bishop of Cork. He said he'd deny them the last rights if they were killed by the black and tans. Barry lined his men of west Cork I.R.A. brigade up, and told them that any one of them could go home, and it would not be held against them. Not one I.R.A. man stepped out of that line. 'You know why Father' I said, 'because every one of these I.R.A. fighters knew lots of good priests who supported them, and assured them their fight was a just war against a foreign aggressor and to fight on. They promised to give the last rites if anything happened to any one of those men. When the I.R.A. drove the Brits out of the southern part of Ireland and became heroes, the Catholic hierarchy trampled over each other to get their photo taken with General Tom Barry! I've no doubt it will be the same here in this part of the country when the time comes. In the meantime Father, do us a favour and keep your political views to yourself. I don't care what you say about us, keep ordinary people out of it, old people especially, they look up to their parish priest'. Barry came in 'These are the same people who put this big house over your head'. He looked over sharply at Barry and said 'Don't you get personal' he said angrily, 'that's out of order'. 'Well, what you did was out of order too' said Barry. The priest then said 'I'm an Irishman too you know, I don't like what's going on in our country' he said 'I hate it'. I stood up and so did the priest. I put my hand out and he took it. I looked at him in the eye and said 'That's the one thing you and I agree on', as I shook his hand in a tight grip. 'I hate it too, but we will fight on and win'. We bid our goodbyes, and me and Barry stepped out into the cold night air, across the road and into the safety of the county Tyrone fields. We picked up the machine guns and small arms we had hidden in the hedge, left there in courtesy and good manners towards the parish priest and his housekeeper, and made our way into the county Tyrone night, and an uncertain future.

The parish priest acknowledged that we called to the parish house from the pulpit at mass the next Sunday. He said he respected our courage and sincerity and the fact that we had called to him in person. The old woman of the house was still a bit annoyed. We didn't call much with her after that. She's long since dead and very happy in heaven I'm sure! I was told that the parish priest rarely ever made any reference to the fight against the Brits in the north after that. It's very possible that he is dead at this time too. I hope he too, went to heaven.

East Tyrone I.R.A. were in action again, trying to stem the flow of catholic murders in the area that had become known as the mid Ulster 'Murder Triangle'. It was a very difficult part of the fight to contend with. While they were fighting the British crown forces, the I.R.A. also had a duty to protect the nationalist population from loyalist murder gangs. These gangs were often helped by the crown forces and crown special forces. 85% of intellegence used by these murder squads came from R.U.C. special branch. The I.R.A. refused to get drawn into a sectarian war against the protestant population. This would be against all it stood for, it never got into doing that. It had to try and pinpoint those British murder gangs, and deal with them, to protect the nationalist population, and in doing so secure and keep our support base within that population. This was always a difficult task. Their aim was to terrorise and cow the nationalist population and undermine our support base. Catholic homes were fitted with special strong external doors to withstand the sledge hammers of the gangs trying to murder them. Security gates, fitted at the bottom of the stairs and secured before the family went to bed. No-one was safe from these British murder squads. They murdered a granny and a pregnant mother of young children in this area of east Tyrone during those terrible years of the conflict. The duty of trying to protect this population, set heavy on young shoulders. The I.R.A. did its best in very difficult circumstances. It is to the great credit of these Irish men and women that they never cowed down, and reared well adjusted happy children. They were very brave very resilient people.

40

RECOMMITTED TO THE STRUGGLE

ME AND BARRY got scouted out of the north after that, and back into county Monaghan for a well earned rest. It was very good to be back there again, amongst the good people of Monaghan. Christmas of '74 was coming up. There were rumours coming down from G.H.Q. in Dublin of another ceasefire, there had been some kind of peace talks again. In the meantime, me and Barry had some socialising to catch up on! Roll on the Four Seasons and The Hillgrove, my two favourite watering holes in county Monaghan! The man who owned the Four Seasons was a republican supporter all his life. An absolutely committed republican Irishman who made no secret of his support for the fight against the Brits in the north and a very good personal friend of mine as well. He came up to me at the bar of his hotel, just after me and Barry had come back from the north and offered me a new chance at life in New York, where he had several hotels and bars in the Big Apple. 'You have enough done, Tommy' he told me, I will organise your flight over and look after you for a job over there, please consider it' he said. 'Don't answer me now, take a few days to think it over'. I told him I'd think about it. He was a very sound man. Oul Hughie was his janitor, handyman and drinking buddy. Alan the hotelier was a hard drinking man; him and oul Hughie would go at it for days! I had a session with them myself into the early hours of the morning. This man was like a second father to me. While Oul Hughie was a hard drinker and good craic, he was also no-one's fool. He was the hotelier's right hand man; his eyes, his ears, his watchdog when he was in America or elsewhere, and was a loyal as one of these canine species as well. Hughie would have gladly died for Alan. It was at one of these social occasions that he asked me if I had made up my mind about New York. He was going back soon and would have to get the ball rolling. He'd put me on the payroll of the hotel, give me all the paperwork I needed with an address in New York, and state I had a job to come back to in Ireland on my return. I knew he meant it all and I knew he really wanted me to go. I also knew he would be very good to me and give me a great opportunity in New York. But I turned it down, I just couldn't go at that time. I was too committed to the fight and to my comrades. I had considered his offer because it was a once in a lifetime opportunity, but I felt I had to refuse. He said he respected my decision but was sad that I had said no. He also said that if he could be of help to me in any way in the future all I had to do was ask. He was as good as his word. The Four Seasons hotel at the time was known as the I.R.A. social club, a description not far from the truth! The managers were told by the hotelier, 'When I'm not here, look after whatever this man wants'. The look on the managers faces when they got those instructions from their boss! It was said that the Four Seasons in Monaghan was famous for the hard-eyed I.R.A. men that were always evident in it! It was famous for the east Tyrone Sinn Féin dinner dance held in it every year. Sinn Féin did the ticket sales and organised it. People came from all over east Tyrone for this annual function. The I.R.A. volunteers of the East Tyrone Brigade area were the guests of honour. Supporters were told to use the Fermanagh and Armagh border crossings for security reasons. The Tyrone crossing could be monitored by Brit security personnel, but the hotel was always packed to the doors for this great night out. Political discussions were rife, and top I.R.A. personnel gave speeches on the state of the fight. A rallying call, a morale booster and a feel good night. It felt good that we had so many decent people committed to us. It was also a commemoration ceremony for fallen comrades from East Tyrone Brigade I.R.A. A time for moral and personal support for fallen comrade's families and friends. A night to remember them and a night to honour them. A night to recommit to the fight to our people and comrades. It was then I knew I was right not to go to New York. My place was here in Ireland with my fellow Tyrone Irish men and women, and I.R.A. comrades, playing my part in the fight against the British occupation forces in the six counties. These nights were always great nights out, full of great memories of wonderful people, who backed their guerrilla army to the hilt. Our county Monaghan supporters came to these nights as well, for these people were also vital to our war effort and could not be done without! The I.R.A. ran its own security for these functions. The grounds and fields around the hotel were manned by low profile, but heavily armed I.R.A. men. There were armed I.R.A. men inside as well. Cars kept back from parking near the hotel, incase of Brit bomb attempts. It was on the run up to one of these functions that a member of the Brit forces was spotted in the area spying for the enemy. He was overpowered, disarmed, arrested and taken out to the border, interrogated by the I.R.A. and then taken into the north and executed by east Tyrone I.R.A. men. Another one was also caught spying around the county Monaghan area. He too was arrested and disarmed. This was a particularly brutal member of the crown forces, a man who was always the hard man interrogator to captured I.R.A. men. When he was being interrogated himself by I.R.A. men, he was a coward! Guerrilla fighters will always respect a brave enemy when captured, a brave man is a brave man, whether enemy or not! Some of them did show courage. I.R.A. men expected to be shot on sight too, and were on several occasions, so it was no quarter asked for, or no quarter given. That was why it was of paramount importance to safely secure the Four Seasons hotel for our night out. We had too many important personnel in the one place to let anything happen! On one of these nights out Bill was head of I.R.A. security at Four Seasons. A tall man and very well dressed for the night, a very intelligent I.R.A. man with a quick wit. A posh lady member of an up market, pro establishment British newspaper came to the doorman and demanded to be allowed in to report on the function. She was told in no uncertain terms she wouldn't be getting in. She demanded to see whoever was in charge as she had been insulted! Bill was sent for. He approached the very annoyed lady reporter, all six foot two of him in his three piece suit and tie! 'What's happening here' he said. The posh reporter from the pro Brit paper drew herself up to her full height, flashed her press card and said very pompously, 'I have been insulted and I demand an apology immediately'. Bill looked down on her with a certain amount of distain and contempt and said, 'Madam, that rag of a newspaper of yours has been insulting us for years and we never got any apologies! Now out of here and give my head peace, I have more important things to be doing than standing here talking to the likes of you'. There was a stunned silence from the posh one and everybody started to laugh. The posh one picked herself up with what little dignity she could, and flounced out of the hotel. It was very funny, a good laugh! It's remarkable how a building can figure largely in your life for no apparent reason. The Four Season hotel was the hotel we picked up the war material from when we ran into the Brit checkpoint, which resulted in us getting captured and having to go on the run. It was the last place I was talking to my father, the last time I saw him alive. Many years later it would be the last place I saw my mother before she died. My brothers and sisters held a lot of their weddings there to facilitate the likes of me that couldn't go north. Alan would be one of my best friends for life. I spent many a good night in it for the craic. I.R.A. men got lifted for shooting it up one night! The trial at the local courthouse fell through when nobody testified to seeing anything. One woman witness was asked by the local justice at the trial was she there when three men pulled pistols and started shooting into the air. She said she was there all night, people were eating chicken, some were singing, some chatting, some dancing and some shots were fired in the function room, but she didn't see anybody and passed no remarks! The courtroom went into stunned silence. Then the local justice said 'Let me see have I got this right. You were at Chicken in the Buff in the Four Seasons?' It was Chicken in the Rough but the justice had made a mistake! He continued on to the woman witness, 'You and your friends were drinking, eating chicken, laughing, talking, singing, dancing, some shots were fired, and nobody passed any remarks?!' This Chicken in the Buff must be one hell of a night out!' he said. The whole courthouse burst into laughter at both the woman witness and the oul justice - even the Garda and solicitors were in stitches, bent over laughing! It was very funny! When everything quietened down again the oul justice said 'If the calibre of witness was going to be the same as the last one - i.e. see no evil, hear no evil etc. I don't think we have a case to proceed with'. The Garda sergeant nodded his head in agreement and the case was dismissed! It was I.R.A. men who were involved in the incident. It was investigated by the I.R.A. These type of incidents were very rare. The I.R.A. men were told not to let it happen again and it was let go at that. The Four Seasons hotel would be the place where an incident would take place later that would lead to me being put in jail again; so it was a busy place for me! War and conflict were not funny things, but some very funny and some humorous things can happen during such conflicts! It is important for the guerrilla fighter to see the humour of his position sometimes. It is said that when a guerrilla fighter loses his sense of humour, it is a sign he should quit!

41

NOT A BUTT BETWEEN US

ONCE, THE UNIT of the East Tyrone Brigade were being left down to the border to ambush the British security forces by an old hill farmer. He was a real character! He also wore a robin hood hat with a feather sticking out of it! He was a real jaunty old boy, full of wise cracks. He use to love having I.R.A. men in his house. 'Bring in the guns and all the gear' he'd say when they'd arrive at his isolated farmhouse. The I.R.A. would lean all the weapons up against the kitchen cum living room walls and we'd sit at the big open fire and have the craic with him. Them bloody Brit helicopters he'd say, can you not get them "gazookoes" things from the Russians and blow them out of the air? The noise of them is scaring my calves and my sheep. It just shows you how everybody's priorities are different! He was running the unit down to an ambush site at the border, at the dead of night. Half a dozen armed men squeezed into his old Ford Granada. One of the I.R.A. men asked if anybody had a cigarette. No answer came. He asked again 'Has anybody got a cigarette?' he said, louder this time. 'No', 'no', 'no' was the chorus of answers that came one after the other from all the I.R.A. men. 'Well, has anybody got a butt then?' the same man shouted. 'No', 'no', 'no' came the answer from everyone again; not even a butt. The old farmer looked out from under his old robin hood hat, his eyes twinkling with humour. 'Lord' he says 'you's are the rarest bunch of men I ever came across' he said 'not a butt of a cigarette between you, and you heading down to the border to take on the might of the British empire!'. He chuckled to himself, and him shaking his head in feigned disbelief. We all saw the funny side of it and fell about the place laughing! The hill farmer had a very quick mind, but not everything is funny in war.

Sophie, was caught by the Brits in possession of war materials and was in Armagh women's prison and was awaiting trial. She was facing a very long prison sentence. It broke my heart to think of her locked up for all those long years. A lovely girl like her, locked up in a British prison. This saddened me a lot. The conflict continued on into Christmas 1974, it was still a very hard fought dangerous situation. Commercial bombs, landmines, ambushes against the British army, R.U.C. paramilitary police forces and the Ulster defence force; the replacement for the old B. specials. One was as bad as the other. Catholic hating, sectarian, out of control, well armed, colluding with loyalists paramilitaries in the shooting of innocent nationalist people. Christmas of 1974 came and I.R.A. G.H.Q in Dublin called a Christmas truce for a week. There was talk it was a goodwill gesture to the British government. A New Year truce might be coming. I hoped it would materialise soon. Christmas in Monaghan was a lonely time. I missed my big family and my mother's cooking and the old home. I was a few years on the run but I was still homesick. If I had of been in some far flung corner of the world, I could head home for Christmas, even if I had to travel for days I'd still make it. As the lovely Christmas song goes 'Driving home for Christmas'. Ironically, I was only a half an hour drive by road from where I was born and reared, but I was further away than the most remote corner of the world. For I wouldn't be home this Christmas and that was that! Distance made no difference, it just wasn't possible. Some I.R.A. supporters came up from Tyrone to Monaghan town and we drank heavily all evening and into the night. The I.R.A. in Monaghan had another wee three bedroomed house rented, with an attic room. I made my way up there to the attic room and went to bed. It was late on Christmas day when I was woke up by Pock Face, an I.R.A. man like Lee Van Cleef, only meaner and more evil looking than the bad guy actor! He shook me awake. 'Wake up, wake up' he shouted in my face. I struggled to open my eyes through the horrors of a massive hangover. I saw his face through an alcohol haze and though for an instance it was oul Nick! The devil himself. 'Here is your Christmas dinner' he said and walked out of the dark gloomy little attic room. I struggled up to the bedside locker, and my Christmas dinner was sitting on it in all its glory. A quarter of a steak and kidney pie, still in its tin. I thought, maybe he had been joking, but he wasn't. He told me afterwards he had forgotten to shop on Christmas Eve. I said to him I didn't mind, I was too sick to eat anyway. We sat talking about Christmas at home by the fire and passed the day away. Pock face loved his children. In safe houses he'd have the children playing and laughing with him in no time. They loved him. He had his five children from his wife and another one from a woman in England. He fathered this child while working there. He told me the English woman didn't want the child when he told her he was going home to Ireland. So he took the year old child home with him to Ireland. He put the wee girl sitting at the table when his wife was feeding the other five. Give that one a bite to eat and a bed to sleep in he said. She's mine as well. He told me his wife just reared her along with the rest. He was an evil looking little bollix, but he had a good heart. I met one of my sisters in the Hillgrove hotel just after Christmas. We chatted and she told me that mammy was in very bad form. She said mammy had no men left to make a big fry for, one of our favourite feeds and was very sad. I asked her who she was at the dance with. She told me his name. He was sound, he was a supporter. I said to Theresa, my young sister, 'I'm going down home to Tyrone with you tonight' she looked at me, 'Are you sure', I said 'Yes, your driver is alright, I have a bit of I.D. in my pocket, I'm going and that is that'. Going home with the crowds from the Monaghan dances was a good time to travel, lots of cars crossing the border at the same time. I got into the car outside the Hillgrove hotel, went down through the border checkpoint and landed home. My mother nearly dropped when she saw me. I said 'I'm starving, I need a feed'. She took out the great big black pan, tears in her eyes and made me a great big fry. My sister arranged for me to sleep in one of my neighbours houses. I got up the next day, went to say goodbye to my mother and headed back to Monaghan town after having to take several detours to avoid checkpoints. I made it back across the border again to safety. My mother had to get run up to Monaghan town to see me. She had to see me safe in Monaghan before she could settle. She stayed a little while and went home. She was delighted to see me and make a big fry, but pleaded with me not to do it again. I knew it was an act of madness on the spur of the moment – exactly what were trained not to do. I.R.A. men on the run cannot afford to get sentimental about personal things. It can cost you your life. It had cost lives! I got away with it, but it was a very dangerous and a stupid thing to do

42

1975
TRUCE – THE INCIDENT CENTRES

A TRUCE AND a suspension of military operations were called at the end of January 1975. Both sides agreed to the truce. Incident centers were to be set up to monitor the truce and deal with flashpoints that could lead to it breaking down. Local issues would be sorted out on the telephone in these incident centers. Any harassment by security forces personnel would be resolved this way. The East Tyrone Brigades incident centre was set up in a house on the Donaghmore road in Dungannon. Myself, Joe and Sean were the I.R.A. men who set up the hotline. The number and code word to be used was supplied to us by I.R.A., G.H.Q. The telephone number I now forget, but our codeword for East Tyrone Brigade was "Percy French". When we rang the hotline for the first time from the little townhouse in Dungannon, we weren't sure what response we'd get. The line was answered by this clipped, very formal upper class English accent. 'Codeword' please he said. Joe replied 'This is Percy French speaking', and the voice said 'How can I help you?' Joe spent a while talking on the phone to "the voice" and then said goodbye. We had a meeting to discuss developments. We had no doubt that we were talking to a representative of the British military, and he knew he was talking to the I.R.A. If any incident in our brigade area was causing us concern we were to ring "Percy French" and the British representative would ask for time to sort it out. We would then ring back and relay if our concerns has been met, and incident was now resolved.

The first incident was a patrol of U.D.R., R.U.C. acting aggressively in a nationalist housing estate in Dungannon. The report had come in from one of our local O.C.'s on the ground. We rang "Percy French", told him what our complaint was and he said 'Tell your supporters not to take any action; they will be withdrawn from the area immediately'. The voice was as good as his word. Soon after, the U.D.R., R.U.C. were withdrawn from the nationalist area. The system worked. Red Joe rang back Percy French and reported that the incident had been resolved satisfactorily, 'It is vital your supporters take no action' he advised. He always referred to the I.R.A. as 'your supporters', never by name; he never referred to himself as British military either, but we both knew exactly who we were talking to, and that's what really mattered. We were happy enough. Word from G.H.Q. was that we could relax a bit but that there was no complete immunity from arrest. There would be no aggressive house searches but no guarantee of safety at road check points. It was as if the British administration in the north couldn't guarantee the behavior of the local based units of the security forces; namely the U.D.R. and the R.U.C. It was as if they had not got them fully under control. It was evident before that year was out that they had little or no control over them. Both these local based Brit units were very much a law unto themselves, but for now the incident centers were working and the truce was safe for the time being. I was hoping that our top men could use the truce this time to get an Irish settlement we could all live with, but it wasn't going to be easy because none of the other parts of the jigsaw were in place.

The Dublin government - a very anti I.R.A. government - resented the British government talking peace terms to the I.R.A. They saw their authority and political position as being under mined and threatened by the ongoing truce and peace talks with the I.R.A. The fall of the Sunningdale agreement the previous year had been a big failure for the whole establishment. Politically it had been a disaster for the whole centre political establishment, north and south of the border. Now they saw the I.R.A. republican movement at centre stage, negotiating with the British government, and they did not like it one little bit. They felt their own little 26 county power base threatened and they were closing ranks fast. This Dublin government was not interested in an all Ireland political peace settlement because, if the politics of Ireland went into the melting pot during such a settlement, the twenty six county political parties couldn't guarantee that they would come back out of that melting pot ever again, and they were not willing to take that chance. So when it was party political survival, or a chance of lasting peace in Ireland, these twenty six county party political leaders chose party political survival. It would take many years before a twenty six county political leader would put peace and Ireland before his own personnel political gain. But many twenty six county governments formed by different parties, one a paler shade of green than the other; paid lip service to the idea of a united Ireland, but deep down they were trembling for fear it might happen. It would be true to state that not only did they not support such a settlement, they actually resented such a settlement being negotiated by the I.R.A. republican movement so much, that they undermined attempts to achieve that settlement, such was the depth of fear and political cowardice in them. This might sound a hard judgment on fellow Irish men but I believe it to be true. The old man in the house in Park Street, Monaghan, the father of the young I.R.A. man who fell at Brookeborough, county Fermanagh on New Year's Eve 1957 and whom is remembered forever in the rebel song 'The Patriot Game' use to say to me when he was talking to me about Irish history, as often as he did, 'The I.R.A.', he'd say, through clenched teeth, 'will bring the British government to the negotiating table, but' he said, pointing his long straight pipe up to Dublin, 'watch Leinster House' he'd say, 'watch Leinster House, as they will stab you in the back, for they don't want an I.R.A. negotiated settlement'. 'They are afraid that if the political system that is partition, goes into flux, that they may not come out of it again! And therefore lose their privileged positions. They don't want real political change'. I listened and took mental note of it all. To them the nationalist people of the north are an unwelcome reminder of the failure of partition, the 26 county political establishment like to believe that they have achived 'the republic'. The conflict in the north forces them to confront the fact that 'the republic' has not been established. They do not like to face such a reality. They would rather the north would just 'go away'. I listened intently to this old Irishman. He was right. Too often, when the people of the south looked north, they saw nothing but 'the conflict up there'. When we looked south from the north we saw the beauty of the rest of our country.

43

BACK IN CRUMLIN ROAD JAIL

THE TRUCE OF 1975 was still holding fast. U.D.R., R.U.C. were hard to keep in line but the incident centres were doing their job, I relaxed a bit that year. It was a lovely summer; I did a bit of fishing for a change in the river Blackwater as it runs along through county Monaghan. I stayed mostly at the wee house in Park Street, I liked staying there. The old man of the house, his son, his daughter and son in law were all dead sound. I was enjoying myself more than I did in years. We kept up the I.R.A. brigade meetings. It was very important to keep the brigade area in good shape. So regular meetings were very important between all the key players in East Tyrone Brigade I.R.A. After one such meeting in a schoolteacher's house in Dungannon, I went over to Sean's house; Sean was married to Bill's sister. After a while in the house he said to me, 'I am going down to Crumlin road prison in Belfast to visit Bill, would you come with me', he said, 'he'd love to see you, come on'. 'I'll get you real good I.D., I have a fella who looks just like you. I'll get you his wallet, it would be a real morale booster for the big fella'. His wife, Bill's sister looked at me, 'Would you go' she said, 'he'd love it'. I thought of how lucky I was that I wasn't in that jail with Bill and then found myself saying to Sean and his good wife, 'Alright, I'll go and visit him'. Sean arranged the I.D., it was very good, I had to memorize the details of it that night, write his name a lot of times to get use to writing it. I couldn't afford to forget and write my own name instead. It is a big danger, when you are using someone's I.D, you have to be clued in at all times. We set off for Belfast and Crumlin road prison early the next morning. It was a lovely summer's morning, sunny and bright. Down the M1, the short enough drive to Belfast. We got into the prison no bother, went through the formalities and found ourselves in the waiting room. As we sat, I thought to myself, what the hell I am doing in here in Crumlin road jail; the jail the Brits wanted to extradite me back to, the one I had jumped bail from! Just then we were called to our visit. Peader was my name; I sat down opposite Bill. Sean said 'Here's Peader'. Bill caught on right away. We had right good craic through the visit; Bill kept looking at us and laughing. It was good to see him. Don't worry about your sentence' I said, 'when there is a settlement you will be out, you'll be out in no time'. Sean was cracking jokes like a stand up comedian and in no time at all the visit was over, I signed my name to get out of the prison and soon enough we were going back up the M1 to Dungannon. I felt great, stuff them I thought, this is my country, I'll go where I like. It was good to get one up on the British authorities, an authority I didn't recognize anyway! Sean played a cruel joke on his wife when we got back to Dungannon and his house. He left me hiding in the car and went into the house all distressed and told his wife, half crying, that I had got caught. His wife almost collapsed at the thought of it. Sean was a very good joker, he could put it over real well. His poor wife, she nearly died. I walked in then and she threw her arms around me like I was someone back from the dead! 'Mocking is catching', I said, when he told me I had come in too quick, But it was a great oul episode altogether! I visited my father's grave through that time too. I stood at his graveside and thought to myself, he was a good man, he loved my mother and his twelve children well, and he was good to us all. My father would have been a peace loving man, conflicts and wars would not have set easy with him. My mother would have been the rebel. My father loved his dogs, his gun, his fishing rods, his fiddle, Irish music, his chess, playing cards, céileing to all the neighbours homes, a good argument, but most of all he was just a big, salt of the earth, decent country man. I was proud of him. I went to Big Paddy's grave too. Hope we can finish the job for you I thought, as I stood to attention at his memorial and saluted him as a comrade and a friend. Slán abháile, Big Paddy, you were a good one. This is the speech I gave during the peace process

If I had to go to the grave of Big Paddy in Dungannon and stand at the end of his grave and say 'Paddy. Can this agreement complete the ideals that you died for? Did you open the door for us so that we can walk through and achieve our goals without any more young men and women going down to an early grave or spending the best part of their lives in jail?'

'And can I take on this peace process, without walking away from your grave and feeling that I let you down because you didn't die in peace? You died in the

middle of the battle.' But at the same time I know that if Paddy could speak back to me he would be willing to say to me, 'If there's a way that you can do it without any more deaths and without any more destruction, without any more tears and without any more suffering', I would say that he would say to me 'You take that way, because I gave my life for the freedom of this country'. I don't know whether this agreement is enough. The end result, if it's good enough, will be when I can stand at your grave and say 'Because of the doors that you opened with your supreme sacrifice, we now have the free democratic peaceful Ireland that we all want'.

44

THE COLOUR PARTY

THE EASTER COMMEMORATION to the Garden of Remembrance in Carrickmore, county Tyrone was held every year in honour of all who died for Ireland's cause. East Tyrone Brigade I.R.A. decided to form the colour party with I.R.A. men who were on the run. We trained in the local hall to get our drill right; many a time I danced in it and courted outside it. This was a different story altogether, as we drilled up and down the dance floor, I.R.A. men getting ready for a public show of strength. How things had changed in such a short, short time. The commemoration day was a huge success. A massive crowd of Tyrone people and others turned out for the ceremony. Me and Barry and a young I.R.A. fella called Patsy made up the front row of the colour party. Red Joe stayed out of the parade in case the Brits might try to disrupt the colour party or the ceremony. Joe would have a red hot reception ready for them! The I.R.A. took over the village of Carrickmore for the day. If the Brits decided to break truce and try to arrest us, or any of the speakers who were also on the run, they would have to get past Joe and his I.R.A. protection party first. Kevin was the main speaker that year. He was only after coming off a long hunger strike in a jail down south. He gave a rousing speech; read the Easter message from I.R.A. G.H.Q. The roll of honour of I.R.A. men who fell in the fight was read out. He did Tyrone proud. We moved on down to the village of Eglish, and unveiled a monument for Dan, the I.R.A. man who died during the mortar attack on the barracks in county Tyrone; the one where Patsy died as well. We all gathered at the local G.A.A. hall at Eglish to march to the grave yard where Dan was buried. I met his wife again, the wee girl I had to bring such bad news to the morning after her husband was killed; I'll never forget that. We spoke a while with her and his family before the colour party formed again. Joe was still our protector, though this was more open countryside and much harder to make safe. But Dan's memorial was to be opened and honoured, come what may! Everything went off well, it was a great day. The memorial was an outstanding piece of sculptured black granite, a fitting tribute to a great soldier of Ireland. Years later this I.R.A. man's nephew Cormac died tragically in his sleep when he was captain of the Tyrone Gaelic football team. A great Irishman too; a very proud Tyrone Irish family. We headed back to Carrickmore later that night and turned up at the commemorative dance in the parochial hall. The Wolfe Tones were playing at this function and a great night was had by all! A real rebel rousing night; everything had gone off safely and Joe could relax at last. He was a great friend and comrade; we couldn't have had a better man looking after our safety. He got all the scouts on the roads organised as well, he told me later he had a scout car on every stretch of the roads, 'If there had been any danger for you all, I would have known and looked after it' he said laughing. I knew well what Joe meant when he said 'I would have looked after it'. He said the R.U.C. and U.D.R. had been the biggest threat to us, as they were breaking the truce more and more, but Joe and his I.R.A. men of the East Tyrone Brigade would have been well able for them! No problem!

The truce was coming under pressure, not from the regular British army but from the local U.D.R. and R.U.C., they wanted to break the truce and get the regular British army involved again, but so far the Brits had stayed very much in the background and were keeping the truce. The incident centres were still doing their job, but the U.D.R. and R.U.C were slow to respond to demands to get out of nationalist areas. They were a threat to the safety of the I.R.A. men operating the truce in those areas. I.R.A. security was stepped up. Internment without trial was being phased out. It was too much of an embarrassment around the world for the British government. The Human Rights Court in Strasburg was on their case. My brother Martin was released when I was in Dungannon on I.R.A. business. He came around to my safe house to see me. I never visited my mother's wee house in the housing estate in Dungannon, because she would be too worried and would want to see me back in Monaghan before she could sleep again, so I never let her know when I was in Tyrone. It was too hard on her. Marty had stood it well, but then he was young and hardy; he had just turned 18 when he was interned, he was now over 21 years old. He had spent his 21st in a Brit jail - no charges, no trial. As the song 'The Men Behind the Wire' says, 'To be Irish is to be guilty'. But to hell with them one and all, we'd be here when they were gone, that's for sure! The one thing I hold against those bastards is how they treated the internees. These men were tortured. Men were taken away by helicopters, blind folded, and disorientated. They were told that the north was now under military rule and that they had the power to do whatever they liked with them. Then they brought them over to the open door of the helicopter and told them they would be thrown out if they didn't give them information. Men were actually thrown out of the helicopter believing they were dead men! The helicopter was hovering just about ground level but these men didn't know that. My brother was one of the men who got this treatment, at 18 years of age! It is to his eternal credit that he didn't break, but it affected him for his life. He could never get on an aeroplane. Places he would have loved to have gone to during his life - family holidays, football matches, horseracing meetings; all had to go by the wayside, because of this torture treatment. It was only recently, and he is over 50 now, that he could bring himself to step aboard a plane. It was in the last couple of years that a business friend of his booked private lessons for him with an aeroplane company, and he has managed to overcome his unnatural fear of flying. He is going everywhere now; can't keep him out of the aeroplanes, he loves travelling!! They were interned in the round shaped tin huts like big open dormitories; row after row of beds, and no privacy what so ever. Leaking rat invested kips. The men burned them to the ground; the problem was that it was winter time! They were left huddling in the cold of the winter for weeks under make shift shelters, while other mobile huts were made ready by their captors. All this perpetrated on these men and not even a charge or a trial of any kind. Is it any wonder Britain had to end this barbaric practice, world opinion forced them to end it. I listened to my brother's account of how he and the others were treated and then we bid our farewells and parted company. It was good to see him free again.

Long Kesh Internment Camp

Republican News Greetings Page

McNULTY – Martin B. (Cage 2, Long Kesh). Happy 21st Birthday Marty and your third in captivity. You're a manly boy. love and best wishes from Mother and all the family x x x x.

SMYTH – Happy Birthday Brian. I always think of you, Hoping your next will be spent in freedom. U.T.P.* All my love and God bless. From Martha and Son, also Mum.

WALSH – T.A. (Remand Prisoner, "A" Wing, Crumlin Road Jail) – Happy 19th Birthday Terry. If all the world were mine to give. I'd give it all and more, just to see your smiling face coming in the door. Love always, Mother and Brother Johnny and all in St. John's Crescent.

---

*Up The Provos

45

UDR RUC LANDMINED!!
AMBUSHED!!

THE TRUCE WAS holding during the summer of 1975 but the U.D.R. and the R.U.C. were out of control more than ever. The regular British army were keeping a low profile and the truce with them was still working. Then the R.U.C. started going after I.R.A. men and arresting them at checkpoints! To hell with this, it wasn't good enough! I.R.A. G.H.Q was getting bombarded with complaints from brigade areas in the north about the harassment of the U.D.R. R.U.C. Then came one of the most unusual instructions ever to be given by the I.R.A. G.H.Q in Dublin. U.D.R. and R.U.C. could be hit with gunfire and with landmines but the truce was holding with the regular British army, and they were not to be attacked, even if they came into the I.R.A.'s ambush positions. So if we had the British army standing on a landmine, units were under strict orders from G.H.Q. not to hit the plunger. If this was a mutual agreement between I.R.A. G.H.Q. and the British army, and I assumed it was, it amounted to the R.U.C. U.D.R. being fed to the wolves, by their British masters. The unit decided to put a landmine in a border road and stage a landmine and gun attack on a patrol of crown forces that came that way every couple of weeks or so. The I.R.A. had good intelligence that an armour strengthened personnel carrier was being used by U.D.R. R.U.C. to secretly patrol the border area and spy and use the cover of the truce to gather information useful to them if the truce ended. This would be the unit's target. They would make up anti personel mines. These were like giant shot gun cartridges. They would get a five gallon tin drum; cut the top of it, fill it one third full with high explosives, next third full of assorted shrapnel, and make cuts down into the side of the drum at the top so that it flapped and closed over. A homemade anti-personnel mine! They made several of these, four in all. The site for the ambush was vitally important. A good place to get them, and a good place for the I.R.A. men to get away. They found that place. It was just where the north meets the south; it was a cul-de-sac where the armoured patrol car had to slow to about ten miles per hour and then turn. They would dig the landmines into the side of the bank that ran alongside the road facing out towards the south. They would hit it broadside with the anti-personnel mines, and then open fire with rifles and machine guns. The firing point was just one small field away, about 100 yards. There was a clump of whin bushes that give them cover from the helicopter. Those helicopters, damn them! hated them with a vengeance. G.H.Q. was doing its best to procure Sam 7 surface to air missiles, but as yet they hadn't got them. To see one of those helicopters fall out of the sky in flames, after all the trouble they caused, would be like a most beautiful dream! But in the meantime they had to watch out for them carefully. So they surveyed their ambush site thoroughly, checked out their intelligence sources and East Tyrone Brigade border unit decided to go ahead with the operation. They were back in action!

The I.R.A. men put the landmines in at night, about twenty of them. I.R.A. flankers, armed I.R.A. men posted towards the north incase a Brit patrol would surprise the men digging in the mines. They had a team digging in the command wire, which led up to the firing point in the whin bushes. Everything had to be very discreet. If the command wire was spied by the enemy or anything else was left careless or suspicious they could suddenly become the ambushed instead of the ambushers. The ambush site had to look the exact same tomorrow morning with the landmine in, as it did yesterday before it went in. It took most of the night to set the ambush site up. Everything had to be clean and tidy, no carelessness, it could cost lives. Just at the dawn break everything was ready. The flankers were brought back to join the rest of the unit. The first team to man the firing point took their rifles and machine guns up under the whin bushes to begin the patient wait for the enemy armoured car. They would man the ambush position from dawn till dusk, using a fresh team every day. They would crawl into the ambush position just before dawn, watch the border road all day and then withdraw just after dusk. This would be repeated until the enemy armoured car came into the trap. Then all hell would break loose! It was the luck of the draw which team happened to be in position when the enemy came. Every team wanted it to be on their watch! They had a safe house on the south side of the border which we were using as an operation base. It was a short walk from the firing point. They had to watch out for the Gardaí as well, they couldn't let them know they were active again. But they were a very experienced guerrilla army unit. They were good at keeping underground and out of sight. I mean they were the East Tyrone Brigade republican army, the best fighting unit in the north, they knew how to operate!

It was summertime and the weather was very good. The border road was quiet, the odd farmer passed, so did the odd smuggler. It was amazing what would be seen on those little country roads at the border! Two farmers meeting and changing livestock from one trailer to another, two other men putting boxes of drink from one van to another, anything that made money from one side of the border to the other was smuggled! It was a way of life here. Good sized houses were built along the border with smuggling money. But most smugglers were local folk doing it as a nixer to help rear big families on small farms. A lot of the same people were helping to get rid of the border, they just used it to smuggle because it was there! If it was gone they would be delighted, most border folk hated the British enforced artificial border. An invisible division, unwanted, and dividing farms, farming communities, parishes, and even houses and fields in some places. It was an injustice, a running sore that was always hated. Some years later, well organised gangs would use the border to make huge money. To use the British border to make money didn't rest easy with a lot of people. Too many good men and women died to get rid of that same border. So the I.R.A. men found themselves sitting patiently from dawn till dusk, waiting for the enforcers of this injustice. They couldn't help but recall the words of the Fox, their staff car driver, and housekeeper, when he said 'the I.R.A. would bring the British army to the negotiating table, but they would still have to sort out the U.D.R. and R.U.C after that!' The orange order, the Loyalist paramilitaries, would have to be confronted and defeated too, before peace would come. So maybe this attack was the start of that confrontation. The Fox Could be right. Two days later, the regular British army came down to the border road and stood right on the landmine, right on top of it! The I.R.A. team followed orders and didn't detonate the landmine and trigger the attack. It was a very hard decision for that I.R.A. team to make, but orders from G.H.Q. were to be obeyed and the Brits had a very lucky escape! The very next day a U.D.R. jeep, one of the armour plated and bullet proof heavy duty models used by the crown forces came slowly into the ambush position. It was about midday when the I.R.A. man who was keeping look out on the binoculars said 'there coming' ,'it's getting closer, get ready, get ready'. I can see them, hit it now'. The ground around the enemy armoured car suddenly erupted into a volcano! Seconds later, the sound of the explosion ripped into the air and echoed off the surrounding hills and mountains like it was a half a dozen explosions. Some of the debris and stones from the landmine went so far into the air it landed near to the I.R.A. unit! Hell, that was a bit close! The sound of the explosion died down and the dust cleared. The armoured car became just visible through haze of the midday sun and settling dust. The I.R.A. men crouched up onto their hunkers and opened fire with the three weapons. The crack crack of the Armailite, the heavier sound of the A.K. on automatic and the thump of the big Garrand rifle rebounding and buckling about was like something out of a war movie. The din was deafening. They fired all of the magazines and clips of ammo that they had handy. Then they decided to withdraw before the British helicopter on the northern side of the border, and the Garda and the Irish army on the southern side of the border appeared. There was still a lot of danger around. New border legislation meant I.R.A. men could be charged with an attack in the southern courts that had actually taken place in the north. So the terrier dog snapping at their heels was still there! A bit of a nuisance, but the I.R.A. couldn't afford any confrontation with the southern security forces. I.R.A. Standing Order Number 8: No confrontation with the Southern states security Forces under any circumstances. This was still in force, and couldn't be broken. They took one last look at the upended armoured crown forces patrol car, heaps of clay and earth up around it. Not a move from it. Job done. The border unit of the East Tyrone Brigade withdrew from the ambush site knowing they had hit the enemy a hard blow. They withdrew safely back to the safe house and watched the evening news on the television. The ambush was first item on it. It said an armoured car had been destroyed. The Brits reported no casualitys. The I.R.A. knew they had hit them hard. It was a very successful landmine and ambush operation carried out by the border unit of the first battalion East Tyrone Brigade I.R.A.

The Man From God Knows Where!

A bunch of the boys whipped it up in the Four Seasons saloon,
The band that played the music was hitting a republican tune,
When out of the night that was cold and dark and into the din,
And the glare, there came An IRA man straight from the border, dog dirty and loaded for bear.

He looked like a man with a foot in the grave,
And scarily the strength of a louse,
But he threw his money up on the bar,
And called 'whiskey' for his thirsty mouth!

There are men, who somehow just grip your eyes and hold them hard in a spell,
and such was he and he looked to me like a man who had lived in hell!!
With his face all hair and the dreary stare of a dog whose day was done,
But he watered the whiskey in his glass and the drops fell one by one.

I got to figuring what he'd done, but questions, no! I'd ask him none!
Then all of a sudden the music changed, then it burst like a pent up flood
And it seemed to say repay, repay and my eyes were blind with blood,
And the thought came back of an ancient wrong, and it stuck like a frozen lash!
And the lust arose to kill, to kill! Then the music stopped, with a crash.

Were you ever out in the great alone, when the night was awful clear,
And how the hills, they hemmed you in with a silence you most could hear,
And only a sound of a car on the road, camped day and night in the cold,
An IRA man in a stark dead world, waiting patiently for the Brit patrol.

And high overhead both yellow and bright the helicopter searchlight swept in bars,
Then you've a hunch what this music meant, hunger, the night and the stars!
But hunger not of the belly kind that's banished with bacon and beans,
But the knowing hunger of lonely men for a home and all that it means.

For a fireside far from this bloody war, four walls and a roof above,
No more fighting and no more death, just the feel of a good woman's love,
Then all of a sudden the night sound changed!!
Listen, it's them! The high pitched whine of the Brit armoured car, as it came up from the country road, and into his deadly lair!

Belly tightened, nerves taught, this is how Guerrilla wars are fought!
The plunger hits, the landmine goes up, witness the death of a patrol of Brits.
The Guerrilla, slipped away into the night, knowing he'd struck a blow for the ancient fight!
Now I'm not a wise as these lawyer guys, but strictly between us two,
The man under the stars, and the man at the bar, was the man from God knows where!

46

THE TRUCE FAILS

AS THE YEAR went on the truce got shakier and shakier. The R.U.C. and U.D.R. more and more out of control and aggressive. The assassination of innocent catholics went on bad as ever. The peace talks seemed to be getting nowhere. The British were taking a hard line on the crucial issue of a date for withdrawal of British troops from Ireland. Internment had been phased out, the Long Kesh internment camp was being gradually closed. A new prison at the Maze outside Belfast was being built. There was word coming down the political grapevine that the British were going to abolish political status for I.R.A. men. The 50% remission of sentence would be taken away, the right to wear their own clothes would be abolished too and captured I.R.A. men would be forced to wear a criminal uniform. The full force of law and order would be used against the I.R.A. The whole political fight by the I.R.A. in the north would be classed as a criminal conspiracy against the forces of law and order of the state. The facts were, that the army, police, courts, prison system, would be used as a legitimate weapon to try defeat the I.R.A.; in other words the whole fight would be criminalised by the British government. This policy decision by the British government would have very far reaching and tragic consequences, as the years ahead would prove. The name of that new prison outside Belfast would be known as the H blocks! The truce with the Brits ended when four British soldiers were killed by the south Armagh brigade I.R.A. This was when the British dubbed that area as 'bandit's country', I'm sure the south Armagh I.R.A. men were not worried - the truce was over anyhow. The British were gearing up for their law and order onslaught against anyone who dared to oppose their military and political role. In Ireland, 1976 was the start of a whole new phase in the war of resistance against the Brits in Ireland. The long war had begun. The law and order and criminalising policy was put into force in 1976.

Long Kesh internment camp was closed down and internees all released. The H blocks new prison was opened, the Diplock non-jury courts were established in Belfast and the two interrogation torture centres were also established, one at the Gough barracks in Armagh and one at Castlereagh in county Antrim. Detention for seven days was brought in for anyone arrested for questioning about I.R.A. activity in the north. The conveyer belt system had now begun in earnest.

The conveyer belt system worked like this; suspects were arrested during raids on their homes. Monday morning was a favourite morning for arrest raids. The suspects were brought to the torture centres at Castlereagh and Gough barracks; statements were either forced out of suspects or forged. The suspects were then brought before the Diplock non-jury courts and given long prison sentences on the flimsiest of evidence and brought to the H blocks. There, they were told that they were common criminals engaged in a criminal conspiracy against the structures of the state. There was no politics involved, they were given a criminal uniform to wear, and told they would now be referred to by a criminal number. The I.R.A. subsequently began to believe that the British had used the year of the truce to gather intelligence. They used the truce for their own ends. The first man they brought through this conveyer belt system was an I.R.A. man from west Belfast. He immediately declared himself as an I.R.A. man, a political activist involved in a justified guerrilla war against British rule in the six northern counties of Ireland and demanded to be treated as a political prisoner. He refused to touch their British criminal prison uniform, never mind wear it. As the H blocks song went, 'I'll wear no convict's uniform, or meekly serve my time, that England might brand Irelands fight, eight hundred years of crime'. The British prison screws in the H blocks grabbed this I.R.A., beat him up, force stripped him, marched him naked down to his H Block prison cell and flung him into it. The British establishment had committed its first act of brutality against an Irish man in the H blocks of Long Kesh; unfortunately it would be the first of a long litany of such brutality. This I.R.A. man, a brave principled guerrilla fighter for his country and his cause, gathered himself up from the floor of his H Block prison cell, took the blanket that was on his cell bed and put it around himself to cover his nakedness. He was the first blanketman. The war in the north ploughed on; there was also a bombing campaign in Britian as well. Men I had met in jail would volunteer to fight in England, a lot of them young southern I.R.A. men, some would become very famous. A new younger group of volunteers was coming through the training camps at this time. I was now past my mid twenties, was classed as a war veteran, an old hand, but well looked up to and highly respected by this new younger generation of I.R.A. fighters. This respect was very important to me, an I.R.A. fighter who had given the best he had for more than six years at the front line of the fight.

I met an old comrade at the Ulster final in Clones that year and we had a good long talk about the war against the British and where it was at. He said 'It's going to be a long fight, a long war. We'll fight for as long is needed' he said, but we'd want to have a personal life as well' he said. 'Don't let your own life pass by as a sacrifice to the cause, we can fight on for as long as it takes, we live here, were going nowhere. We can fight on and have a life as well. The fight is safe', he said, 'We have new volunteers coming through, our people as still rock solid behind us'. The Brits are digging in for a long hard fight, but we will dig in down there with them, no problem. We'll fight for as long as it takes, in the meantime we'll have a life for ourselves along the way. We have a well established guerrilla army, plenty of young ruthless fighters, a solid support base, and we'll give the Brits as long and as dirty a fight as they want! Bring it on, we will win out in the end, after all, it's our country, we live here'.

This was typical of the straight forward way of this man. A straight forward, honest, deeply religious Christian type of man, who rarely ever cursed or swore. When I'd walk into his cell in Portlaoise jail in the mid seventies, he'd unashamedly have a string of Rosary beads hanging from the top of his bed. He was a very dedicated, strong, capable man, who showed good leadership qualities from very early on. These qualities stood him in good stead later on when the peace was called with the British, and he became one of the chief negotiators on the Republican side. He carried a huge amount of street cred, and this was vital. In his dealings with the British and the representatives of the Protestant people of the north (including Ian Paisley), these direct speaking qualities, 'where a spade was a spade' earned him a huge amount of respect, both from his own people and his former enemies.

Just then the teams came in for the Ulster final, a lovely summer's day in Clones with Tyrone and Derry playing Gaelic football. No more politics we agreed; lets enjoy the football, 'Up Derry' he shouted, 'Up Tyrone' I roared! We had been friends for years now, but today we'd oppose each other on the Gaelic football field. No doubt tomorrow and for a lot of tomorrows after that, we'd be back to fight the common enemy again! Two proud Irish counties Derry and Tyrone. 'Up the rebels, and to hell with the begrudgers', I laughed; it was good to have come through this far, still living free on this lovely summer's day. I fought on with the east Tyrone I.R.A. border unit that year. It was getting harder to survive in the south. The Garda under the pro-Brit Dublin government had become more in our faces than before. The Derry I.R.A. men had a few run ins with them along the border roads, there was a lot of ill feeling building up between them. The young hand-picked border Garda were a more aggressive bunch. One of them said to us in a local hotel 'I don't know what you I.R.A. men are fighting for, I was out at the border today, I saw nothing but mountain and bogland and gorse bushes'. One of the Derry men, a bad tempered wee man called Mickey, put his face up into the young Garda's face and snarled, 'It might be mountain, bogland and gorse bushes, but it's ours, and we intend to have it all back, by whatever means it takes, and you would be wise not to stand in my way. If I ever meet you on that border at night…' he said menacingly. 'Cool it'. Mickey. He was pulled back by his mates. He moved off muttering under his breath about Free State traitors!

A few weeks after that we all went to the Four Seasons hotel for a night out. Tyrone men, Derry men and Monaghan men as well. Good supporters these Monaghan men, mostly Sinn Féiners, political back up men. The craic was good! There was also a group of young Gardaí in the Four Seasons that night, a bit unusual; they mostly kept to the other hotels in Monaghan town. The Four Seasons hotel was known as the I.R.A. social club, and groups of young Gardaí normally stayed away from it, but there were up to twenty of them there that night. Just as the night ended, Mickey went over to one of them and argued with him. The young Garda busted Mickey's nose with a box. Then all hell broke loose! The I.R.A. men and the young border Garda got stuck into each other; it was something you would see in a cowboy film! 20 to 30 young men making the dancefloor into a battleground! I saw Wee Tommy in trouble with two fellas beating the shite out of him; I jumped in to help him when I got hit on the back of the head with a fist, I turned around and lifted the man who had done it off his feet with a box under the chin. Then I got hit again on the side of the head. Wee Tommy was stuck in the middle of two more young fellas knocking the meat out of him again. I busted one of them to give him a breather. Louie, John, Joe and Barry were all in the middle of it. The local Monaghan men got stuck in as well. It spilled out onto the front car park. A Garda in a red jumper faced up to me, a good fighter and we traded a good few blows. He was a tough boyo! Just then, the sirens from half a dozen Garda cars screamed up the driveway of the hotel, skidded to a halt and a swarm of uniformed Garda with batons drawn swooped upon us like locusts. I got split open on the forehead with a baton; I was dazed with the blow, the blood going into my eyes. At this stage, I was arrested and thrown into a patrol car and found myself in a cell in Monaghan Garda station along with Wee Tommy and Mickey. They were both covered in bruises and blood, but they made for the two Garda who threw me into the cell; they wanted more fighting. They looked at me and start laughing, 'You look like you were in the ring with smoking Joe Frazier' they said, 'You don't look like the Mona Lisa yourselves' I said, 'not that you ever did!', Mickey had a face like a bulldog at the best of times, a crabbit, bad tempered little bollix, but with the fighting heart of a lion. Wee Tommy was the same, he'd fight till he dropped. The Garda brought us all to the local court the next morning and we were charged with an affray and let out on bail of £200 each!

The fight was the talk of Monaghan town. No-one was seriously hurt on either side, a few from both sides were in hospital getting stitched up or suffering from mild concussion. But no-one got glassed, bottled, knifed or kicked to death. We just didn't fight like that in those days, it was good clean hard fighting. Even some of the young Garda we met afterwards who were involved in the battle said they enjoyed it! They said it was a great fight, they gave as good as they got! No hard feelings about it they said, it was already local folklore! When we were brought back to the to the local court just before Christmas the case was referred to the Special I.R.A. court in Green Street for early January. I knew me, Wee Tommy and Mickey were in trouble. The other I.R.A. men had all managed to escape on the night of the fight and avoided getting arrested. A group of the Monaghan men were referred to the I.R.A. court in Dublin as well. On the morning of the court case in Green Street Special I.R.A. court all the Monaghan men got off with a fine but me, Wee Tommy and Mickey all got six months each. We found ourselves in a cell in the I.R.A. jail in

Portlaoise. I had cell on the opposite side of the jail this time. When I got up on my cell bed and looked out my window, there was no farmer, no of field of barley to be seen but there was a lovely old fashioned cottage just over the prison wall. It looked real peaceful and homely, it was lovely. Wee Tommy was in the cell next door to me. There was a heating pipe running through each cell. There was a gap between the pipe and the wall; this enabled you to talk to the man in the next cell if you got down beside it. He was always down at the pipe, talking, telling jokes and discussing the news and politics. Time was harder here this time. There was a lot of tension between long term I.R.A. prisoners and the prison wardens. Searches were carried out more often, it was much more tense but we'd only do four months out of the six months sentence, we'd be out in springtime, so the tension didn't mean that much to us. The long termers called us three the visitors; they reckoned we were only in for a visit. I read a lot and listened to the radio a lot and kept to myself a good bit. I had a lot to think about and this short term in prison was forcing me to do it. Wee Tommy got on well with everybody. He got friendly with a top Sinn Féiner who was also a school teacher by profession. He was spending a lot of time in this teacher's cell. Wee Tommy confided in me that the reason he was spending so much time in this teachers cell was that he had left school illiterate, and this teacher was teaching him how to read and write. He was giving him school lessons in his cell. He asked me to keep his secret as he would be embarrassed for anyone else to know; I laughed and assured him his secret was safe. This man, who was a few years younger than me, would fight on in the I.R.A. for many years to come and fight hard. Then he would go to America, New York, become head of the Tyrone men's association there, as well as being heavily involved with Clann Na Gael in New York. A bricklayer by trade, the same as myself, he would be involved in the building trade in New York and become a self made millionaire! He'd come back to Ireland in years to come and buy a hotel in Donegal he used to be barman in. He'd also meet lots of very famous New Yorkers, amongst them the Cardinal of the catholic church of New York, who presented him with a plaque for good work done for the Irish community in the Big Apple. Not bad for a 22 year old I.R.A. man who left school illiterate, and was now next cell to me in an I.R.A. jail, getting taught how to read and write! Wee Tommy was a great character! His life and mine would intertwine a lot, both before he went to New

York and afterwards. In the meantime, he was in the cell next to mine and was annoying the hell out of me! Since he'd learned how to read a bit, he was coming on real fast - he was now reading a cowboy book, a western! Every now and again he'd be down at the pipe asking me the meaning of this word or spelling out a word and asking me what word it was and what did it mean - he took great pleasure out of reading. After he'd asked me the meaning of a word, from his western, he said to me, 'McNulty you know, this reading is nearly as good as being at the pictures!', I lay across my bed and laughed my head off at Wee Tommy, one of life's real characters! When they made him they threw away the mould!

The winter was going by fast. My release date was the twenty sixth of April, I would be out for early spring, a lovely time of the year; I love the spring time. A new beginning, full of the promise of life. What promise did life hold for me I wondered, as I lay on my bed at night. Every time I'd gotten out of jail before I'd head back up to Monaghan and report to the East Tyrone Brigade I.R.A. for active service, now this time I wasn't so sure. I'd been a long time at the face of the battle, I'd seen a lot of good men fall in the fight, a lot of good men and women go to jail for a long time. My brother Joe had got captured by the British army during an operation for the East Tyrone Brigade's border unit, he was now a blanket man in the H blocks, he was doing ten years. I was heading into my late twenties and had come through a lot and very important to me I had come through it well. I'd never let anybody down, and I'd never let myself or my family down either. They were all still proud of me. I always did my best to be decent and right to all. I was a bad enemy all right, but I was a good loyal comrade and friend. I'd also met some great people along the way, people who'd kept me in their homes. It might have been our safe house, but it was also someone's home, the risks these good people took for me and my comrades will never be known. They often took as big a risk as I did. I owed them a great debt. I'd been on the run, away from my own home since the spring of 1971. I'll owe those people who looked after me for the rest of my life. So as I lay in my prison cell in the spring of '77 I knew my front line active service with the first battalion east Tyrone was coming to an end.

47

ORDINARY WORKING MAN:
MY OWN BUSINESS

I ALWAYS KNEW that when my part in the struggle was over I'd go back to my trade as a brick layer. I'd never been interested to being promoted to the higher ranks. J.B. offered me that back in Monaghan but I wasn't interested. I knew someone had to do the administration of the struggle at the higher level, but it just wasn't for me. I have great respect for those who did take it on; for they could not have been done without. I remembered the talk at the Ulster final some years earlier. 'We want to get ourselves a life' he said, 'It's going to be a long war'. I would still support the fight against the Brits; I'd support those younger I.R.A. men who were on active service especially those still fighting with the East Tyrone Brigade. I knew then, that when I left the prison on the 26th of April 1977, I'd go to Dublin city and get myself a job as a brickie. I got up on the end of my bed in the small cell, and watched the man living in the wee cottage just on the other side of the prison wall. He went to work every morning on his bike about eight o' clock. His dog, a collie, would watch him until he got out of sight. His wife would mind the children, and hang out the clothes to dry. He kept a lovely garden; spuds, vegetables, flowers and bushes. When he would come home from work in the evening, the smoke would be billowing out of the chimney of his little home in a welcome; his dog would run down the road to meet him and his wife and children would come to the cottage door all excited to see him. He'd go through the open door and I'd picture the big open fire beckoning him with its red warmth, his dinner steaming on the table for him, and I wondered if I'd ever be lucky enough to get what he had. He had all I ever wished to have in this life. I got down from the end of my bed and said a wee prayer, that some day, if I worked hard enough, I'd be lucky enough to have what he had. I left that prison at 7 o'clock on the 26th April 1977 picked up by Hughie the Builder, and two other Tyrone men. Noel from Carrickmore, who was going to New York that morning, and another young Tyrone man called Aidan also from Carrickmore. I'd sent word to my former comrades of my decision to go to work in Dublin, and they wished me luck. I had £11 left in my personal account in the jail which they gave me on the way out. They offered me a bus ticket and a small amount of prison money but I declined the offer of both; put my £11 into my pocket, got into Hughie the Builders car and the four of us headed into Dublin city. I was back on civi street!

Me, Hughie the Builder and Aidan went for a meal and a beer in Dublin city. Hughie the Builder's wife was a lovely woman. She was very good to me, and they treated me as one of the family. Mickey the Gangerman was Hughie the Builder's main man. A tough building worker, a real McAlpines man. He worked hard and was a good man to his wife Kathleen and his children. Hughie had wee children as well. They were good, decent, hard working Tyrone men who were good supporters of the fight in the north, and were looking after me because they knew my history in Tyrone. They knew I had fought a good fight and were there to help me get my feet back on the ground in ordinary life. I was on a small housing scheme of about 10 houses. As to my trade as a bricklayer, it was like learning how to ride a bicycle, once learned, never forgotten. I worked hard for Hughie the builder and earned my wages, good wages at that, two hundred quid a week was good money in 1977. Most ordinary workers would earn half of that, brickies were very well paid. A lot of brickies came from the north in those days. Most council housing estates in the north were all built with red brick; there was a lot of these red brick estates in the north, so we northern brickies had a lot of practice building brick. We were very proud of the fact that we were good at our trade. I'd get up in the morning about seven, get breakfast and be in work for eight; we'd finish about five and go home for dinner in Hughie's house. His wife was a really good cook. I was well fed, had a good bed to lie in, had money in my pocket. Me and Mickey had become good mates; him and his wife Kathleen were very good to me too. Aidan the young lad that came down to the prison the morning I got out, worked for Hughie as well. He was into everything Irish - G.A.A., Irish music, Irish history. He was very interested in the fight in the north, he loved finding out about my time there. He later joined the East Tyrone Brigade and fought well.

I spoke very little about my past life. I was still very security conscious, I knew a lot. When an active service man's time at the front line was over, it was not a problem to leave and return to ordinary life, but you were expected to keep your secrets strictly to yourself. The mantra 'Loose talk costs lives' was still very strictly adhered to. I found it very difficult to adjust to life in Dublin, I missed all my old comrades. I knew I had done my bit but I still missed them and what had been my life for so long. I was lonely, I felt isolated. Sometimes I felt guilty that I wasn't still fighting, I felt I had abandoned the fight and my old comrades. I knew I shouldn't feel like this, but I couldn't help it. I had called up to county Monaghan to meet my old comrades. They had been with me in my decision. No-one was expected to stick to that kind of life forever. The ones who understood best were the ones who had shared the hard times with me! They knew the kind of toll that type of life takes from you. They knew only too well cause it took the same toll from them. Soon after I made my decision to leave, many of my old comrades made the same tough decision and left as well. There was a whole new generation of younger fighters anyway, we were veterans, old veterans in their eyes. I'd met some of those young fighters when in Monaghan, and they appreciated the fact that we had left the east Tyrone battalion area in very good shape for them to carry on the struggle. I felt good about all of that. I realised that it would just take time to adjust to my new life. After a while in Dublin I got my own flat. I got the bottom of a small terraced house in the Kilmainham area of Dublin, Prospect Terrace, Kilmainham. I enjoyed living there; I had come to love the anonimity of living in Dublin. The fact I could walk down the street, get lost in the crowds and no-one knew who I was, was a relief to me. There was no special branch constant surveillance - they had lost track of me at this time, even though they would catch up again later! But at this time I loved the feeling of freedom Dublin city gave me. I felt safe again, for the first time in many years. I was beginning to enjoy my ordinary life. I got a love of Dublin city then that I never lost. I will always have a soft spot for Dublin even if I am a country man at heart, it was always good to me. Hughie the Builder had got a new contract; houses that had been built in Dublin in the sixties with no solid chimneys were now getting them installed. A home improvement grant from the Department of the Environment covered most of the cost of this work. I could be working in Tallaght or Lucan, so my place in Kilmainham was handy for both places.

Hughie the Builder then asked me to run the Lucan side of the job for him, he was splitting from a business partner of his and things were a bit messy. He didn't want this partner in on the Lucan side of things so I was running Lucan for him as a separate business. I got my own work team and was doing a good job for Hughie, it was payback from me to him. I was glad to be able to work hard for him, he'd been good to me. I was earning good money, I was able to live well and still save a good bit of my wages. I'd put it in the Bank of Ireland in Lucan every Monday. I was going on the old country advice given to me growing up. Make a bit, spend a bit and save a bit! Good down to earth mentoring, it was to stand me in good stead! I was with Hughie the Builder over a year now. Aidan was one on my work team. Another Tyrone man, a young fella called Kevin from the Dungannon area of county Tyrone was my other main man; a very sharp young fella he learned everything he was shown very quickly. Him and Aidan got on well. I nicknamed him Kevin the brain; he loved to show off as to how smart he was - he loved being first, no harm in that! We worked well for Hughie the Builder and I gained a lot of experience. It worked well for both of us.

I was now enjoying working and living in Dublin, life was getting good, easy going after all the years of turmoil. It was good to feel ordinary again. I hadn't socialised a lot that year, I had just been finding my feet. I had a few pints of beer in the local pub The Patriot's Inn at Kilmainham, near the old jail. At least I was on the outside looking in this time, not the other way around!! I was sitting in my flat one evening reading the Evening Press and happened to come across an article about corporation houses in the Finglas area of Dublin city. The tenants of these houses were marching on the corporation offices on Capel Street in Dublin, protesting about the lack of heat and damp conditions of their houses, all because they had no chimneys in their houses. They were demanding the corporation built the chimneys into their houses. This could be very interesting I thought. I got into my car, a Mark 3 Ford Cortina and went across town to Finglas. I asked someone where St. Helen's area was and they directed me to it. I knocked at a door and asked where the chairperson of the tenant's association lived and they brought me to it. A lovely, friendly Dublin woman came to the door and smilingly asked me in. I explained to her over a cup of good tea that I had seen the report in the paper of their protest at the corporation housing department's office in Capel street. She raised her eyes up to the heavens and sighed 'It's been a long fight with them' she said, 'but I think we have won, were getting a grant to cover most of the work. The rest will be put onto our rents over ten years but the housing authority will pay the builder in the meantime. So the builder will get paid in full when the job is completed and passed by the housing inspector'. Sounds good I thought as I listened. I told her that I was a builder doing private houses in Tallaght and Lucan. I explained that I was interested in doing chimneys in their area. I assured her that I knew how to do them and do them properly, her and me got on well. She lived in a four block of terrace houses. I'd needed to do the four at the same time, which would pay well. 'Would you do mine first' she said anxiously, 'we have a lot of damp and small children, it's not healthy for them', I agreed to do her four block first and she passed it with her three neighbours. I had to get planning permission from the local housing corporation for the chimney installations, which I applied for with an architect the next day. It would take a few weeks to come through. The woman chairperson had things to get in place with the Dublin housing department and then we would be in business! I went to the Bank of Ireland in Lucan and explained what I was going to do. I had some money in the bank but not enough to keep a new business going until the corporation finance department would come through with their first payment, that could take up to eight weeks. The bank manager listened carefully to my proposal and then checked my account, 'You save regularly' he said, 'that is why I am going to do business with you. Get your first four houses completed, get them passed by the inspector, get the finance department of the corporation to write to me here at the bank confirming your installations are passed and in the pipeline for payment. Get the cheque made out to your company and to Bank of Ireland Lucan and I will put the full amount of your payment into your account immediately'. I shook hands with him and we were in business! He also gave me a small amount of an overdraft. It would still be tight enough to survive until I got my first installations passed but I'd manage. The job would need to be done perfectly otherwise I would in big trouble. I'd have left a good paying secure job and if I'd messed up I could lose the lot! I'd have no money and no job! It was a chance, a risk, but then in the big picture of my life it wasn't really much of a chance or a risk. I laughed to myself, it was wee buns compared to the risks I'd taken in the past, but it was a good opportunity to do well and make some big money and I'd work hard at it to make it a success! I loved hard work and the challenge.

I approached Kevin about leaving Hughie, and true to form, he wanted a share in the business to leave! He would see if he could raise several thousand pounds from his family at home in Tyrone, and if he could, he wanted a partnership with me. The money would leave the business secure, I thought. He was a very efficient organiser, and could be very gruff in his attitude to people, but he'd be a good site manager and he'd get the job done, and done well. It would give me more time to look after the bylaw approvals, get new jobs, form a limited company and get an accountant etc. It could work between me and Kevin I thought. I shook hands with him. Get the money and we're in business I told him! Kevin got the money and I got one of my brothers to buy an old angle cab B.M.C. lorry from a head stone man in Dungannon. The old lorry had been cared for like an egg, it was perfect for the job. it was also handy money and we now had a lorry! My brothers who were in the building business in the north also filled it with building tools - some scaffolding and planks and a few very useful bits and pieces. They were so delighted I was still alive and kicking and going into business on my own! My mother was so happy, her prayers were been answered! Joe was still in the H blocks of Long Kesh, but at last I was safe! Me and Kevin had now everything in place. I went out to Finglas and told the woman we would be starting her house in ten days time, on Monday morning at 8 o'clock sharp. She told me she would have her house and her neighbour's houses cleared out and ready. She was delighted, so was I! Aidan had agreed to work for us, so we had a team. I told Hughie the Builder of our business plans, and that we would be leaving him. He wasn't too pleased. He said he would be sorry to lose us, we were a good team but he did wish us luck in our new venture. I thanked him and his good wife for all they had done for me. I told him that if we were successful in business and could ever do him a good turn, he only had to ask. He thanked me for that and we parted company in good form. I said goodbye to Mickey the Gangerman, it had been good to work with him. He was as tough and as hard as building workers come, but he was a good man with a big heart. Him and I remained good friends for life. His wife Kathleen was a lovely person, a happy couple with lovely children.

Our new business was a huge success and grew quickly. We rented a yard on the Cabra road beside Finglas. It was a part of the old unused farmyard attached to the deaf and dumb school. We had it rented from the nuns, it was a big yard and very useful. Getting bylaw through for every individual house was slow and time consuming. The corporation building overseers sat with us full time on our first four block of houses. They checked everything we did thoroughly but they soon realised that we were an experienced crew and let us alone to do our work. The people in the four block were delighted with their new fire and fireplaces with hot water at the sink and three radiators in the bedrooms upstairs - it was heaven to them. The corporation inspector passed the installation no problem. The finance department sent the letters of confirmation to the Bank of Ireland Lucan and the funds were put into the company bank account. The bank were happy with the arrangements and so were we. Kevin was doing a good job, the site was running smoothly. We were swamped with tenants in the houses wanting their chimneys in. We were known as the northern chimney men. All the tenants wanted us to do their chimneys. We had a very good reputation; so good in fact that the Dublin corporation housing department gave me a block bylaw approval. I didn't have to apply for individual bylaw's anymore. I could go in to any one of the hundreds of houses in Finglas south and do their chimney installation without an architect or all the time consuming paperwork. It was great to have gotten that! I think the corporation housing department were so pleased to have the tenants off their backs and a good efficient team to do the installations that they were delighted to speed the jobs up and avoid unnecessary paperwork or delay. Suddenly me and Kevin had a very successful business to run. We rented a big house in Glen Hill Park area of the north road for our workers, I moved in there myself. We bought ourselves two brand new Ford Escort cars, a new Volkswagen pick up. We also set up a new plant for making fireplaces in the yard we had rented, instead of having to go into Dublin and buy four or five fireplaces for big money every week. We were now manufacturing our own, it made a lot more sense. We ran our business in a very professional manner; we always came in on time, paid our men, paid our suppliers and made good money.

It was now 1979 and the war in the north was still as bad as ever. I kept in touch with Wee Tommy; he was still an active I.R.A. man with the East Tyrone Brigade. He'd come down to Dublin for a rest every now and again and work on a part-time basis with me. I was delighted to be able to look after active service I.R.A. men, as I had been looked after in the past. I felt I was doing my bit again, only in a different way. I'd be a back up man to the East Tyrone Brigade active service I.R.A. men. The fight against the Brits in the north was still going strong and I was still a part of the fight. I gave more active service I.R.A. men part-time work with my company. I would regularly go to Monaghan town, book into the Four Seasons hotel and meet up with old comrades. I got to know some new ones and have a few beers with them and also give them some well needed pocket money before I left town. I knew how much that meant to me when I was in their place, it was now great to be able to do it for them. I would always oppose British rule in my country in whatever way I could. I'd always back the northern Irish people trapped on the other side of a British imposed border, their fight would always be my fight. I'd never forget that.

The British Ambassador to Ireland was landmined and killed around this time, on the outskirts of southern Dublin city. The Garda special branch and southern security forces went mad. My job in Finglas was raided and all the workers arrested and brought to the Brideswell Garda station. They were taken out of the vans and lorries; taken from behind the mixers and the job left abandoned. They also raided the house in Glenhill Park and arrested any one who came there. Just after this had happened the special branch cars followed me down the north road to the traffic lights at the old Premier Dairies, jumped out of their cars armed with UZI sub machine guns and pulled me out of the car and promptly arrested me. I'd heard about the explosion of the landmine and the assassination of the British ambassador, so I knew why I was being arrested. Seemingly, the special branch had made a list, along with their British special branch helpers, of all the men from the north who were experts in the fields of landmines, and I came up as one of them! How I wonder, did they come to that conclusion!! They questioned me for a day and a half. Then this man, a British man, came into my interview room on his own. He said he was from the British embassy. He said he was in a position to offer me unlimited money if I could tell him who killed the British Ambassador. He offered me a new life in whatever country I wanted to go to, and told me that I'd never have to work again. I sat looking at this asshole for a minute. Did he not know how much I enjoyed my work? Never work again - that didn't interest me one little bit! Turn traitor, for any amount of money! The insulting British stupid bastard! I looked this sad spectacle of a British bagman in the eye, and told him to fuck off out of my sight, as he made me sick. He was startled, pulled back a bit, and got the hell out of there. I laughed to myself. Some people think money can buy them anything. Stupid bastard! Me and my men got out of there and went back onto the job. Now there are jobs where the like of this might do your company serious harm, but not Finglas south! We became overnight heroes! Seemingly the women of the houses heard that the workers who were working in their homes had been arrested. They were onto the Bridewell Garda station continuously, demanding the northern builders, as they wanted their 'bleeding chimneys finished'. Those type of women, when they are angry, would scare anybody - not a bit of wonder the special branch released us! They were scared out of their wits! I'd rather face the British Paras than face those working class Dublin women when they were angry! The Dublin special branch tried to do my company harm with the corporation but they couldn't. It was the tenant who lived in the corporation house who had the say as to who did their installation - no-one else, and they were having no-one only the northern builders! You can't beat working class people! The job in Dublin was going well and I was making good money. It was a change to have real money after all those years with the I.R.A. where money didn't matter. I kept going to Monaghan and socialising there and meeting the active service I.R.A. men and looking after them with a good feed, a few drinks and a few quid! Years later, they told me that when I came into the Four Seasons, the word would spread like wildfire - 'McNultys in town!' I enjoyed the craic up there.

The brutality in the H blocks prison was getting worse and worse. My brother Joe was getting a hard time. They were now on the dirty protest, living in filthy cells with no clothes, no sanitation and no visits. They injured my brother badly during a cell search and he had to be brought out of the prison to the Royal Victorian hospital to be treated for injuries including broken bones. I knew Joe's form and I feared they would kill him in there. Joe was as tough and as game a man as I ever met in my life and I had met some tough ones! 12 screws could come into his cell and he'd fight them all until he wouldn't be able to move a muscle. They would have to kill him to beat him, and I was afraid that was just what they would do. I really feared for my brother's life in that hellhole of a prison. A new British Prime Minister had been elected in Britain around this time. A woman called Margaret Thatcher, a real right wing, domineering British tory. Her connection with the H blocks would become infamous for its callousness and cruelty. She became one of the most hated and despised British Prime Ministers in Irish history. Even her own working class British people would despise her. She would become a mortal enemy and a war criminal as far as the I.R.A. would be concerned. There were demonstrations right across the north and south in support of the H block men and in protest at their inhumane and degrading treatment. I attended those demonstrations and kept up to date with what was happening in that terrible hellhole! It was 1979 and that year in the summer, Lord Mountbatten and 19 British soldiers were killed on the one day. It was the biggest single loss of life for the British army since World War II. All known I.R.A. men and sympathisers around the country were arrested. My men and myself were all pulled in again, it was getting to be a habit! We got out again after a day or so. I watched Prince Charles of Wales at his favourite uncle's funeral. Lord Mountbatten had been his mentor and hero. His grief was evidently very real and deep. I hoped he realised that the grief of the British Army's Irish victims, including the Bloody Sunday victims, was as deep and as real as his was. The grief and profound sadness at the loss of an uncle or a father for a working class Irish family was, as great as the loss of a member of the Royal British family was to him. As commander in chief of British armed forces, I hoped Prince Charles would reflect on the amount of sadness and grief his army had brought on the Irish people over nearly 800 years.

48

MY OWN HOME

I HAD NEARLY enough money saved from my company to buy my own home. I was looking out for someplace that would suit me; I didn't want a city house. I wanted some place in the country, preferably with a plot of ground with it to run my small building business and fireplace business from, somewhere north of Dublin city would suit me. I was in Monaghan for the weekend again and was heading down the road towards Dublin on the Monday morning when I saw a For Sale sign on a small country house about 25 miles outside Dublin city in county Meath, between Slane and Ashbourne. I was flying along in my new big Renault 18 TS. I braked and pulled around up at the old gate and jumped over it. It was an old cottage on about an acre of land, enclosed by high mature hedges. A lovely, big plot of land along the main N2, it was just what I was looking for! The cottage was old and in need of repair but it could be lived in. It had electricity, water, an outside toilet but I had often lived in worse during my I.R.A. days! It was one of about six similar houses with a shop just down the road. I decided to buy it right there and then if the price was right. I rang the estate agent from Dublin and made an appointment to meet him the next morning at the cottage. The couple who owned the cottage lived in England. He said he would ask them that night for the best price they would take. The next morning I was pleasantly surprised, the price was way below what I would have paid. I did a deal there and then and paid a deposit. The estate agent promised he would get the deal closed as soon as possible, he was as good as his word and six weeks later I got the key to my own cottage! I'll never forget the feeling when I opened the door and walked into my new home. I had been away from my own home on the run since the spring of 1971 and it was now the spring of 1980 - almost 10 years without a home of my own. Living with other people, very good people, is still not the same as your own home. I knew for a long time now that I wasn't going home anytime soon, it was going to be a long drawn out conflict in the north. I needed a home of my own and now I had one. At 30 years of age it was very important to me to have my own place. I looked around inside - three small bedrooms, a small kitchen and a small sitting room with an old wood burning stove. It was perfect! I walked around the big field with the high hedges and I felt so good, this was all mine! I'd do it up and build a workshop for fireplaces, a showroom for selling them directly to the public and a yard for my building gear, scaffolding, van and so forth. I thought of the man in his little cottage over the I.R.A. prison wall, the man who had everything in this life I ever wanted, and I felt I was getting there! It was just three years since I was in that prison cell, now I had my own wee house and field! I was getting there with the basic lessons that I grew up with - hard work and an ambition to succeed! Ability, ambition and hard work, a winning combination every time!

That year I started a major renovation to the little cottage and field. I kept some of the cottage walls and built a four bedroom house around the shell. All the trades men whom I had given good well paid work to over the last three years, returned the favour with good workmanship done at minimum cost. John Joe had settled in the same area of county Meath as me and he had a digger, a J.C.B. He was after selling an old family farm in the north that was left to him by his dad. His did trogan worked for me on that old cottage and field; he just wouldn't take money off me. A very decent man, old comrade and friend. Wee Tommy was a brickie by trade, and him and another I.R.A. man from Tyrone, Tommy, a brother of the man Noel who was in the car the morning I was picked up outside the I.R.A. prison, was a brickie too. He gave great help also. His brother Noel who went to the States the morning I had got out, was killed in a tragic car accident outside New York city coming home from work, R.I.P. Tommy married a lovely girl from a well known republican family in county Meath area and settled in a nearby village. John Joe married a local girl as well. Quite a few I.R.A. men on the run would settle in this part of east Meath. The man who was injured in the attack on the British army barracks in county Tyrone, had made a full recovery; he had spent a long time in hospital, but he recovered and went back on active service with the border unit. Him and Barry were both plasterers by trade, and I done a deal with them to come down from Monaghan and plaster my renovated cottage. Harry from Carrickmore in Tyrone did the roofing and joinery. A wee man called Sally the Electrician did all the wiring for me. Pascal from Dungannon and his apprentice Shane, who done all the plumbing for the chimney contract in Dublin, did the plumbing for me. One of the hardest drinking whiskey men I had ever encountered in my life! I often wondered how he survived. Sleepy Eyed Peter from Fermanagh was my handyman on the job, he kept everything right on the site. You would have thought he wouldn't get safely down to the little country shop a few hundred yards away, so sleepy and laid back he was. But he went off to America for 30 years and did well for himself. A great lover of Irish music and a musician himself who played the fiddle, he was a real character. He had a little Morris Minor van and kept his fiddle and a bottle of Poteen, which was made by him and Big Joe a mate and comrade of his from Fermanagh, in the van. Sometimes he'd just stop the Morris Minor, take out his fiddle and bottle of Poteen, take a slug of his raw Poteen and then proceed to play his fiddle! Him and Big Joe were both I.R.A. men with the Fermanagh brigade I.R.A. We did a joint operation with the Fermanagh men one time. Our first man in that Fermanagh area sent word back that he had met the I.R.A. men from that area, he said there were just two, and of them one was a poteen brewer! He was talking about the fiddler, an unforgettable character! So the craic was ninety at the renovation of the little cottage. The local shops and pubs did well as they were always either hungry or thirsty!

Old Hughie and Alan, the man who had offered me a new life in New York in 1974, called by one day. I was delighted to see them. They congratulated me on the job I was doing on my new home. Alan was doing a big job on a hotel in north inner city Dublin at the time. He instructed old Hughie to deliver all the plastering materials for my cottage project free of charge from Gypsum in Sheriff Street, where they had a main depot. He said it was an appreciation of the effort I had put into the fight in the north. Alan remained my friend and mentor all my life. When he died of cancer years later I felt I had lost a father for the second time. He was a great man to have on your side. It got to be a feature of my little cottage in the Balrath area of county Meath on the main N2, that anybody who was anybody, in the republican movement, stopped in my fireplace shop to say hello and have a yarn. It was to be a famous calling house. The Garda special branch would love to call as well, when they got to know who lived there! I used to say that if an I.R.A. man farted in Cork, they'd check to see if the smell was in my fireplace yard at Balrath in county Meath! They were to raid my place in Balrath for everything that happened in Ireland. But sure it was great to be so popular, at least I'd never be robbed or burgled, it was like having your own security company full time! They never left my stretch of road, even my suppliers got to know them! So I worked away at the cottage at Balrath, and the chimney contract in Finglas at the same time. The chimney contract was still profitable and doing well and the little cottage at Balrath was coming along well, but one thing that wasn't going well – that was the situation inside the H blocks of Long Kesh outside Belfast.

The captured I.R.A. prisoners on the blanket were getting a terrible time of it, under Thatcher's British government. There had been a hunger strike just before Christmas of 1980. 7 I.R.A. prisoners of war had gone to death's door when Thatcher's government had done a deal with them. She later reneged on the deal, and now in the early part of 1981 there was talk of a second hunger strike in the H blocks, but this time it would be different. On the first hunger strike all the I.R.A. men had started on hunger strike at the same time, so they were all approaching death's door together. This time there would be several weeks between I.R.A. men starting hunger strike, so that if Thatcher's government reneged on a deal with the first hunger striker, then they would be faced with another dying hunger striker a few weeks later, and so on until the I.R.A. men's demands to be treated as political prisoners was achieved. It was a daring plan that would demand the highest of courage and commitment from the brave I.R.A. men.

49

MY BROTHER JOES STORY
THE H BLOCKS – BRITIANS HELLHOLE

IT WAS TENSE, very tense in the back of the prison van on route from Crumlin road prison to the H block of Long Kesh. Myself and my comrade, Aidan had been given a sentence of ten years each by a be-wigged diplock judge, sitting on his own (without a jury); and as he put the hammer down, he didn't even try to hide the total hatred and disdain he had for Irish republicans.

A jumble of thoughts, emotions and feelings cascaded through my mind. The abruptness of the court case. We refused to recognise the court, I had the utter contempt and anger in me that a unionist judge could wield such unbridled power against us. Republicans in such a court had no chance of justice, it was as easy as shooting mice in a barrell the corrupt orange judiciary excelled in meeting out harsh penalties to anyone who challenged their authority on the status of the six counties.

It had been ten months previous that we were captured by British troops on the border between Clogher Co. Tyrone and Co. Monaghan. At 6.45am on a sunny early July morning, we were allegedly making repairs to a landmine whose wiring had become dislodged when a force of about ten British soldiers with blackened out faces jumped out of the ditch screaming all sorts of treats and obscenities. We were bundled to the ground and put face down in the dirt while a very loud and heated discussion between the Brits ensued. The ordinary squaddy wanted to shoot us on the spot, but their officer in charge said we were captured prisoners and would be taken into custody. The younger Brits countered that we had possession of a landmine and were planning blow them up without mercy, so why should they not be given the go ahead to execute us. They had a point, but the Brit officer won his argument. After an hour, they called a helicopter in to take us to Clogher barrack and then to

Castlereagh interrogation centre. It was probably the longest hour of my life, but in a calm strange sort of way we were resigned to our own fate. If the same circumstances had occurred in the eighties (shoot to kill Thatcher policy) then I must certainly wouldn't be writing this, and my co-accused wouldn't be alive either. So we lived to tell the tale, so to speak, unlike a lot of our other comrades who lost their young lives in the fight for Irish freedom.

My mind jolted back to the present grim reality, and I took a quick glance at the four prisoners whose pale and stressful faces said a multitude of unspoken words, as I'm sure mine was likewise, as I felt extremely tense. Fear of the unknown is probably the ultimate sanction that the human psychie has in its armament, and it was employing this weapon to its maximum effect. We had heard in the Crumlin prison about the kickings, brutality and beatings that had been inflicted on helpless blanket men and the mind will always multiply that fear tenfold, because it cannot figure out the unknown in a rational way.

In 'The Crum' we were given political lectures by our own O.C. He was a huge frame of a man, with a beard that seemed to cover most of his face, tall and heavy set. He was an imposing figure, good with words, and could ram home his point with great authority. We were told that any sentenced prisoner who went to the criminal blocks was forsaking all their republican beliefs, and if you donned the prison uniform you were no better than a turn coat, and you would cease to be a republican in the true sense of the word. Harsh words, strong words. Words that didn't do any justice to the human frailty. That all humans, even with identical republican ideals, are essentially individuals, and have different thresholds on mental endurance. The British government had indeed set the battle lines. When it withdrew political status from republican prisoners in 1976; which in effect, was saying to the world that our struggle for Irish freedom was only a criminal conspiracy. The stakes could not have been higher. In my own mind I was determined not to wear the criminal uniform (monkey suit) and had been mentally preparing myself for this undoubted ordeal for a considerable period of time. I inhaled deeply on my last cigarette, one of the small luxuries a jail prisoner has, because I had my mind firmly made up that I would stop smoking the day I went on the blanket. Prisoners on the blanket could get some tobacco smuggled in some days but there would be days there would be nothing.

For a forty-a-day man, days without would be torture on its own, so I quit completely. I have never smoked a cigarette from that day thirty years ago. It's a dark cloud that doesn't have some silver lining!! I also learned the Irish language in the H Blocks, and I am fluent, which is a source of great pride to me. So if for nothing else I am grateful in some small way to, it for those small blessings.

We were taken out of the prison van and escorted into a H block. It was the dreaded H block 3 that had the infamous reputation as the cruellest and most brutal regime of all the blanket blocks. The screws then offered me the last chance to wear the criminal uniform, which I refused. I was stripped naked and after a few slaps and punches I was escorted to the cell and handed a blanket. This was my living space for some years to come.

The first day on the blanket I thought of my mother who I had seen a few days earlier in 'The Crum'. She looked smaller than ever and the concern on her gentle face said a thousand words. The worry lines around her eyes and forehead showed that she had had many sleepless nights, and it was with a heavy heart that I told her that I would not be accepting visits on the blanket, and for her not to worry, as I was strong and determined, and that I would keep in good health. She gave me a hug and I never saw any of my family again for almost 3 torturous years. I couldn't afford to be too sentimental, as you had to suppress your inner most emotions and keep yourself case hardened to the task in front of you, (this might sound utterly callous) but that's the way it was and had to be. You had to be divided from soft emotions, to survive in this ruthless environment.

H block 3 was a truly horrific place to be. The protest escalated to daily brutality and almost starvation, to intimate body searches over mirrors which left some prisoners bleeding from the anus. Human waste was being put on the walls because prisoners were being callously beaten whilst going to the toilet. Wing shifts were a running battle and some prisoners were physically sick hours before a shift. There was a prison boss in H 3 called Ken who delighted in handing out extreme violence at his command.

Some big, strong, decent, honest, republicans couldn't hack this cruel regime, and went up to the (criminal) work blocks as they were called. I never held it against any prisoner who at least gave the protest a shot. When I heard that our big bearded O.C. in 'The Crum' did recognise the court, got a light sentence, and went straight up to the criminal blocks without even trying one day on the blanket, I was sickened. I held him in utter contempt, as he was supposed to be a leader who gave political speeches, but who took the easy option in self preservation. It was my first lesson in not believing all within your own ranks, and not to have a robotic mind on anything.

The first hunger strike was called and I forwarded my name to participate in it. We were told in no uncertain terms that you would probably die but it didn't deter me as I was determined, as a totally committed republican, hardened by a brutal regime, and willing to go to the death if necessary. Nobody knows their limitations until tested, but I was content with my state of mind at the time to see it though. This hunger strike failed because the Brits back tracked on the promised demands. About twenty of us were put on the hunger strike for the last five days for a final push for our demands, but it was called off when Sean McKenna went into a coma.

Bobby Sands was camp O.C. and after the first hunger strike he used all his undoubted skills to try and get enough of our demands to end the blanket protest, but he was met with total and utter intransigence from the prison bosses and the British government. On the first day of his hunger strike Bobby Sands made a speech to the rest of us on the wing, and he told us that Thatcher probably wouldn't compromise and that we were listening to 'a dying man'. How truthful those prophetic words turned out in the next terrible months.

At one stage previously I had shared a cell with fellow Tyrone man Martin Hurson. Although I never knew Martin on the outside, it was always a big advantage to get moved into a cell after wings moves with someone from your own district. 'Hurson Boy' as we called him, was great craic and great for morale on the wing. There used to be sing-songs to while away the long nights. Hurson was the worst singer you ever heard! He would get up to sing one song and finish up singing seven or eight - everybody was booing and telling him to stop but he kept on. It was all part of keeping our spirits up and Hurson Boy was an expert at that! A highly religious fella he was faithful and said at least two to three rosary prayers a day. I always went for a wee sleep or rest when he was praying, to afford him as much privacy as possible in the cramped circumstances we were in. He got great strength out of his prayers, and after a rosary he would get up totally and utterly rejuvenated, and could face anything the system could throw at him. I didn't pray much, but I was a bit envious of the total comfort, strength and inner peace he took from his praying.

In December '78 there was a huge rumour going around that some men were going to be force washed. Unfortunately, it was true and our cell was the first cell to be hit. The screws battered, kicked and punched Hurson out of the cell and the ferocity of the attack was sickening in its intensity. In a strange sort of way it was nearly worse listening to a brutal attack than being on the receiving end. I was then forcibly removed from the cell, slapped, kicked and punched in the most violent manner. I was taken to an ice cold bath, held down into it and my hair and beard shaved off with cheap shears. The screws scrubbed our bodies including our testicles with deck scrubbers and then shaved the remaining hair of our heads and faces with a blunt 'seven o'clock' razor, which severely cut us in several places. I lost some teeth, had a dislocated jaw, nose broken in three places, and numerous flesh wounds, when I was thrown back in my cell. Hurson Boy was already back and he was in extreme pain. He had a disk kicked very badly in his back, which was making him writhe in total pain. They also broke three toes as they pulled him through the grills, and his head and body were a mass of cuts and bruises. I looked at my comrade and with his baldy head and no beard. I could hardly recognise him with all the cuts and blood. Hurson Boy said to me through gritted teeth 'Joe, they're going to end up killing us'. I said 'I think your right' as we comforted each other with our pride and determination not to yield to such a corrupt regime.

But it got even worse when the prison doctor whom we called 'Mengles' (after a notorious Nazi concentration camp doctor) came to our cell. He ordered Hurson to be taken to the prison hospital. About ten minutes later, the screws charged into the cell, lifted Martin unceremoniously onto a canvas stretcher slapping and punching again. I shouted encouragement to him and as I watched from a hole in the side of the cell door. The screws proceeded to kick Martin on his badly injured back up through the canvas stretcher. The screams of pain from Hurson Boy rebounded throughout the wing and I cursed this God awful place with every ounce and sinew of my body. It was the last time I saw my friend and comrade Martin Hurson alive in this earthly world. He died on the hunger strike. I was then taken to the Royal Victorian in Belfast under a blue light to get treatment for my injuries. I didn't put my name down for the second hunger strike, because I could not mentally peak again, and unless you were 100% sure in your mind, it wasn't the place to be, as there was so many fundamental principals at stake.

In H3, as the hunger strike was coming up to 30 days, before Bobby was taken to the prison hospital, there is one aspect that will never leave my mind. That was the smell that came from a hunger strikers cell. As Bobby was 3 or 4 cells down from me on the same wing, the smell was a permanent fixture on the wing at that stage. It is enormously difficult to describe this smell, (during the hunger strike there was no dirt protest). It was like a hospital type clinical smell, not a foul odour, yet it assaulted your nostrils and senses in a strange and sinister way. Maybe it was the smell of death, but I have been in the presence of death and dying people and never experienced this before. It was years after that that the starkly obvious explanation hit me; when a sick person is seriously ill part of the vital organs are closing down and the body is not functioning in its normal fashion and that in its own way will bring natural odours to the fore. This was entirely different in every aspect. These were healthy, vibrant, strong-able bodied young men, with not a disease of any kind amongst them, and most importantly everything to live for; loving families, partners, young children that they longed to see growing up. These were perfectly healthy men in their prime dying, but fighting tooth and nail to stay alive at the same time. A totally unique situation; hence the unique odour that surrounded their presence. Perfectly healthy men in their 20's dying was a medical contradiction that the powers that-be couldn't fathom in their closed minds.

I often think of the hardship I had in life - brutal interrogation in Castlereagh, the torturous H blocks - but everything pales into insignificance when you delve into the unquenchable spirit of these men and their unbreakable valour and courage. Any soldier, should he be a freedom fighter, or a member of a standing army, is brave to a certain extent, because he is risking his life. But these men died a thousand deaths. A soldier in action gets shot dead and it is often in a split second, and if he/she is injured they are taken off the battle field. These men got a hundred bullets every day for months, and it was indeed a long, slow and painful death for them. Hurson Boy in particular couldn't keep water down after 43 days. The water cleanses the body and keeps the toxins washed out of your system. When Hurson Boy couldn't hold the water down, the toxins attacked his brain and he died screaming and delirious with terrible pain. At 43 days on hunger strike he was still relativity strong physically. You have to realise, that all Hurson Boy had to do, was lift his hand for a sign that he wanted treatment, but he wouldn't give in. Such bravery is away, away, beyond the call of any duty. I still question the tactics of one man out in front on hunger strike, because if one dies, then the next in line, see it as his duty to follow through, even if he personally thinks that there is no chance left to broker a deal. So they finished up dying for each other.

Personally I believe that the hunger strike should have been called off sooner, to save some men's lives. To conclude (and I can say this without contradiction) that every hunger striker, blanket man and volunteer that I ever talk to, joined the republican movement to fight for a united Ireland, free from British military.

There is one monument and only one, that is a fitting tribute to the 10 hunger strikers (and indeed all the volunteers that died for Irish freedom). This is not a monument of stone, steel, wood or marble, or indeed any man made material. The only epitaph that is worthy of such unbridled bravery, unbreakable spirit, steadfastness in the face of a terrible enemy, is a free peaceful agreed Ireland. Anything less would be unthinkable for men of such valour and calibre. May their brave and gentle souls lie in peace, a peace they couldn't find in this world of injustice, cruelty and brutality. Their noble spirits will be with me always, an inspiration in life and in death. Sleep your peaceful sleep where there is no pain and suffering. You all deserve it.

PS: It would be remiss of me not to mention the hunger strikers families who had to sit day and daily, and watch their strong sons, brothers die in such horrific circumstances. Their courage and anguish must have taken a great toll. My admiration to all of them; for their dignity and resolve in the most horrendous circumstances.

50

THE VISIT

TERESA SAT IN shock transfixed by the sight of the human being in front of her. Had she not have known that she was in the H blocks prison in county Antrim and that the person she had asked to visit was her brother Joe, she would not have recognised the bedraggled, gaunt eyed, dirty haired and long bearded, smelly, blanket covered, skeletal like person, that sat in front of her, in the visitors room of the infamous prison. It was only when he spoke that she knew it was her brother. He was a terrible sight. He was on the blanket protest refusing to wear a prison uniform and because he wouldn't wear a uniform, he was denied any clothing. Hence the prison blanket were his only clothes. They were now being denied the basic human right to go the washroom to shower and shave, unless they put on the prison uniform. Joe refused to put the Brit convict uniform on, so here he was in front of my sister Teresa like some sort of pre historic man out of the caves! Not having got his hair cut, a shave, his teeth cleaned and his face or body washed for months, and covered only in a dirty blanket. The tears rolled down her cheeks as her mind went back to their childhood days growing up amongst the fresh green fields of Tyrone by the side of the clean, clear waters of the Lough. She gazed at the long beard and the tears kept rolling down her face. Her mind went back to the little country shop, McKenna's. We always walked the few miles to or went on the bikes to shop for our mother. Me, Joe, Ned, Barney and Marty were all in our mid teens and attempting to grow beards for the first time. None of us resembled one of the Dubliners! But Joe was fair-haired, so his beard didn't show up all that well. He was forever wanting people to notice it and was very pleased when people remarked on his new beard! He'd stick his chest out and prance around!

Me and Teresa, who was with us lads on the way to the shop, hatched a plan to play a joke and embarrass Joe in the shop. Teresa went on ahead a bit and got into the shop first, and told the shopkeeper to help her with the joke on Joe. Kathleen laughed and nodded; we lads all walked into the little shop with its cement floors and wooden counters and shelves, and its very distinct smell that only a little country shop has. As Kathleen was serving us she looked at me and said 'Did you forget to shave Tommy, or are you growing a beard?' I said 'Yea it's a beard. 'Well it's not as good a beard as Ned's', she said 'that's a lovely dark beard Ned', Ned nodded his head in agreement. She served away at us, then it was Barney and Marty's turn, the two youngest, 'I see you two boys are trying it too' she smiled, 'you are a bit young yet, but it will get better with age'. At this stage Joe pushed his way into the counter and gave his order to Kathleen. He waited until she came over to the counter to him; stuck his chin out and waited for Kathleen to notice his beard and say something to him. Kathleen looked him in the face, gave him his order and moved on without saying a word. Me and Teresa looked at Joe with his chin still stuck up in the air and could hardly keep in the laughing. Kathleen was the same. Joe was disgusted! As we filed out the door of the country shop and headed home up the wee country road, we kept talking about the beards and how Kathleen noticed all of them, except Joe's. We gave him a lot of slagging on the way home. When we were near home, me and Teresa told all the rest of them, including Joe, about the joke we had played on him with the shopkeepers help. We all fell about laughing and after a while Joe saw the funny side and joined in the laughing too. We told everybody else when we got into the house and all of us had another good laugh at Joe's expense.

And as she looked at this human being in front of her, who was the same wee brother, the tears kept rolling down her face at the loss of those lovely, innocent, happy, carefree days, of not so long ago; but now sitting in this prison visiting room it seemed like an eternity. Little letters of communication or comms as they were called were swallowed by the visitor. She put her arms around her brother and gave him a hug. The comms were passed to the visitor in an exchange like this, and they swallowed it. No modern flush toilet for that visitor for a day or two! They had to watch like a hawk and wait for it to be passed through the body to retrieve the vital information it contained. Teresa left the prison with a heavy heart.

I was at my house in Balrath when I got the comm from the H block. My brother impressed on me the vital need to get maximum awareness and support for the hunger strikes. He said the hunger strikers would be the frontline soldiers of the fight against the Thatcher government and the brutal prison H block regime. He stated that the fight between the H block blanket men hunger strikers, would be a fight to the death. Do all you can to support us in the H blocks and especially the hunger strikers he wrote, this is a battle we have to win. I knew the minute I read the comm that this was going to be a serious fight. I vowed then that I would do all I could to support the H blocks and the hunger strikers in their brave fight for political status.

51

THE G.P.O. VIGIL

WEE GEOFF WAS an I.R.A. man from Tyrone. He sold the 'An Phoblacht' the republican newspaper all around the pubs and hotels and streets of north Dublin city. A political activist all his life, it was him I approached to get set up a H block committee to organise, support and fund for the hunger strike campaign. It was decided at that meeting, that on the first day of the hunger strike we would set up a H block stall at the G.P.O. in O'Connell Street Dublin. We'd put up a poster of Bobby Sands, sell books and leaflets and collect funds. The stall would be manned by two main people delegated by the H block committee to do so. They would be there for two days and two nights. During this time they would do the two days and two nights without food in support for the I.R.A. men on hunger strike. The first two main people would start the morning of the day Bobby Sands went on hunger strike. This stall would be kept going continuously until the hunger strike ended. It was to be a LONG and a very tragic spring and summer of 1981. 'I'll wear no criminal's uniform or meekly serve my time, that England might brand Irelands fight, eight hundred years of crime'. On the 1st March 1981 in the hellhole prison of the H blocks of Long Kesh just outside Belfast in the county of Antrim, Ireland, Bobby Sands, I.R.A. man, political activist, political prisoner commenced his hunger strike to the death. We set up our stall outside the famous site of the Easter Rising, the G.P.O., on O'Connell Street, Dublin. Our stall would end up more like a grotto of sorrow. Myself and wee Geoff did the first 48 hour shift at the G.P.O. It had been announced officially by the I.R.A. that one of their members in the H block prison had started to refuse food in his cell and was now officially on hunger strike. The passersby at the G.P.O. were mildly curious about the photo of the fine looking young man who was on hunger strike. We also had supporters stopping and asking what they could do. Me and wee Geoff told them to go home to their own part of the country and set up a H block support group and many of them did. On the big support marches in Dublin during the hunger strike many of these good people came to our stall and told us they had done as we had asked. We felt good about that. I was fulfilling my brother Joe's request, that he had asked in the little comm, before the hunger strike had commenced. It was as little as I could do.

Bobby Sands was about a month on hunger strike when the sitting M.P. in the British parliament for Fermanagh and Tyrone died suddenly. A man called McGuire - R.I.P. It was decided to nominate Bobby Sands, hunger striker as the nationalist Irish population's candidate for those two famous Ulster counties. All other nationalist parties' candidates stood aside to give Bobby Sands, the hunger striker, a clear run. Supporters from all over Ireland descended on the two counties to canvas for the young hunger striker. All my men working on the chimney contract were given time off to go to Fermanagh and Tyrone to canvas. The hunger strike support was more important than anything else; we expected everybody to help. The good Irish people of Fermanagh and Tyrone didn't fail the young Irish man from Twinbrook estate, Belfast city, now dying on hunger strike in Thatcher's hellhole of a prison. They voted en-masse for him - all thirty three thousand of them, and elected him as their member for the British House of Parliament at Westminister, the same house of parliament that Prime Minister Thatcher presided over! Bobby Sands, on hunger strike for to be recognised as a political prisoner, was now an M.P. in Thatcher's own parliament, surely this must save his life. The good Irish population of bordered off Fermanagh and Tyrone, had thrown the young hunger striker a lifeline. Surely even the cruel hard hearted bitch that was Thatcher couldn't deny the Irishman of Belfast his political status now. For God sake, he was an M.P. elected by 33,000 first preference votes, enough to elect about half a dozen T.D.'s to Dáil Éireann. Surely the Charlie Haughey led Irish government would raise a racket to the high heavens, come out and publicly endorse the young hunger striker's political status. But alas, it never happened. When Bobby Sands M.P. hunger striker, was dying an agonising death for his political principals, Charlie Haughey was too busy putting brown envelopes in his pocket, to worry about or support the young Irishman in the H blocks of Long Kesh dying for his political principals. I'll never forgive the Haughey led Irish government for their lack of political courage. They could have embarrassed Thatcher's British government all over the world. It may not have worked, but as a fellow Irishman they should have at least tried. Haughey failed as an Irish leader and an Irishman to look after his own. I then thought of Fergal O'Hanlon's father, in the little house in Park street, Monaghan who use to point his straight pipe in such belief, 'Watch Leinster House, they'll stab you in the back' he had said wisely. He was right. First Jack Lynch in 1969, now Charlie Haughey in 1981. I was involved in the Civil Rights Movement and the Provisional I.R.A. in the north. I'll knock the myth, for that is all that it ever was, of Charlie Haughey's I.R.A. credentials. They don't, and never did, exist. I know; I was there. Bobby Sands had more principals in a single strand of his hair, than Charlie Haughey had in his whole body. He was the second Dublin leader to let the northern population down at a critical time. But this was not a reflection on the Irish population south of the border, who would, when the opportunity arose, elect hunger strike men as their T.D.'s in counties south of the border in Monaghan, Cavan and County Louth. It wasn't the southern people's fault. They were led by men of no courage or principal. Bobby Sands, Irishman, I.R.A. man, H block blanket man, political prisoner, H block hunger striker, M.P. for Fermanagh and Tyrone, man of principal, died after 66 days of hunger strike. A true hero of an Irishman and I was proud to be a comrade. A man who would never be forgotten. I took a black marker at our little grotto outside the G.P.O. in O'Connell street, Dublin city and wrote R.I.P. across Bobby Sands poster that was hanging on the G.P.O. wall. The same walls and pillars that are still pockmarked with the bullet holes of the British guns, when James Connolly defended his post during the 1916 rising. I looked at the poster of the young hunger striker R.I.P. and James Connolly R.I.P. Both killed by the same British system. Connolly would have been proud of you Sands, I thought and I saluted him. The funeral of Bobby Sands was one of the greatest political funerals in Irish history. Thatcher's government must have looked on in dismay as the young Irish hunger striker from Belfast was buried with full I.R.A. honours. The I.R.A. colour party, the I.R.A. firing party and the hundreds and thousands of mourners that came from all over Ireland and all over the world. Streets were named after him in other countries across the globe, a silver cross was sent by the Pope in Rome as he lay on his deathbed, and all the respect and honours accorded to him from all over the world highlighted the effect he had had on ordinary decent people. Thatcher must have thought to herself 'I can't defeat him. Even though he is dead, by his very death he is winning a huge victory over me and my government'. Bobby Sands was known as a hero worldwide. But he wasn't the only hero that long summer of 1981. 9 more young men would die on the H block hunger strike before that long summer would end. It took a head of government of unbelievable cruelty and callousness to preside over the deaths of all those young brave principled Irish men, and not be moved to act. And to make it worse Thatcher's British government granted political status to the I.R.A. prisoners of the now infamous H blocks, almost as soon as the hunger strike ended. The I.R.A. political prisoners of the H blocks of Long Kesh won their right to be classed as political prisoners, at a terrible cost of human suffering.

My brother told me something years later. That after the deaths of Sands as M.P. and Keiran Docherty as T.D. the rest of the men on hunger strike were dying for one another. The bible says 'Greater love no man can show to give up his life for another'. Love and bravery was in abundance in that hellhole of a British prison, that was the H blocks of Long Kesh in 1981.

I had just moved into my wee house at Balrath in County Meath, when the young Derry man Tommy McElwee was nearing the end of his life on the H block hunger strike. He had six sisters, all lovely dark haired young women, some of them were students at the University of Derry and had staged a long walk to Dublin in support of their brother and his comrades. They would go so far every day, and then stop in houses along the way, provided to them by supporters. When they came into County Meath, as their walk was from Derry to Dublin on the N2, the road my wee renovated cottage was on, they rested in my humble abode for the night. I volunteered my new home as their stopover in County Meath, before completing the journey of support for their brothers life the next day. They arrived at my house about nine o'clock the next evening, all 30 of them, most of them young students. They had already eaten their evening meal and all filed into my wee house and sat on the chairs, sofas, floors and beds, just wherever they could get a place to sit. My house was rough and ready as I was only moving in, but the walkers were all happy to make the best of it. Tired, weary, sad, but with the indomitable spirit of youth, they began a sing-song to keep up the spirits of the group and especially Tommy's sisters. They were lovely girls and thanked me again and again for my hospitality. I assured them it was given freely and willing, their fight for their brother's life was also my fight. I went down to the local pub, me and Wee Sally the electrician who wired my house, and brought back a huge carry out of beer and spirits for the weary walkers. They were delighted. We got a load of cigs as well, needless to say the pub owner was happy! The party really got going then. The students were a lively and talented bunch, great craic altogether. They nearly raised the roof of my newly renovated cottage – I thought that I'd have to bring the roofers back! It proved that the spirit of youth cannot be beaten, they were great!

Just at that time a very daring escape had taken place at Crumlin road jail in Belfast. Seven I.R.A. men made a daring daylight escape from that heavily guarded British prison for I.R.A. remand prisoners, before they were moved on to the infamous H blocks. These I.R.A. men's photos were all over the newspapers and TV's. They were been hunted by security forces on both sides of the border. They had been nicknamed the Magnificent Seven! They had become legends in the nationalist community of the north. Someone had quickly written a song about the Magnificent Seven and the students in my wee house were singing it at the top of their voices. It was good for morale, but I had an even bigger morale boost for them. Two of the Magnificent Seven were being kept safe in a house in the Skyrne area of County Meath not far from the famous Hill of Tara – the Hill of Heroes. But there weren't all dead heroes residing in that area that night - there were two there that were very much alive! They were a man called Pete from Tyrone and a Belfast man. I said to one of my men 'take your van around to the safe house and bring the two magnificent here to the party'. Shortly after he came back and we brought them into a wee shed at the back of the house. I went into the party which was in full swing and called for silence, as I had something important to say. When I got them quietened down a bit I told them I had two very distinguished guests to bring in to join the party. I said that these men were in great demand all over the country and that we were very, very privileged and honoured to have their presence. So without further ado I opened the back door of the wee house and in walked two of the most wanted I.R.A. men in Ireland! Two of the Magnificent seven! The roar that went up from the Derry students could have been heard in Derry!! The Magnificent Seven two, paraded around like celebrities, especially Tyrone Pete! He loved the young women all over him - he loved himself anyway, thought he was God's gift to women at any time, but now that he had achieved fame and notoriety, he lapped it up! They stayed until the party ended in the wee small hours. Next morning, me and Wee Sally went down to Seán's at the little country local shop beside us, and bought him out of eggs, bread, milk, butter etc. before he had his wee shop right open. He had to call all of his suppliers to stock him up again! I told Sean who we had in the house and he threw in some extra food and gave me a small cash donation as well. He said he hoped the walk would save young Tommy McElwee's life. But alas history would tell that it didn't. The young man from Derry died from hunger strike soon after. Me and wee Sally cooked everyone of them a breakfast before they set out on the road to Dublin.

I never had the pleasure of meeting any one of them again, but when I watched Tommy McElwee's lovely dark haired sisters carry his coffin out of their local church in Derry, a short time afterwards, I sat in my wee house in Balrath in Meath and I could still feel their presence in my home. But it was like looking at different souls, all their youthful cheerfulness had gone from their faces. Faces full of sorrow and pain at the loss of a brave young brother.

I looked at these lovely girls carrying their brother's coffin, after an agonising death on hunger strike and I hated Maggie Thatcher with a hate I never knew I could feel for another human being. But then I didn't count this cruel hearted monster a human being. No human being, especially a woman, could have presided over such a summer of sadness. It was a crime against humanity. It was a war crime, and in my mind, she is still a war criminal. We maintained the wee grotto vigil through the whole summer of 1981. We were disturbed temporarily during the day of the riots outside the Dublin British embassy, when a long suffering people's anger and frustration boiled over. This riot was not against the southern state, it was just pure frustration and anger at the continuous trickle of death coming out from under the big steel doors of the H blocks of Long Kesh, all summer long. We were briefly disturbed by a handful of overzealous special branch men, but we set up again immediately. The ordinary Gardaí in Dublin never interfered with our Grotto at the

G.P.O.; we got on well with them and the public. I remember some of the main people who manned the G.P.O. vigil. Una from Carrickmore County Tyrone went to the U.S.A. and settled in San Francisco. Her friend Bridget went home to settle. Wee Geoff was knocked down and killed by a car on Dorset Street, while selling An Phoblacht. R.I.P Geoff. I can't remember all of their names at this stage of my life but they were all great people. The hunger strike ended with a great sense of loss and sadness. In a way, we felt somehow, we didn't do enough to save them that summer. It was our best but it wasn't enough. We took down posters of the dead hunger strikers with R.I.P. wrote across every one of them; the 11th and 12th posters were up as well. Even though they hadn't died, they nearly did, and were prepared to die. It was one of the most heroic examples of human courage ever. We took down our little table and cleared up the area outside the G.P.O. and took everything back to our little H block committee office. We didn't know whether to be glad or sad. We didn't know whether we had won or lost. We were glad the suffering had been ended, but the same question was on everyone's mind - where did we go from here? Though I do believe that the Sands election success was the start of the Sinn Féin political strategy which led to the Good Friday Agreement.

A few years after that, Pete from the Magnificent Seven; so full of life at the party in my wee house that night, was shot dead by the S.A.S in a village in Co. Tyrone, along with two brave comrades. The S.A.S. set fire to their car while they were still in it. A terrible scene.

52

LIFE AT BALRATH

DURING THAT YEAR I also sold my share of the building company in Dublin. The chimney contract had done its job for me, I now had a home and a fireplace company beside it, and I now had lost heart in working anymore with the chimney contract. I had neglected it quite a bit during the hunger strike and the election campaigns for Kieran Docherty in Cavan Monaghan, and Paddy Agnew in County Louth, and also at the vigil at the G.P.O. The long absence hadn't helped the business but I didn't care one bit. I was proud to be part of the history of the H blocks campaign; it was now time to move on. I sold my assets in the building contract to my partners, Kevin and his brothers. They were chomping at the bit to get running it themselves. I was happy to get out when I did, the little chimney business had been a huge success for me. I now had a home and a business in a lovely part of County Meath. I was looking forward to living and working there. The little house was already a well known calling house for everybody involved in the continuing fight in the north. I was happy I was going down there to live.

I already knew my new neighbours and got on very well with them; they turned out to be the best neighbours a man could ever have. Paddy and Nanney lived next door on the Dublin side of me, a lovely couple, they had a traditional fireplace with crook and hob. Their welcome was every bit as traditional as their little Irish cottage, warm and friendly. There was a man who lived with them called Emmett the Dread. He religiously got drunk three times a day! He was from landed gentry stock who was reared in the big country house. Mullafin House on 100 acres. He had sold the family jewels and was now proceeding to drink and gamble the whole lot! He was about as obnoxious and bad tempered a man as you'd ever want to meet when drunk. He'd pull himself up to his full height, hook his thumbs inside his braces - he always wore a shirt, tie and suit, look down his upper class nose at you, 'My name is Emmett' he'd say loudly and aggressively, waiting for everyone to bow and scrape in front of him. But he also had a disarming way with him - he could be very good humoured and funny. You could love Emmett the Dread and hate him all at the same time. His own family didn't like him for the way he was drinking his wealth. The family on the Dublin side of Paddy, was the Maguire family. A real big Irish good natured, friendly family. Their dad, the Bull Maguire, died while cutting logs for the family fire just across the road from his cottage in the wood, just before I moved into the area. I'd heard he was a great character. The mother was a friendly woman, quiet spoken and sincere, never a bad word to be spoken about anybody. The daughters would have been teenagers at that time, Susan, Caroline and Pauline; the two young cubs would have been 9 or 10 years old. The nickname 'The Cubs' stuck with them for good - Peter and Brian were always known as 'the cubs' after I had christened them so. A lovely family. The last family on the Dublin side were living in a bungalow, set diagonally towards the road, their name was O'Connor. The woman of the house ran a playschool from her home. It was more like pre primary school course than a playschool. The children who went to this lady's playschool were always way ahead at primary school. The man of the house was Tom, a great G.A.A. sportsman and a big, hearty, good natured neighbour. A real helpful neighbour, a real good Christian man with a deep faith in all that is good about life. Him and his sons were into handball, one of the most ancient Irish sports, and were Irish champions. His eldest son Walter was a great rival of the great hand-baller from Kilkenny with the nickname Ducksy. Their contests were the stuff of legends. A great Irish family, very good mannered and quiet, hardworking and honest. Down the little country laneway beside Connors there was another little house with a family as well. Just next door to me was John and Kathleen, a young couple who had just moved in. A very quiet couple and great neighbours. Next to them on the Slane side was a Traveller man and his wife and two small children. A trader; he sold carpets and small bits and pieces of things to make a living. Martin O'Brien, as decent a man as you'd ever meet the length and breadth of Ireland. An inoffensive quiet family, I was on good terms with him and became good friends.

The next cottage on the Slane side was the last one. Old Molly Maguire lived there with her son Ben. She was eighty years of age and had a memory like a computer. She was a great storyteller and loved to talk. I learned a lot from her, sitting at her table by the window while she made tea and sandwiches. Her old, white solid fuel cooker was always stoked up really hot. She lit it every day of the year - winter or summer. It was the little engine of her home; she couldn't be without it for even a day. Fermanagh Peter was the first to make friends with her. She used to give out to him for his drinking but she was very fond of Peter. She didn't take to Shane the apprentice plumber, he was too young and cocky. She insisted all the workers came up to her for tea, she got to know them all by first names and made friends with them all. 'A great bunch of fellas' she'd say, 'a credit to their mothers'. She loved talking to them, sometimes she'd have kept them too long for their tea break; the men's excuse was always 'I just couldn't get away'. The minute you'd try to go she would start another story and it would last a half an hour! I knew the men weren't to blame, the old lady Molly, just loved the company. She knew all the local history and just loved to tell it. She told me about the land commission people who were brought into that part of county Meath by Irish government, given a small land commission house, a small farm, farm stock and farming implements. These people were all from the poor counties of the west of Ireland; lots of them Gaelic speakers. The land they got had been taken back from British landlords, known as absentee landlords, for they were rarely ever seen. It was a good idea and lots of these west of Ireland people settled in county Meath. Thousands of them; mostly little nests of them, up long lanes or little side roads; they were always grouped together. Like settlers. The scheme was a good one, to take the land of the landed gentry and give it back to ordinary people. The government made one big mistake though, Molly told me, they forgot to give any of these farms to the ordinary county Meath people. The very people who had been servants to these landlords. These Meath working class people had to bow and scrape and serve the arrogant upper class landlords. Molly told me they owned your job and the little house that you lived in. If you lost your job you lost your home as well. These landlords used and abused a lot of these native county Meath people. When the land commission farms were given out and the government passed these Meath people by and gave all the farms to the west of Ireland people, it caused a bitter feeling between these working class Meath people and 'The Westies' as the Meath people called them. That lasted for generations. 'It was hatred for each other at the height of it' said Molly. Very, very bitter indeed. The western people formed little groups of their own, and became like little communities within the community. The native Meath people disliked that. It took 50 years for this to solve itself out and the two communities eventually came together. Married into one another, played football together and the younger populations forgot the past and the bitterness faded away. Molly was a very well read woman and could have been an historian. She had a very sharp memory and just loved to tell her stories, about the Royal County of Meath. This name had nothing to do with the British royal family she'd hasten to say, but had all to do with the nearby Hill of Tara, where the Irish kings and queens of ancient Ireland gathered to the Hill of Tara to feast and enjoy themselves and make laws for the people to live by. This was Ireland's own Royalty she'd say proudly, nothing to do with England. She told me about the Hill of Slane where St. Patrick lit the Paschal fire. The mounds of Newgrange which was a thousand years older than the Egyptian pyramids, and older than Stonehenge. She explained about the sun coming through into the burial chamber on the longest day, solstice day. I had a great interest in Irish history, music, culture, and games. G.A.A. especially; I loved playing it myself. Molly was a great old teacher, I was the willing listener. I loved going to her little home and sitting there for hours. Another neighbour played the bagpipes. He was called 'The Customer'. A real character. He had a big family and lived to be nearly 90 years old. He was a very healthy man and I asked him one night what his recipe was for a healthy, long life. His eyes twinkled and he said, 'That's easy. Three meals a day, and a female at night!!' I loved it.

My little fireplace business at Balrath, 'Balrath Fireplaces' I called it, had taken off and was doing well. I had employed two young lads from the area, Seamus and Thomas, the 'Juices' as they were known. Their father Jimmy was a lifelong republican. His sons had taken after him. Their mother was a real Irish woman and very proud of her family, they reminded me of my own family back in county Tyrone; hardworking, decent people. Jimmy the father was a very outspoken supporter of the I.R.A. fight in the north, also a great critic of the Irish government for not doing enough to help the six counties Irish population. Being so outspoken, he was not always popular, but he had deeply held republican views all his life, and he got grudging respect for that, even from his political opponents in his home area. Seamus and Thomas were good apprentices to the fireplace makers trade, or slabbers as they were known within the marble and granite trade. Good hardworking, honest, well reared young men, I got on well with them and became lifelong good friends and neighbours. We manufactured our fireplaces, brought some from a Tyrone man based in Boyle in County Roscommon. This man was known as 'Horse' and I used to go over to his factory on a regular basis. I enjoyed the trips over to his place. I'd sometimes stay the night and me and the 'Horse' would have the craic. He was a very shrewd and astute businessman, ruthless in his ambition to be rich and successful but a great man to work marble and granite. He made some lovely marble mantelpieces, his trademanship was well known within the circle, I learned a lot from Horse. Hardens of Gowron in County Kilkennny were generations in the marble trade and old Jim Harden was known far and wide for his Victorian and Georgian white Italian marble pieces. We did good business for years; I also bought and restored old antique marble pieces. I advertised in Dublin golden pages for buying old fireplaces. I did a good trade from them as well. I use to love restoring old pieces and bringing them back to life. Seamus and Thomas were getting good at their job and they enjoyed working at 'Balrath Fireplaces'. Chris from C&R Fireplaces in Navan was in the trade for as long as me and longer, we were the only two fireplace manufacturing companies in County Meath at that time. A real gentleman in his business and personal life. Chris and his staff were, and still are, great friends of mine.

53

MARRIED & FAMILY LIFE

THIS WAS LATE summer 1981 and I went to a party at John Joe's new bungalow near Skyrne; he had settled down there and I met the woman I would marry the following spring. Bridie and me got on well from when we met; fell for each other and by early 1982 we were planning our wedding! It was a bit of a whirlwind romance but I got on with her and her family, especially her father Eudie. He was soon selling fireplaces for me, doing sales man from his own little car! He loved a drop of Jameson and many a good session we had in the village of Killmesson and Swan's of Skyrne. He was a real gruff Meath man, no airs and graces, he either liked you or he didn't. Fortunately for my future marriage prospects with his daughter, he took a liken to me, and duly gave his consent to my marriage plans. I decorated the wee house at Balrath early that spring of 1982 and with the help of Bridie and Rosie, Nina and Ann, her sister's, we got it into good shape by St. Patrick's day of that year. The wedding invitations had gone out and the wedding was set for the 3rd of April 1982. The wedding was in Dunsany church in County Meath. The reception was in the Russell Arms Hotel, now called the Newgrange, in Navan and we booked a room in the little hotel in the village of Duleek County Meath for that night, before touring Ireland on our honeymoon. We were all going back to the very popular pub in the village called Big Tom's so called after the owner. A big man with a heart as big as his belly, a very well liked man, Big Tom's pub was great crack. So we were all heading back there after the hotel session was over, to finish off the day's craic in Big Tom's of Duleek. The wedding day went off well and all of Bridie's family were all there in all their finery. My big family all came down from the north, and a group of I.R.A. men from the border came down as well! My mother was delighted, as were my brothers and sisters. They got on like a house on fire with each other and the two families had a great days craic. The I.R.A. guests numbered about six, Aidan and Dinger, two of my old workers from the chimney contract in Dublin, who had joined the I.R.A. on active service with the East Tyrone Brigade, and had often stayed in my house in Balrath. Jim the Councillor from Monaghan town, a completely dedicated I.R.A. fighter with the border unit, as was Tyrone Pete the escaped prisoner from Crumlin road jail. His best friend and comrade from the Lough Neagh area of county Tyrone, Lawrence. They were a tough crew, I was delighted they had come, it was a connection from Tyrone I.R.A., a unit I had spent so much time with. They all had been to my house in Balrath and had all stayed there. They all got on well with my new wife and she liked them all and looked upon them as friends! The northern people and the Meath people were similar, straight up front, no bullshit type of people and I think that's why they got on so well, a spade was a spade with both of them!! Like it or lump it!!

The wedding party moved from the hotel in Navan to Duleek village, all went to Big Tom's pub. Some of the local lads were there including Daithí from Mulafin Engineering, an old Meath family who ran a small engineering business fixing old farm machinery or any type of old iron works, or steel fireplaces or grates. Old Benny and Coyte, the father and mother, were two great characters and I was often in their house at Mulafin. Norge, the brother of Daithí went off to Australia about this time. Daithí was in Big Tom's that night and joined the Wedding party with one of his best mates Johnny the Diggerman. Johnny was a big good natured 20 stone man who wouldn't hurt a fly. He was the eldest of a big family from a local housing estate, whose father had died young. Johnny had taken over the role of father, and was very protective of his brothers and sisters as he was the eldest. I knew Daithí and Johnny, Bootsie, Norge and a few more of the local lads well, a good bunch of fellas. The I.R.A. team had moved on to Big Tom's as well and Dinger had taken shine to one of Johnny the Diggerman's young sisters. Dinger was about 20 years old and she was about seventeen; which was fair enough. Dinger was a tall, young black haired well built lad, and looked a bit older than his age. Johnny was keeping a close eye on his young sister! He didn't look all that pleased with young Dinger, but that didn't worry Dinger or the young one, they were oblivious to Johnny and were evidently enjoying themselves, as was everyone in the pub! It was about 12 o'clock midnight when all hell broke loose!!! Johnny had confronted Dinger about making out with his young sister. Dinger was having none of it and told Johnny to get lost! He told him on no uncertain terms that she was the girl he wanted to be with, and visa versa so that was that! The party was still flying; everybody was looking forward to a late drinking session, as Big Tom's was a well known late house. Dinger and Johnny were both angry at the time, and were wrestling and fighting. Dinger's I.R.A. comrades were trying to pacify him, as were Johnny's friends, trying to quieten things down. Suddenly, the lot of them fell onto a low level table! When they were helped up and separated, it was noticed that there was a lot of blood on the table. I looked at Dinger and the blood was pumping out of his neck like a geyser!! I didn't need to be a doctor to know this was a very serious injury! Johnny was shocked, as was everyone else. Dinger fell to the ground in slow motion just beside the counter! The pool of blood on the tiled floor was getting bigger every second. This was bad. Suddenly my sister, a nurse and my sister-in-law, also a nurse, stepped forward and asked for space to attend to Dinger. The emergency services were called on 999 and a hushed silence came down on a packed pub. There wasn't a sound as the two nurses fought to stem the flow of blood from young Dinger's main artery. They were doing a very efficient job as medical professionals do in times like this. They knew the best thing to do, and after what seemed like an age, the ambulance came and got Dinger onto a stretcher and took him away to the hospital in Drogheda about 10 miles away. My sister and sister-in-law went with Dinger in the back of the ambulance. I hoped to God that he'd be alright. Some of my family and friends persuaded me to head down to the Village Hotel with my new wife. There was nothing anybody could do anyway, just hope for the best for Dinger. Johnny had been taken away by some of his friends, crying that it had been a terrible accident. He was distraught and he was also terrified! He knew Dinger and his friends were I.R.A. men! But Dinger's comrades were more worried about him than confronting Johnny. The hotel was lovely and quiet and we had a night cap to relax and then went to the bridal suite!! An eventful day it surely was! Never a dull moment!!

The next morning myself and the wife went over to the hospital in Drogheda to see how Dinger was. He had 'died' twice in the back of the ambulance during the 10 mile journey from Big Tom's to the hospital! But he had survived after getting six or seven pints of blood. He was now sitting up in his hospital bed with all his comrades around him! He had made a miraculous recovery!! My sister and sister-in-law and the ambulance team had done a very professional job. They had saved his life!! Dinger was sitting up in bed weak and pale looking, but chatting away! Jim, Aidan, Pete, Lawrence and a few more were standing around his bed when we approached it. They made room for us to shake Dinger's hand and to wish him a speedy recovery. He told me he had felt himself slipping away twice during the journey from the pub to the hospital in the ambulance. When Dinger was going through his training before he left my fireplace company to go on active service, he had asked me if I had any words of advice for him before he joined his active service I.R.A. unit. I just looked this young man in the eye and told him, no matter how dire or hopeless looking any situation is you find yourself in, never give in, always believe in your strength and ability to get through it. Hang on in there no matter what. He told me when he felt himself slipping away in the back of the ambulance, he thought of what I had said to him and he acted on it. He believed it helped to save him; I laughed at him and said 'No problem Dinger, glad to be of some help'. The good natured banter went on at Dinger's bedside for a while. He got almost all his blood replaced; he had lost so much through heavy bleeding. Suddenly his I.R.A. comrades went into a little group at the end of Dinger's bed and started whispering and pointing to Dinger in his bed; very worried looking. Dinger got annoyed and said to them 'What the hell is going on', Jim said very solemnly 'Dinger, we have a problem with you now, we may have to dismiss you from the I.R.A. unit', Dinger looked up annoyed 'I was only in a fight for god sake, if every I.R.A. man who was in a fight was dismissed there would not be many left, so get lost'. Jim said 'Seriously, you could be a serious security risk now Dinger, you got most of your blood replaced, you could have gotten some Brit's blood, or an Orangemans blood, or a Garda special branches blood - we don't know who you are anymore, so how do we trust you?', Dinger looked at them, shocked in disbelief, not knowing for a moment if they were serious or not. The look on Dinger's face was precious! All of a sudden his I.R.A. comrades started to laugh at him! A relieved looking Dinger started to laugh too, as did everybody else. It was a very funny episode at that hospital bedside!

Myself and the wife left to go on our honeymoon around the south of Ireland. Before I left, Jim told me they were going over to Duleek to assure Johnny that there was no hard feelings. The whole thing was just an accident; all's well that ends well. As he shook my hand and wished me luck in my married life on behalf of all his comrades he said 'Seriously, we could have well been organising an I.R.A. man's funeral, it was a close thing'. Myself and the wife headed off around Ireland, relieved that our wedding day hadn't turned into a tragedy. That's all that we would have needed! But it was a lovely spring day and everything was good.

My first daughter was born a year later. I loved her from the second I saw her. It was great to be a daddy! I felt now that after all these years away from my own family I now had a family again. It was just great. I felt the very same way when my two other daughters were born over the next few years. Very, very special times indeed for a man and a woman; when they are reproducing. It is fundamental to life itself to reproduce. I looked upon them with such pride! I gelled into being a daddy very easily, maybe because, being from a very big family myself, I found it easy to help look after them. My wee fireplace business was providing me with a good enough living; even though the eighties was a very tough time in Ireland. A lot of tradesmen left Ireland for America; most of the men who worked on the renovation of my own home had all left to get work in the States. Most settled there and never came back. Some did come back though, most notably Wee Tommy and settled in county Donegal. We remained good friends, myself and Wee Tommy, even through all his years in the States. He had got to be a very much wanted man, on both sides of the border during the late seventies and early eighties. He had been very active against the Brits in the north. It was best he went for a while or something would have happened to him; but Wee Tommy, the fella who learned to read and write as a political prisoner in Portlaoise jail in the early seventies, became a millionare in the U.S.A. in New York's building industry. He told me after he got his first week's wages in New York of $1000; he went downtown in New York and went mad! He said that after all the troubles in Ireland, and all the restrictions that had been brought into his life, he felt like a little calf let out for the first time in the spring! He felt like one of them! He kicked his legs up into the air, went downtown New York and had a ball! He settled down and did very well, running his own construction company. He got very high up in the Irish community in New York, and met some very famous people. He got to be a real success story, fair play to him. All the men whom I knew that went to the states all done well for themselves. But then, they came from hard working, honest Irish families, and were well reared. Their involvement in the I.R.A. was just an accident of Irish history. The war in the north just happened in our time, it could have been some other generation, but it wasn't, it was ours. But the success of these former I.R.A. men when they got to New York and other U.S.A. cities, was proof that it was there in them all the time. It just took a country like the U.S.A. that gave them fair play, to bring out the best in them. I stayed in Ireland, I love Ireland too much. I'd be homesick within a month! I was happy rearing my wee family in co. Meath, Life was good.

Children of the Conflict

During the conflict, weddings and important family occasions were moved over the border to facilitate a family member 'on the run'. When I watched these young people enjoy themselves and dance away into the wee hours of the morning, I was often amazed at the beauty of them all. How happy and confident the 'Children of the Conflict' were. they were a great credit to their parents who raised them in the midst of all the troubles. Some of them had kept childhood friends from the Protestant community. Childhood friendships that had survived all the difficulties that may have destroyed them. One of these friendships are two women, now in their mid-fifties, who are still as close today as they were when they played as childhood neighbours and friends. It is, indeed, lovely to see that.

The Protestant people of the North were prisioners of its own history too. They are a very decent, deeply Christian people. Recently I walked around the graveyard of the old Church of Ireland just outside the village of Mullagh in county Cavan. Inscriptions on some gravestones date back hundreds of years. Some are so old and weathered that the letters are barely legible. There are some gravestones which are just pieces of ragged stone taken straight from the mountain and stuck in the ground to mark the grave of a family member. I was shocked and saddened to discover a Famine plot. The inscription on the piece of old granite read that 320 men, women and children from the parish of Mullagh were buried there, victims of the Great Famine. As in the conflict in the north, there were no barriers to the suffering of a people when historical tragedies strike.

Just up the road, a little closer to the village, stands the Catholic church. I took time and walked aroound it as well. It struck me that a number of the family names were the same in both graveyards. Both churches having a history steeped in centuries of existing side by side through good times and bad. Good Christian neighbours. Mullagh mountain overlooks both churches and the lough, which is beside the Church of Ireland. It's a beautiful, peaceful part of Ireland. On the top of the mountain is a huge, ten foot high cross, erected many years ago. It stands in testament to the similiarity of the two Christian churches and their people living side by side in peace and harmony, in this part of the ancient provence of Ulster. Some day, hopefully, all nine counties of this historical provence will be able to co-exist together in mutual respect and friendship as the people of this lovely old village have done for centuries.

The two women at the wedding tell me it can happen.

54

THE BRIGHTON BOMB

THE WAR IN the north continued into the middle eighties, it had intensified in the English cities. An I.R.A. hit squad had been given the task of assassinating the hated Thatcher. They almost got her in the attack on the Conservative Party Conference in the Brighton hotel. She was very lucky to escape that attack, which killed and badly injured several members of her government. The British security forces knew that an I.R.A. hit squad were smarter than they were, and couldn't be stopped. I remember the I.R.A. statement, issued by G.H.Q. I.R.A. to Thatcher after the Brighton bomb. 'Thatcher you were lucky this time, but remember Thatcher you have to be lucky every time, we only have to be lucky once!' She had insulted the Irish leader at that time, Garret Fitzgerald, when he put forward a political solution. At each proposal he had made, she contemptiously threw each part out, 'That's out, that's out, and that's out' as she dismissed his efforts with the utter disdain only she could show an Irish leader. Shortly after the Brighton hotel bomb, she did a complete u-turn, and in 1985 she signed the Anglo Irish agreement, giving an Irish government an official role in the political governing of the six counties. The first time a British government did so since partition. The Irish leader who she signed the Anglo Irish agreement with, was none other than the man she had insulted with her 'Out, out, out' speech, Mr. Garret Fitzgerald. I would rename the 'Anglo Irish agreement' of 1985, a landmark shifting of British government policy towards the north, as the Brighton Bomb Agreement! So much for the so called Iron Lady, who presided over the deaths of the ten brave hunger striker's. When it came to nearly dying herself, at the hands of the I.R.A., she wasn't so damned brave!

55

THE BOMB & THE BALLOT BOX

THE SINN FÉIN Ard Fheis in 1986 was a watershed in republican politics. The old leadership of Sinn Féin had managed to hold onto on to the power right through the seventies and into the middle eighties, but there had been unrest and unease at their leadership for some time. The I.R.A. had fought the British to the negotiation table on two occasions, 1972 and 1975, Sinn Féin had no success either time. The northern I.R.A. leaders were unhappy with that. It was time for a change of leadership, a shifting of political power within the republican movement as a whole. It was the election successes of Bobby Sands, Kieran Docherty and Paddy Agnew that proved, that the I.R.A. and Sinn Féin could make political gains alongside each other, contrary to what the belief had been for years. It was time to seek political power north and south of the border and for the first time, blend the armed I.R.A. and the political Sinn Féin together, and fight on both fronts at the same time. The hunger strikers had shown that this strategy could work. The old republicans, who owed their alliance to the first Dial of 1918, were trenchantly opposed to any change. But at the Sinn Féin Ard Fheis of 1986, they lost out. After a very heated and acrimonious debate, the proposals of Gerry Adams and Martin McGuinness won the vote. It reminded me of the heated debates in the cells of Portlaoise prison when we'd almost come to blows; but this wasn't a debate in Portlaoise I.R.A. jail, this was at the Sinn Féin Ard Fheis in central Dublin and this debate was for real. But it was drawn upon the same divisions, that were evident between I.R.A. men in the cell debates many years ago. These men's attitude was, don't let points of principal defeat your cause, find a way around them, over them or under them, but don't let points of principal stop you from winning! The famous phrase, 'The ballot box in one hand and the armalite rifle in the other hand' was coined that day. I felt it was time for a more pragmatic approach to the war in the north and the drive for negotiating a peace settlement. There was no point in being tied up in old historical dogmas. I was sorry to lose some great old comrades and friends, but I felt this was the way to go. The policy of the political struggle and the guerrilla fight alongside each other had won the day, but at a price.

56

THE RAIDS AT BALRATH

ALL THROUGH THE eighties my home at Balrath was raided when anything of any importance happened in relation to the northern conflict. The search for Don Tidey, the kidnapped German industrialist – raided. The search for Ben Dunne – raided. The hunt for the Border Fox – raided. The search for Dominic McGlinchey, the so called 'Mad Dog' – raided. When the Eksund, the ship loaded with I.R.A/Libyan weaponry was apprehended on the high seas – raided. The search for the weapons already shipped in before the Eksund – raided. The search for Shergar – raided. Why any of those people, including the poor animal, would be stupid enough to choose my house as a hiding place is beyond me! It would be the last place I would hide out if I were a wanted I.R.A. man. It became a long standing joke about the Irish special branch detectives involved in the political scene, that they would raid the old 'reliables', and bring in the usual suspects. I think it was like clocking in to their superiors. We raided such and such a house, at such a time, that house later, that house the next day and so on, there is my timesheet, that is how I spent my time, now pay me my wages! The fact that four shiploads of weaponry was landed of the coast of Ireland, distributed to secret dumps the length and breadth of this country and only the Eksund developed engine trouble and was apprehended by chance, says enough about the real level of intelligence within the Irish and indeed British political special branch! Their real level of intelligence was non-existent! Even with all their prolonged searches and the 'operation mallard' where they swept the country from top to bottom, produced nothing. The I.R.A. intelligence system was way ahead, and much more efficient. When they were raiding the likes of my wee house in Balrath, the I.R.A. men who were active at this time were running rings around them. But it was upsetting for my wife and children to be targeted continuously like that. I resented this behaviour from the special branch men, some of whom I got to dislike personally. It was all so stupid. I mean, there were safe houses for the I.R.A. in county Meath, and not one of them was ever raided. Not one! Northern counties were twined with southern counties. Tyrone was twined with Meath. Anything the Tyrone I.R.A. men needed, it was Meath I.R.A.'s job to get it for them. The Meath special branch didn't even know that. I disliked those special branch officers for the harassment on my family. It was unnecessary and vindictive. I got on well with the ordinary Gardaí. The local Gardaí were grand. I knew some of them very well and respected them; had a drink with some of them now and again. Some of those Gardaí, now retired, I would count as my friends. I think that, by and large, the Gardaí are a very good people's police force. As one member of the ordinary Garda said to me one day 'Tom, even the Gardaí who oppose your political beliefs will give you one thing, that since you came into county Meath, you worked hard and honest for a living. There is not a dishonest bone in your body; you are a good hardworking decent honest man'. I felt good about that, it was the truth. It was how I was reared.

57

MORE BITTER LOSES

PETE AND LAWRENCE, who always called to my house at Balrath through the eighties, were killed in action in County Tyrone. The British S.A.S. ambushed them in a car in the village of Coagh, near Cookstown and riddled them with bullets and then set their car alight, and burned my two good friends and comrades to ashes. They were both buried with full I.R.A. honours. Jim who always called at Balrath, and often stayed over, and was very fond of my children, and often expressed the hope he would live long enough to have some of his own someday. But that wasn't to be; he was killed by British soldiers at the attack on Loughgall British army R.U.C. station, along with seven other I.R.A. men from the East Tyrone Brigade. Several of these men would have stayed at my house at Balrath. One of them worked with my brother in the family building company. His unopened wage packet was there for him, but he was dead. Several of these young I.R.A. men were from Cappagh village, in County Tyrone. This village graveyard had so many young men who died in the northern conflict that it prompted the parish priest to say at their funerals, 'There is something radically wrong with a society that buries their youth first'. Over 50 young I.R.A. men, from the East Tyrone Brigade, died fighting. All young men from good, decent Irish families. R.I.P. He was right. I helped carried Jim's I.R.A. coffin through Monaghan town with other Tyrone and Monaghan I.R.A. men. Jim, my good friend and comrade, was buried with full I.R.A. honours in Monaghan town graveyard, his town, the town where he was a Sinn Féin councillor while still a teenager. Lawrence was buried with the same I.R.A. honours at a small graveyard near the Middleton border in County Monaghan. I was proud to carry his coffin as well. All the rest of the Loughgall I.R.A. men were buried at different graveyards throughout County Tyrone. It was a very sad time, but none of these I.R.A. men would have complained, they knew they could die in the fight at anytime. It was believed that an informer, who supplied a safe house for I.R.A. men, sold them out to their British enemies. How this person watched these young I.R.A. men go to their certain deaths that summers evening, I don't know. It's not a bit of wonder that informers are shot, when the terrible result of their treachery is witnessed. The informer is so difficult to deal with during a conflict. The informer is sometimes a comrade, and almost always from the same community of those whom they are informing on. The familys of the informer within their own community are put in a terrible place. they find themselves treated like lepers almost overnight. Often these familys are good supporters of the guerilla army in their midst. An impossible place for a family to find themselves in. It's a stain on their character that can last for generations. A lot of these informers were victims of the 'Dirty Tricks' department of the British security forces, including MI5, and R.U.C. Special Branch. Their 'handlers' used them ruthlessly for their own ends and then abandoned them to their terrible fate when their 'cover' was blown. They were then led out for execution by their former comrades, as was well depicted in the movie "The Wind That Shakes The Barley". The disappearance of these informers probably looked like a way out of an impossible dilemma. The terrible tragedy is that the young informer, and the young men tasked with this terrible deed could well have gone to the same school and played football together. There were no winners in this scenario, only the British security forces 'Dirty Tricks' department.

The war in the north continued, as did the war in Britain. The 'Persuaders' as the I.R.A. team in Britain were known, were hitting English cities. The war in the north had been going on now for over 20 long years. It was a long time, a very long time. My brother Joe had been released from the H blocks and couldn't settle at home had gone to the U.S.A. I supplied the necessary paperwork for him to get out of Dublin Airport. He came home for the Loughgall funerals. I picked him up at Dublin airport. He was home for a month. He met a girl, married her, got himself a lovely home and four lovely children, and never went back to the U.S.A. It is indeed an ill wind that doesn't blow some good! When my brother Joe was getting out of the H blocks after 8 years of hardship, the Governor of the prison approached him at the gate the morning of his release, to offer Joe the customary good advice given to all prisoners getting out of jail. Joe cut him short and looked him in the eye and said, 'Mr. Governor, what brought me into this prison of yours was a set of beliefs that I had. A set of beliefs worth fighting for. That's why I joined the I.R.A. Since I came to your hellhole of a prison you did your best to break me. You tortured me and my comrades. Your jail took the lives of ten of my best friends, all this to break me and my set of beliefs. Now, Mr. Governor, I have bad news for you, the beliefs and principals that brought me here are stronger within me now than when I came here! Now, to hell with you, your jail and the British administration in Ireland, Mr. Governor. Open that prison gate, I have my time done, I want to hear none of your weasel words'. At that the Governor opened the gates of the infamous H blocks and my brother Joe walked out, still a proud Irishman, 'I'll wear no convict uniform, or meekly serve my time, that England might brand Irelands fight, eight hundred years of crime'. Good man Joe! As oul Jemmy would have said, "you were 'a manly boy'".

58

THE CEASEFIRE

GOING INTO THE 1990's it was on the I.R.A. grapevine that Gerry Adams and John Hume were involved in talks that might lead to a peace settlement with the British. It was early days but it was happening. The hated Thatcher was thrown out of power in England by her own M.P's. John Major was more amiable to peace. Peace could have got nowhere with Thatcher in power in Britain, but now with a new British Prime Minister there was a slim chance that peace might be possible. The talks between Adams and Hume continued, but there was another very important man secretly involved in these talks. This man was the new Irish leader in Dublin. A man called Albert Reynolds, who came to power in Dublin when Mr. Charles Haughey was ousted from power. Mr. Haughey, who presided over the Hunger Strikes without protest, who presided over the extradition of young Irish men over the border to the Brits, again without a murmur. A man who dishonestly helped himself to Irish people's money. A self serving man that Ireland was better off without. The new Irish leader, Mr. Albert Reynolds, would prove to be the man who wasn't afraid to break the mould, think outside the box, and put the good of the Irish people north and south before his own political ambitions. A southern leader of this calibre was a long time coming, but Mr. Albert Reynolds would prove to be a man of great integrity, political foresight and courage. Albert Reynolds brought Sinn Féin in from the cold. He realised that a conflict situation couldn't be solved without the participation of one of the main protagonists. The southern media and political establishment, scared out of their wits at Reynolds new approach, were screaming at the tops of their voices in fear and apprehension at bringing the 'terrorists' into the political system. John Hume got a lot of vilification through the southern establishment and media, but he publicly stated he was in search of a permanent peace settlement, with all sides involved and he didn't care who it pleased or didn't please, he was going down that road. The same southern media hated Hume, as he was a very hard man to get at. St. John, they used to call him disdainfully. They could get no dirt on him, and how dare he talk to Gerry Adams! Yet Adams represented the people of west Belfast, a large section of Irish people in one of Ireland's biggest cities. His vote would have elected several members of the Dublin government. He also represented the key constituency of west Belfast where a lot of the war was fought. How were you going to achieve peace if you wouldn't even talk to, or acknowledge the public representative of these marginalised group of Irish citizens? A 'voice over' had to be used by news reporters when talking to this public representative, his voice wasn't allowed to be heard in public, in the southern media and television. They had a stupid law banning this public representative or any elected Sinn Féin representative, of this section of the Irish people, from being heard or being allowed to properly represent constituents. The likes of this nonsense wouldn't be seen in South Africa. It was stupid, vindictive and wrong to treat an Irish elected representative like that. Albert Reynolds lifted the media ban on Sinn Féin, and was vilified for doing so by the now hysterical media, southern political hacks, and west Brits. The old man in the wee house in Park street, Monaghan came into mind again, with his straight pipe pointing down the Dublin road, 'Watch Leinster House, they'll stab you in the back. They don't want political change in Ireland. Their only political concern is to maintain the status quo. They are political liars speaking out of the both sides of their mouths, who, would, undermine peace efforts, if it served their own personal political ambitions'. But the right man at the right time had happened. Albert Reynolds was a Dublin political leader who was to put the good of the Irish people ahead of his own personal political ambitions. Reynolds wasn't afraid of political change in Ireland, he had the courage to welcome that change. When Albert Reynolds, John Hume and Gerry Adams took a photo call on the steps of Leinster house, their three hands touching in a show of political solidarity, I knew then that peace had a chance. I hoped it would. The vital difference between this attempt to settle the conflict and the sunningdale attempts was that the people most involved in the conflict, were included.

59

BACK IN DUBLIN

MY OWN PERSONAL life was going through a rough patch at this time. I had got into business a bit too deep. I got involved in constructing houses when the housing market suddenly collapsed. It was causing a lot of stress between myself and my wife. The political raids on my home had taken its toll as well. The result was that we separated and I moved back into Dublin. I had developed arthritis in my hips from all the heavy lifting of fireplaces and building materials. The move to Dublin worked; it took the pressure off my family home and gave me and my wife a chance to sort things out. We were finanically secure, so it wasn't too bad. It was lonely at the start, being on my own again, but as I was down at Balrath nearly every day. I didn't lose touch with my children. They also spent a lot of time with me in my apartment in Phibsboro. They got to know Dublin very well during the six to seven years. Myself and my children always remained very close. I looked after them well, we went holidaying, camping, stayed in hotels, B&B's and Mosney. They loved Mosney, just over the road from their home in County Meath. I took them to all the G.A.A. matches; we never missed an Ulster final in Clones, Co. Monaghan and always supported County Tyrone and County Meath in all their Croke Park matches. They got to love Gaelic sports and they still do. We had always two chances of being in Croke Park; Tyrone and Meath. If one wasn't doing well the other would be! My ex-wife and I managed a good working relationship, we looked after the children well but we never got back together. I was determined my children would get a good education; they were brainy children and would go far if they got the chance. I was going to make sure they got every chance to get to where they wanted to be in life. In the meantime, myself, my ex-wife, and our three lovely children got on with life. It wasn't ideal, but it worked.

60

I.R.A. CEASEFIRE: THE PEACE PROCESS BEGINS

IN 1994 THE Irish Republican Army called a ceasefire with our British enemies. I had gone to all the peace meetings called by Sinn Féin all around the country. I spoke in favour of a peace process if we could get one established. The British would have to co-operate to make it work. They were still a bit reluctant, but Sinn Féin believed they would come on board. It was the Irish and the Americans, who were the driving force behind the start of the peace process. It was acknowledged that the peace process would be a drawn out, prolonged affair. It would not happen overnight, after 25 years of Guerrilla war in the north and in England. The south had suffered too. The southern volunteers were great men. One of then stood out for what courage and bravery is all about, Martin 'Doco' Doherty gave his life outside The Widow Scallons pub in Pearse Street in Dublin City. He confronted armed British undercover agents and single handedly stopped them from planting a bomb in the crowded function room, where 200 republican supporters were enjoying a night out. He saved dozens of lives by sacrificing his own. He was a hero. The peace process could have been set back for years had this attack been successful. Doco's courage had saved the peace process and given it a lifeline. It wouldn't matter how long it took, as long as it was a genuine effort on both sides. The soldiers in the frontline of any war are always the first to welcome peace. Ask any soldier; be he from a conventional army or a Guerrilla army, he would always welcome peace, provided it is a just peace for all involved. The fighting soldier has a lot to lose by the continuation of conflict - his life for one; that's why he loves peace. The dream of his girl, and a chance to be with her, and set up a home and a family, kept so many soldiers going, through very tough times. It's his lifeline. Some make it to that Promised Land, and some don't. The ones that survive conflicts, don't know why it was them who survived, rather than their comrades who didn't make it. It's one of life's great imponderables that just has to be accepted; that's how the cookie crumbled. The northern people were delighted that a ceasefire had been called. The Irish heroic population of the six counties had gone through 25 years of terrible conflict, and were war weary. They wanted to give peace a chance.

61

MY MOTHER

MY MOTHER WHO never once complained about the burden she had to bear in the fight for the North. Long nights not knowing if her son's would survive the conflict or not. This generation of mothers and fathers suffered a huge amount. She was happy to see peace. My brother's building company had renovated the old family farmhouse into a lovely, little, country cottage with all the mod-cons and my mother or 'Granny Mac' as she was known as by this time, had moved back home and was very happy to be in her own home again. She never called the house in the housing estate in Dungannon her home, it was just a house that was necessary to have because of circumstances. Home was always the little old house by the Lough in amongst the Glens of Tyrone. Glenadush was the name of our townland, the glen of the bushes. It lived up to its name every spring and summer. The whin bushes would turn bright yellow all up over the hills, it was a lovely old place to live. The sun would sparkle off the water of the Lough, the whin bushes with their huge splash of yellow, the green of the thorn hedges and the green of the fresh grass - it was nature at its best. Granny Mac was so happy to be home. I always met her in the hotels along the border, the Four Seasons in Monaghan town, the Glencarn in Castleblaney and the Great Northern in Bundoran in Donegal, were the favourites. These were always very special occasions. I wasn't going to make the same mistake I made with my father, thinking they would be there forever. I knew that every one of those occasions in those hotels were special. I loved those family gatherings. We, the family, ran a surprise 70th for Granny Mac, she loved it once she got over the surprise. It was held in the Glencarn in Castleblaney. All the big, wide family circle turned up in honour to Granny Mac. This lovely articulate, very astute old lady, who had come through so much with such resilience, she was special. My daughters went up to Tyrone to visit Granny Mac and stay with her during the summer. They loved Granny Mac; they loved her little cottage in the County Tyrone countryside. Granny Mac always had a few little chickens or little kittens or little puppies, it was a magic place for grandchildren. The memory of those visits is still very alive with my children, years later. She loved County Meath as well. I took her to the Hill of Tara, the Hill of Slane, Newgrange, and the Battle of the Boyne site near Drogheda. She loved Ireland and everything about Ireland. The language, the music, the dance, the G.A.A., every bit of Irish history was fascinating to her. She kept scrapbooks of newspaper cuttings, her own remarks written on a little piece of paper and attached to the newspaper article. She wrote about everything; that's how she passed her time; she was a gifted writer and could write for hours on end. We have kept a lot of her writings; these writings are very precious to her big family. Granny Mac's wee cottage at the lough was a very special place. Even the adults in our huge family circle said, if you have a problem troubling you, after a visit to Granny Mac, talking to her by the fireside, knowing that whatever you discussed never left that fireside, was always a way to lessen the burden of any problem in life. If she couldn't solve it, you always felt the burden was lighter when you left, than when you came. She had a great understanding of life and was full of the wisdom you can only have by rearing 12 children, reared during those troubled years, and surviving it all. Granny Mac said she went to many jails to visit her own sons and the sons of neighbours. But she said God spared her from having to go to the graveside of one of her own. For that she said, she was always grateful to God almighty. So many mothers of the conflict had to make that heartbreaking journey to the graveside, on all sides of the conflict. When a British soldier would die in an ambush in the north my mother would say she could understand why he died, but, he was still somebody's rearing. She always had compassion for their mothers and fathers, he was somebody's son. She went to all the funerals of I.R.A. men whenever she could. Innocent Catholics shot by loyalist murder squads as well. She prayed for the Protestant victims of the conflict too.

She felt for them all.

62

CANARY WHARF

THE CEASEFIRE BROKE down temporarily and a huge bomb went off at Canary Warf in London docklands. It caused millions and millions worth of damage. A mortar attack on Downing Street sent the British government scarpering under a table at 10 Downing Street. I'm sure shit was touching cloth under that table! I'm sure the smell down there wasn't great! It was a shake-up the British Government needed, for soon after that the ceasefire was called again. This time the British joined the Irish and Americans in the peace process and were genuine participants. Why was it that the British seem to need those kind of lessons? There were some innocent casualties in the bombing campaign in England as well. Two young boys died at one stage, a terrible tragedy. The innocent casualties of war. These deaths of innocent people who are not participants of the conflict; are so unfortunate and tragic. The innocent always get hurt in war, that's why I have grown to hate all wars. I never ever want to see another one in Ireland. I hope Ireland and Britain can find a final peaceful solution to our conflict

63

AN OLD COMRADE CALLS

ONE OF THE south Armagh men called to my house at Balrath. He asked me where I stood - did I support the I.R.A. ceasefire? I said I did, he said he didn't. I knew this south Armagh man well; he was an old comrade and friend. I said 'we fought a 25 year guerrilla war for the Irish people, left on the wrong side of Britain's unwanted border. We brought that population from being on its knees back up onto its feet. With the help of an honourable number of Irish people, north and south, Irish Americans, and the Irish in Britain. We survived 25 years, because we had the backing of all those people. We fought a downtrodden people's war. These same heroic people who suffered so much, now want to give peace a chance to succeed, and deliver the rest of the political changes by political means. Our war on their behalf has opened the door for our political people to walk through. Without the sacrifice of the I.R.A. men and women who fought and died in this conflict, that political door wouldn't be opened. Our movement is now out of war gear, and shifted into political gear, and that's what the people want. If we're not fighting a peoples war, who's war are we fighting? A personal war of some kind? There is no moral grounds for a war like that. I won't have anything to do with it. You will get yourself up a political cul-de-sac that you will never get out of, but I won't be up there with you. If a minibus load of young people came to this county right now to be trained as I.R.A., I'd send them all home immediately. I wouldn't send my own to fight in a conflict no-one wants, so therefore I wouldn't enable anybody else's to fight either. The war is over'. He looked at me with a kind of sadness and said, 'We were some guerrilla army, man, I'm sad you don't see it my way', 'I don't', I said. 'You must have a people's war or no war'. He got into his car and left my yard. He never came my way again.

The Omagh bomb happened some time after this and I know that this man was turned sick by it. I'm sure that this man wished he had taken my good advice that day at my wee house at Balrath. He was a good man; I was sorry to see him going down the foolish wrong way. These men became known as 'The Dissidents'.

64

THE PEACE PROCESS CONTINUES

SOME OF THE British security forces bitterly opposed the peace process. They called it destabilising! A special envoy was sent by President Bill Clinton to help in the search for a lasting peace. This patient man's political skills would be very important to the peace process. The protestant people of the north had to be brought into the peace process as well. This very skilled U.S.A. envoy would be able to do that. So we now had a political situation in the north, where the Irish political leader in Dublin, the British Prime Minister, the President of the United States of America and the leaders of the Irish population north of the border including Adams of Sinn Féin, the S.D.L.P.'s, John Hume, the leaders of the protestant people in the north all prepared to work together. Albeit, it was very slow at the start to seek a peace settlement after eight hundred years of conflict. This was to be expected. I wished them well in that peace effort. The I.R.A. ceasefire was solid. The decommissioning of I.R.A. weapons followed some time later. I was happy with this. If there's no war, you don't need weapons of war. If all weapons of war were destroyed the world over, I would be a happy man.

65

GRANNY MAC

I WENT TO Monaghan at Christmas of 1997 to meet my mother in the Four Seasons Hotel. We had a lovely day; we had a traditional dinner of turkey and ham. My brother Malachy's wife was there with a friend. They went into Monaghan town to do some shopping and were away half the day. It gave me and my mother a chance to catch up on old times.

We talked about the big family growing up on the lough, the old neighbours; a lot of them now dead and gone, and the effect the conflict had on everybody. She said that my having to go away on the run was very sore on the oul man. He missed you a lot, she said, even though he'd never talk much about it. I missed you myself, she said. You were good about the house. You were a big loss, but I'm thankful you came through it all safely. The British army raids on the old home was very hard on both him and me, she said. A terrible invasion of privacy. When they left after a raid, there was a terrible smell and atmosphere. It took days to go away. The last raid before he died took a lot out of him, and then only days after his funeral they came back again and took Marty, at 18 years of age, and interned him. When they produced that dreaded yellow form at the end of a raid, then I knew some of my boys were going with them. Me and Shemie, Malachy and Pat fought with them in the living room when they arrested Marty. I pounded the officer in charge on his chest, I screamed was it not bad enough to have killed my husband, did they have to take my youngest son as well? He pushed me away and I fell onto the floor. Shemie, the boxer, hit him then, and I thought he would be shot. One of the soldiers did fire a shot and I fainted. Shemie gathered me up in his arms and took me to his bungalow. The soldiers were shouting halt at him, but he kept going on. The wee girls were screaming with fear. Anita, the youngest at only seven years old, was under the bed. She always hid under the same bed. She talks to this day about their big boots on the bedroom floor. Rosy, Teresa and Kate, who were only a few years older, used to stand around that bed to protect her. When the Brits would go to search under that bed, they'd say, 'my wee sister is under there, leave her alone'! It was terrible. But they arrested Marty even though one of the older boys offered to go in his place. Marty spent his 21st birthday in Long Kesh internment camp. No judge, no jury, no trial. Then they tortured him as well! It was a very hard time. Shemie's wife Kathleen got so scared that she refused to live in their new bungalow, and they moved out. I couldn't blame her. It was a good job they did, because soon after that, a loyalist murder gang came to kill them. Thank god they had left. The day after the murder gang came, I moved out. I had to. I was afraid for my girls and what might happen them at the dead hour of night. They were getting too scared and couldn't sleep. Every sound was scary for them, dogs barking, cars coming up the lane, anyone knocking on the door, all these wee simple things got very scary. So I took my four daughters aged 9 – 14 and moved into the safety of a housing estate in Dungannon. But it was never home to me. I was glad of it for my daughter sake, but my home was at the lough. It was heartbreaking, after 28 years there. All my children, except the youngest, were born in that old home. Such memories. I walked out there any day I could and lit the fire and kept it clean. I always knew I'd be back there, and years later, when the sons building firm done it up lovely for me, I moved back immediately. It was so good to be home. It was never raided again, thank god! Anita came back with me. The other 3 had got married and had their own homes. Anita was happy with me there, and some years later she got married and moved down south with her husband. They are happy there. I am so grateful to god I was spared the ultimate heartache of having to bury one of my own. My heart goes out to those mothers who buried their sons and daughters. Some families buried one, some two, and some even buried three. The terrible pain of lying awake at night, knowing your children were in constant danger.

She expressed gratitude that it was now being resolved by the peace process. Joe had met Celine, a lovely girl, and settled down. He'd had a very difficult time getting back to any kind of normality after coming out of the hellhole that was Thatcher's H blocks, but he got away from it all for a few years in the States. She said those few years had been good for him. He seemed content and happy. She was leaving him the old home, as everyone else had a home. The eldest son, the driving force behind the family business, had got stomach cancer a few years ago, he'd had a very serious operation to remove his stomach, but he survived and now had the all clear. He was back at the helm of his family business, and he and his sons are very successful. Another brother lives by the Lough in his family bungalow. He always loved fishing and hunting with his golden Labrador dogs. Pat never got involved much in politics. He lived just a field away from Granny Mac's cottage. Granny Mac told me that day in the Four Seasons Hotel it was great to have them so near. My next brother Malachy was an electrician by trade. He served his time with an old tradesman from Dungannon. Malachy got his time served and when his old boss died prematurely, Malachy then started his own business and was very successful at it. He bought old houses in Dungannon, and in Belfast University area, renovated them and had them rented out. A very astute, successful man Malachy had a lovely home in the town of Dungannon. He always drove a top of the range car. He was a good driver but drove way too fast. He had a red Honda souped up motorbike when he was a teenager and he'd take the light from your eyes. The speed of him!! But he was also a very good careful driver; he wasn't a road hog, he just loved speed. He and Ann had two sons and two daughters. Granny Mac relied on Malachy. He was very good to Granny Mac, as they all were.

Marty and Joe run their own business. They are doing well for themselves. My eldest sister is a primary schoolteacher in Belfast; her husband is also a teacher, a lovely couple, they live in Belfast with family. My next sister went to England quite young, got married there and set up a home for old people. This suited her for she had always a very caring, kind, good natured way with her. She had a family in England. She and her husband divorced and she came home with one of her daughters, a lovely girl, and settled back home in Dungannon. My twin sisters married two local fellas. John is a mechanical fitter who runs his own business. Sean is an electrician and they live in a lovely renovated cottage style house just outside Dungannon. The twins have lovely families and are very close as lots of twins are. My youngest sister lives down south. Her husband runs his own business. He does very well. My other sister married Paul, a big fella, six foot or more. He is a bricklayer who builds bungalows and houses. They live in County Armagh. So, me and Granny Mac had a lovely time taking stock of where the big family reared at the Lough were, now that the conflict was at its end. 'Not one of you brought shame through the door', she said. It had been tough at times, but we came through it well. My mother told me she still missed Johnny, as she called my father, she still missed him every day she told me. There never had been anyone else before and after she met him, he was the only man in her life. He was a good man she said, he'd always done his best for her and his big family at the Lough. She still missed him and always would, and this was from a woman who would be eighty in a few days time, on the 7th of January. Her birthday was two days before mine, hers on the 7th and mine on the 9th of January. Granny Mac would be eighty in a few days but she still had a mind as clear as a mountain stream. She had an operation for a goiter in her throat a few years ago, it was pressing on her wind pipe and restricting her from breathing, so she opted to get it out. She was told it was a dangerous operation at her age, but she said she trusted these young surgeons and doctors with such God given skills, so who was I to doubt their ability to make me well? The operation was a complete success. When she was coming through after the anaesthetic she was hallucinating a bit. She thought that she was at home and the people beside her were British soldiers who had taken over her home! When Big Marty and Joe came to visit her she gave out stink to them, about the big strong sons she had reared, and them letting British soldiers take over her home! 'Get them out of my home' she told Marty and Joe in no uncertain terms, who did they think they were taking over her place? It was a throwback to the British army raids on the old family home. When she came through properly, she laughed with Joe and Marty and the nurses. When the family approached my mother before she left the hospital about whether or not she was able to look after herself when she got home, she looked them all sternly in the eyes and told them, 'When I am not able to look after myself in my own home, I'll let some of you know. In the meantime, I am well able to look after my own affairs. I'm just looking forward to getting out of here and going home. I want to thank those wonderful doctors for doing such a good job'. That operation was a few years ago and here she was, sitting in the Four Seasons Hotel, and no bother to her. She told me that day she loved living in her wee home, where everybody called. She had over forty grandchildren and several great grandchildren at this time and she told me she had a special place in her heart for every single one of them. That didn't surprise me, for this remarkable old Irish woman had a heart as big as County Tyrone. 'I want to live there for the rest of my life' she said 'and be a burden to no-one'. Ann and her friend came back to the Four Seasons just then and we had a pot of tea between us in the foyer of the hotel. Then we made arrangements to meet the Saturday after her birthday in about two weeks time, with the rest of the family, in the Four Seasons Hotel, for a celebratory meal. Looking forward to that day we bid our goodbyes. My mother gave me a big hug and said how good it was to meet and talk over old times. It had been a lovely day.

My children came to my apartment in Dublin and spent the New Year with me. My children loved Dublin at Christmas and New Year, it was a change from the country life in County Meath. They had made friends with a couple of children in Phibsboro and got on well with them. I had a comfortable two bedroom apartment with kitchen, bathroom and shower. My children loved it. One night in my apartment at New Year, I lifted my phone to call Granny Mac to wish her a Happy New Year. She was delighted. She spoke to my three daughters in turn and when I went back on the phone again she thanked me for the call. She said it was the best Christmas, New Years present she could have asked for. She really loved her wee grandchildren from the south of Ireland and they loved her. I wished her a Happy New Year and Happy Birthday and looked forward to seeing her after her birthday in the Four Seasons Hotel. She was very happy and content with herself. She was really enjoying her old age.

A LETTER FROM MY MOTHER

Glenadush, August '96

Dear Tommy,

Thanks for sending your lovely family down here to Glenadush. They are lovely children and a credit to both of you. It wouldn't be life if it hadn't its crosses. But never let it get you down, theres too much good to live for. Donna, Carrie and Tracey are very precious to me. I hope they'll always come to see us here. The family is still very united. We lost a lot, but we gained more. Some day theres a bright star and it will shine on an Ireland. You have a great past here. We think of you all every day. Bridie is a great mother to the children and you are a wonderful father. Keep looking up and God bless you all.

from Mammy, to
you With much Love

x x x x x

66

THE DREAD

OLD EMMET THE Dread had lost his little cottage home next door because Paddy and Nanny had died and left the cottage to one of their sons. The son needed the money so he sold the cottage. Emmet the Dread found himself with no home. He had trouble with his eyesight and the long years of drinking had taken its toll on his health. He was very annoyed having to leave the area and be housed in Navan or some other town by the local housing authority, where he knew nobody. He was distraught. His own family did not want to know, as he had drank the family jewels. But he was an old man, who had lived in the little cottage next door a lot of his life. He must have some rights. I told him not to agree to move out. I would talk to the son who was selling the cottage. I phoned the man in England and said I would give old Emmet a place to put a mobile home in my yard and give him a place to live for the rest of his life. I said to the man 'You buy old Emmet the mobile, I'll give him the site to live in it, that way you get selling your cottage and get your money, and old Emmet gets a place to live until he dies'. It worked! Old Emmett got his new home in my yard, sold an odd fireplace for me here and there, and everyone was happy! So between one thing and another at this New Year of 1998 I was happy enough.

I had done a bit of travelling too. I went to New York and loved it, the city Alan the Hotelier offered me a new life in all those years ago. I went down to San Fransisco to visit Una and her husband and Sheamie from Dungannon, and I stayed with them for several weeks in 1997 and really enjoyed myself. I liked the States for a visit, but I was glad I didn't go to live in it. I love Ireland too much to live anywhere else. It's the best country in the world. I had also gone to the Canary Islands a few times and enjoyed the sunny climate. I was on one of these holidays in the Canary Islands when my old friend Alan died of cancer. I was very annoyed I wasn't able to go to his funeral. His old right hand man Hughie died around the same time. Life was still good, I was making enough money to meet all my commitments, family and otherwise, and my children were doing very well at school and would go far, they were getting a good education.

67

DEATH OF GRANNY MAC

MY MOTHER TURNED eighty on Wednesday the 7th of January and I was looking forward to meeting her on the Saturday. My own birthday was on the Friday. I got a phone call at about 3 o'clock on my birthday, two days after my mother had turned eighty years of age. It was my brother Malachy. 'Tommy', he said, 'there is no easy way to say this, but Granny Mac died about an hour ago'. I was devastated. I wouldn't believe what my brother was telling me. My beautiful old mother was dead. I told my brother Malachy I would meet him at the Glencarn hotel in Castleblaney at 6 o'clock. 'I'll be there', he said. I left down the phone stunned. Granny Mac is dead, I thought. I have to say my last goodbye to her, in her wee cottage by the Lough. I didn't mind so much not being able to be at her funeral but I had to say goodbye to her in person. To hell with the Brits. There is some things a man has to do in his life, no matter the cost, and this was one of them. I was going home to say goodbye to my mother at her wake, no matter what. Only her immediate family would know for the next few hours that she had passed away, now was the time to go. When her death was in the papers tomorrow it would be too late. British security forces would then know and it would be too dangerous. So it was now, this evening, or never. I pulled into the car park of the Glencarn Hotel and waited for my brother Malachy. Him and his wife Ann drove into the car park at about 6.30. I asked Ann to get into the back of the car and I got into the front with my brother Malachy. 'I'm going to say goodbye to Granny Mac'. He looked at me intently and said 'Are you sure?' I said 'Malachy, I'll thumb a lift if I have to'. 'That's good enough for me' he said, 'Let's go'. He said he had come up through Emmyvale and Aughnacloy and the roads were quiet, no checkpoints. I said 'Go back the route you came'. We headed down through Monaghan town, into Emyvale, crossed the cursed border at Aughnacloy and down towards the Ballygawley roundabout. We then took the old Ballygawley road to Dungannon, down through Parkanaur and Quinn's Corner, down the old twisted road by Castlecaufield and around the shores of the old Lough where I was born and reared. Up the old lane and down towards the old farmhouse, now the little country cottage, a cottage I had only seen photos off, I had never been free to visit.

There were loads of cars already there, as the wake was already on. Malachy went onto the cottage first to tell my brothers and sisters who his visitor was. I went in through the door of my mother's wee cottage, through the kitchen and sitting room full of neighbours and friends. They all said hello and nodded in recognition at me. I made my way into the bedroom where my mother was laid out on the bed in lovely bright clothes. I knelt down by her bedside and gave her a hug and a kiss. I said some silent prayers by her bedside. I spent some time in there, paying my last respects to this remarkable old Irishwoman who was my mother. One of my sisters came over and put her hand on my shoulder and said 'Tommy, are you alright?', I said 'Yes, I'm fine'. I gave my mother one last hug and kiss. I then got up went to the end of her bed, buttoned my coat, came to attention, saluted my mother and stood there at attention and respect for this great old Irish woman, who had suffered so much for Ireland and backed the fight for the north with every fibre and bone in her body, and always had a word of encouragement for her sons and daughters no matter what the hardship was. She never faltered in her unswerving belief that Ireland was entitled to self determination and freedom. As I stood at the bottom of her bed, as a soldier of Ireland, an I.R.A. fighter, I was so proud to call her my mother. As I turned from the bottom of her bed I said my final goodbye and left that room a happy man. It didn't matter I wouldn't be there for the rest of her funeral, I had paid my last respects, said my final farewells in person, that was enough for me. My three lovely daughters would represent me at the rest of the ceremony. I walked back through the kitchen and sitting room, greeting my old neighbours and friends as I went. I went outside, walked over to the old gate down to the Lough field, looked around at the Lough and the fields and said goodbye. This old home by the Lough would never be the same again. It was the end of an era. I walked back from the gate, past the old cottage, up the old laneway where I had walked to school with my brothers and sisters, got into my brother Malachy's car and went back to

County Monaghan. We almost ran into a British army checkpoint. But we avoided it and drove back to the Glencarn hotel. My brother Malachy and his wife Ann went back to my mother's wake and I went back to Dublin.

That's how my life had been for many, many years now and I accepted that was how it was and that was that. I never complained. Many of my old comrades never made it this far, I was one of the lucky ones that had survived to have a life and family of my own. My three daughters and their mother went to Tyrone for my mother's funeral. It was an old Irish traditional funeral. Granny Mac had left detailed instructions how her wake and funeral was to be carried out. She would be laid out in her bed in nice clothes, light the house fire and keep the house cosy and warm. Have tea, sandwiches and drinks for everyone for two nights. Then she would be put into her coffin just an hour before she left her home, taken to the old church of Donaghmore, leaving her home at 9 o'clock for 10 o'clock mass. Irish traditional airs would be played on the fiddle in memory and honour of her husband Johnny who played the fiddle in a Céilí band, and so many nights in our old home – "The Old Rustic Bridge", "The Cúilin", "The Lark In The Clear Air" and "Danny Boy". My eldest daughter read a goodbye letter from me on the alter. I was very proud of them. I could not have been happier as to who represented me at my mother's funeral. The grandchildren and great grandchildren really loved their Granny Mac. After the initial shock of seeing her dead, they were playing around her bed before her wake was over. Granny Mac would be very happy with that. All through their school and college days, if there is a very important exam or any crisis in their lives, my daughters always say a prayer to Granny Mac. It always works! The day of my mother's funeral was the loneliest day in my life. I got up from bed in my Dublin apartment at about 8 o'clock. I made a bit of breakfast and sat around at a loose end. I had no plans made out for the day, except I would go to mass in St. Peters church, Phibsboro for 10 o'clock. It was just across the road and it was Sunday. I sat there in my chair thinking of all that had happened me since I was a child growing up in County Tyrone. So much had taken place, so much had happened to very ordinary people. So much not of their own making, just an accident of history, no-one could have written the script for this story, no-one could have foreseen what tragedy would take place. It felt a bit unreal, as I sat in my apartment in Dublin city, as my own mother was being prepared for her last journey by the rest of my brothers and sisters, way up in County Tyrone. I thought of all my family and old neighbours and friends. It was too much for me. The grief overcame me, great waves of grief and sadness wracked my body, coming up from the depths of my being, uncontrollable and unstoppable. It was as if the grief and the sadness of all that had happened overflowed and was out of control. I think I was grieving for my father, my mother, all my comrades and friends who had died in the conflict in the north. It was an unbelievable overflow of sadness and grief. It finally subsided and I made my way to St. Peter's Church Phibsboro and asked the priest who was saying mass to mention a person's name for me in the death notices. He said 'Ok, who is this person?' I said 'Annie McNulty, Dungannon, County Tyrone'. 'What is the person to you' he asked, 'My mother' I said. He looked intently at me, 'Why aren't you up there?' he asked, 'It's a long story' I said, 'but I would be happy if you read out her name and dedicated the mass to her'. He said he would and then in a great act of kindness I'll never forget he said 'Come to me after the mass is over, I want to make you a cup of tea and hear your story', I thanked him and said 'I will do that but don't expect to hear the full story', 'I don't expect to' he said, 'I have relations in the north, I'm very interested in the history'. He read my mother's name out at the mass. My mother would have loved that, her being prayed for in Dublin City. We went into a room in the church after the mass and he made tea and we talked and discussed the history of Ireland way into the evening. He was a great help to me, on one of the most difficult days of my life. He kept me grounded and kept away the loneliness and got me through a very tough few hours. A real decent Christian man, was that priest. A pity all Catholic priests didn't follow in his example; the church wouldn't be in any kind of difficulties. I'll never forget that man's concern for a complete stranger in a big city. The good Samaritan will never be dead while that man lives.

I met members of my family the next day at my house at Balrath. We went for a tour of all the historical sites in County Meath. It was good for them and good for me. I went to the Glencarn in County Monaghan and had a meal with them. We're a great big close family, a Clan more than a family and we knew how to close ranks and support each other through hard times, we'd had plenty of practice down the years. Back in Dublin I met Marie. She lived in Coolock, Dublin. She is a lovely woman and we hit it off right away. She had four young children, two boys, and two girls.

We are partners 13 years now. We've had some great times together and really enjoy ourselves. I feel that I have 7 children! We have been very good for each other. As our children grew up, she helped me with mine and I helped her with hers. She is a very important part of my life. She has a lovely home in County Cavan now and I spend a lot of time with her there, it's a lovely part of Ireland.

68

THE GOOD FRIDAY AGREEMENT

THE GOOD FRIDAY agreement was negotiated and passed into law that year. It was a watershed in Irish history. If it could be implemented in full it would be a big step forward for the whole island of Ireland. The Good Friday agreement allowed for a return of Parliament in Belfast, a power sharing government where each tradition had an equal share of power. A hard pill to swallow, the very return of Stormont in any shape or form was a difficult move for me. But this one would be very different I was assured. The Irish nationalist people of the north would have positions of real power in this Belfast Parliament. Their position as Irish people in the north would be guaranteed by law and copper fastened by the Dublin government. The Irish people of Tyrone would have the same rights to be Irish as the people of Tipperary or any other Irish county. There would be cross border bodies to lessen the impact of the border. Cooperation in every area of everyday life, north and south, would bring the two parts of the island together again over a period of time. The island had been run by two different sets of political systems for over fifty years, it would take time to get the political lifeblood of the island running through one set of political veins again. Then there would be a Council of Ireland, its membership drawn from the Dublin government and the Belfast Parliament to make decisions for the betterment of all the people in Ireland. Money would come from the E.U., the U.S.A., the British Government and the Irish Government to fund all these plans. Britain also withdrew its absolute rights to the six north eastern counties of Ireland and agreed to a vote to be taken on the border. A majority vote to end the border that would have to be honoured by the British Government, internationally guaranteed. This was a long way from the hated Thatcher's assertion that the six counties were as British as London or Birmingham. I hated that assertion by right wing British conservatives. This assertion was a grievous insult to any Irish man or woman. How dare they state that! Apart from the geographical impossibility, it got right under my skin big time! That was gone now. So much for Thatcher's 'out, out, out!' The British had conceded that the border wasn't written in stone, that the six northern counties were very different from London and Birmingham. This was a great victory in itself for the Irish people as a whole, the border was temporary. It could be phased out over a period of time and gone altogether, sooner rather than later. The claim by Dublin over the north was abolished to reassure the protestant population, another bitter pill to swallow. The position of protestant people of the six counties would be guaranteed by the British Government in the interim period. It was hoped that the Belfast Parliament, the cross border bodies, the Council of Ireland; the funds to revitalise the north's and border counties economies, all this co operation would bring the two peoples of the north, the two parts of Ireland and the two countries of Ireland and Britain into a much more peaceful and co operative era. It would help to reassure the protestant people of the north that their real future for themselves and their children lay within the island of Ireland, in mutual respect of each other's religious and political beliefs. It was recognised that this would all take time and patience but I believed that this ambitious plan could work if implemented in full and in good spirit. To lay to rest the conflict of 800 years between Britain and Ireland was something well worth waiting for. We owed it to our children and our childrens' children to win this peace. I believe that every Irish man and Irish woman who had fought and died for the freedom of Ireland in every generation of those 800 years, deserved nothing less than the full freedom of Ireland as their memorial stone. An agreed Ireland, ruled by the people of Ireland, for the people of Ireland, free of any British political or military interference. A total withdrawal of all British soldiers from the island of Ireland, was and always will be a vital part of any permanent settlement of this age old conflict. If British soldiers remain on any part of this island into the future, then there will always be a group, however small, that will feel justified in taking them on in a military fight. Every generation of 800 years has thrown up its fighters; and the presence of British soldiers on this island will only make certain that it will happen again. Padriag Pearse, at the grave of that great old Fenian O'Donavan Rossa, spoke possibly the truest words ever at any Irish Patriot's grave, 'Ireland unfree will never be at peace'. I think everyone in the corridors of power, especially in the corridors of power in Westminster, would be doing Ireland and Britain, and all Irish and British people a great service, if they finally act on this historically appropriate statement of fact. For fact it is, and will always be, whether we like it or not. The absence of British soldiers in Ireland, any part of Ireland, an unarmed community police force drawn from the two communities, would render even the most hardline republican with absolutely no remnant of a cause left to act on. No British soldiers, they couldn't shoot what isn't there. An unarmed community police service, how could anyone justify going out to shoot or attack in any way an unarmed community police service with absolutely no political input or position whatsoever? A political input by the Westminster Government, after these two vital conditions were met, would have to exist for a considerable period of time to keep the protestant unionist population of the north feeling happy and secure. It would be up to us, the Irish people north and south, to win over the protestant Irish-British population of the north to the position that their children would be better off in an agreed political Ireland. Respecting the catholic Irish and the protestant Irish, equally in every way. Civil and religious freedom for catholic, protestant and dissenter. The Proclamation of 1916 was a document way before it's time and ranks with the best human charters ever printed. An agreed Ireland, were everybody worked for the good of everybody else. The protestant state for a protestant people, north of the border would be a thing of the past, as would be the catholic state for a catholic people south of the border. A catholic state that the protestant people of the north had every right to be afraid of. The special position of the Catholic Church, the blank cheque it received from the old Free State political set up, turned out to be a much abused blank cheque indeed, one that the catholic population of Ireland had every right to fear, never mind the protestant people! A total separation of state and religion is the only way. Practice of, and religious beliefs must be by freedom of choice. These freedoms and choices must be guaranteed by the laws of Ireland. Recent history of Ireland has shown that there is political corruption in both parts of Ireland. It was not confined to the north. Every citizen of Ireland, north and south deserves a better political deal into the future. Ireland must be run politically for the benefit of all it's people, with an honesty and transparency that has been sadly missing for a long, long time. None of the patriot dead of Ireland, protestant patriots, or catholic patriots, would have been happy with the way either part of Ireland was ruled politically since partition. Sean Lemass and Albert Reynolds being the exceptions south of the border. Or perhaps Terence O'Neill in the north? Terence O'Neill being the Northern Prime Minister who met Sean Lemass at Stormont in the mid-sixties to try and bring co-operation to both parts of Ireland. Ian Paisley, the Arch-Bigot, was the man who destroyed this effort to steer a peaceful way within the island of Ireland. This man was an anti-Irish, anti-Catholic, anti-everything that might have been politically good for this island, north and south, for most of his life! He'd have no problem supping at the same table as Lord Brookborough of 'Protestant state for a Protestant people' fame. Also, Mr. Craig, Home Affairs Minister of the Stormont government, who stated he would 'liquidate the enemy', the 'enemy' being the Catholic Irish population of the northern state. Mr. Brian Faulkner, also a leader of the Stormont government, the man that brought in internment without trial, and then ordered the torture of the same innocent prisoners. Mr. Paisley fitted in perfectly with the likes of them, when he incited thousands of his supporters to wave gun licences above their heads in an implicit threat to the same Catholic Irish population. His speeches of hate incited young Protestant men to join loyalist paramilitary groups. So when Mr. Paisley and his good wife sit on the 'Late Late Show', letting the people of Ireland see how good and Christian and friendly he is, forgive me if I can't help thinking, that if it wasn't for the likes of Mr. Paisley and the aforementioned leaders, the conditions for the conflict in the north may never have materialised, and the conflict may never have been necessary. I hope, as he basks in the glory of his new found Christian love of his Catholic neighbour, his 'Late Late Conversion' in more ways than one, that he spares a thought for all the suffering his 'Speeches of Hate' caused for a lot of people, Protestant and Catholic, north and south of the border. Still, it's better "late late" than never, and we have to be thankful for small mercies! But I still can't help thinking, how different Irish history may have been, if Mr. Paisley had backed Northern Prime Minister Terence O'Neill and Southern Prime Minister Sean Lemass in their efforts to promote political and economical co-operation between the two parts of this island during the mid-sixties.

John Hume was one of the politicians who put the welfare of the Irish people before personal political position. He was a leader of the Civil

Rights Movement of the late sixties in Derry City, and was part of the ill-fated march that would go down in history as Bloody Sunday. I hold great respect for civil rights leaders throughout the world; Martin Luther King, Nelson Mandela and Ghandi. John Hume would have found a place on the same platform as these great civil rights leaders. He took a different road to the likes of me. He stayed a bit aloof from the conflict on the ground. I was sometimes envious of these people, who could find a peaceful place to stay when the fight in the north was in full flight. I just couldn't find that safe haven, and like a lot of other people, went from civil rights to military fight. He was always a voice of reason during those terrible years and peaceful men like him, can have a vital place during times of severe conflict. Hume became very important when he became convinced that peace in the north was possible in the early nineties. He sacrificed a lot for that peace. He was very strong, and very genuine in those years. The Adams, Hume, Reynolds talks were the catalyst that started the long peace process. That photo of the three of them clasping hands on the steps of Leinster House was iconic. Peace was more important to this man, than personal political gain, I respected him for that. Adam's was a vital cog in this wheel as well. A very astute politician, with a very sharp political mind and very, ambitious. Realistic, economic and social policies that ordinary people can identify with are crucial. Adams has been hugely important in bringing the peace process to where it is. Derry Martin and Gerry the H block jail escaper, were vital for their 'street cred'. They were very important parts of the jig-saw that would deliver the good Friday agreement. With these men it was, "you get what it says on the tin", and they got respect for that, even from their former enemies. The future of Ireland, for her children and children's children, will depend on good decent hardworking, patriotic leaders, north and south, east and west, who will put the people of Ireland as a whole before personal political gain.

Albert Reynolds was certainly one of these men. The peace process in the north would not have existed without him. Reynolds had the foresight and the courage to act outside the box, and bring Sinn Féin and the I.R.A. in from the cold. He was castigated in the southern press, and by the political West Brit hacks of Dublin 4. As was John Hume, they hated Hume for talking peace to Adams. But he stuck to his task, in the face of huge criticism, and everyone now knows the end result – These men's courage and tenacity resulted in the Good Friday Agreement. Reynolds was a big loss to southern Ireland during the economic boom years. His business acumen and vast experience in business would have been invaluable in seeing the problems coming ahead. He would have had the ability to take the steps necessary to counteract the worst effects of the economic recession. Ahern did not have this ability. He just courted popularity and surfed on the crest of the wave during the boom years. He had no vision of the future. Reynolds would have had the ability to see clearly ahead. He could have been the Lemass of modern Ireland. Dick Spring, his Labour Coalition partner, shafted the best modern day leader Ireland ever had. It's to their eternal shame. Ireland's history will judge them harshly. I believe that the issues that brought down Albert Reynolds' government could have been worked out had he had the loyalty and backing of Spring's Labour party.

The political aspirations and fears of the Irish people have been exploited by ruthless, self-seeking, corrupt, greedy politicians north and south, for long enough. No more Ian Paisleys, no more Charles Haughey, no more greedy corrupt bankers and political elitist capitalist robbers, native and imperialistic, who exploited our political and religious differences, so that they could rule us and steal from us. But these greedy capitalist conniving political rulers, foreign and home grown, didn't only steal from us, they robbed our children's future as well. Let Ireland confine those failed political thieves to the waste paper basket of history, and get honest, decent, hardworking Irish men and women to lead this beautiful little country to a peaceful, prosperous, contented happy future, where all the resources of Ireland are put towards the well being of Irish people as a whole. North, south, east and west, protestant, catholic and dissenter!

I turned sixty that year. I never saw anything but political turmoil in my lifetime. I want it to be different for future generations, I believe it will. I still live in my wee home in County Meath. My three beautiful daughters have grown up to be well educated, happy and contented with good careers of their choice. I have lived at Balrath with my daughters and finished rearing and educating them as a lone parent for the last number of years. My ex-wife, we are now divorced, did it for the years before that, so that is fair enough. I have enjoyed everyday rearing my children. They are the apple of my eye, I am so proud of them. My brother Malachy died in a tragic drowning accident in April 2002, God rest his soul. Martin, Gerry, and the powers that be within Sinn Féin, did their best to get me clearance from the British to help in the search for my brother's body, and attend his funeral in County Tyrone. But they had to inform me that the British would not co operate and that they would arrest me on sight. Some things never change! They have very long memories when it comes to the likes of me. Their memories are not so long when it comes to the Paras of Bloody Sunday or the soldiers who led farmer McElhone out into the meadow to murder him or the G.A.A. man murdered at Aughnacloy British army checkpoint, or all the other innocent victims of British army violence. Not one British Para or member of the British security forces did one day in prison for their actions. Again I met my family in the Glencarn hotel in Castleblaney during this very sad time. It was five agonising days before his body was recovered from the Lough. It was a terrible co incidence that Barney, one of the big family reared beside us at the Lough, a taxi driver, was shot dead behind the wheel of his taxi the same day as my brother Malachy's body was recovered from the Lough. They were both buried on the Saturday morning, one after the other. The men who shot Barney, neighbour and I.R.A volunteer, whoever they were, wouldn't have been worthy to tie the man's laces. Barney was one of the bravest and gamest men I ever met. To me and to lots of other's he was a true soldier of Ireland. Again I spent the exact time of Malachy's funeral in the church in Castleblaney at mass, and wandered through the adjoining graveyard as my brother was buried in nearby Dungannon, County Tyrone. The British side of the Good Friday agreement didn't show much compassion for me, or my family, or Barneys family, as Ned, my best friend and comrade couldn't attend his taxi driver brother's funeral either. The O.T.R's or the 'on the run' I.R.A. men, on the run from the British administration in the six occupied counties, during the war against the corrupt six county state, are the forgotten prisoners of the conflict resolution peace process. Legislation going through Westminster parliament to give the O.T.R.'s an amnesty was blocked by right wing British conservatives and the unionist party of northern Ireland. This leaves me and others like me exiled from my native County Tyrone indefinitely. I was forty years exiled from my wee home at the Lough outside Dungannon County Tyrone that year. The last Christmas I spent at home with my 5 brothers and 6 sisters and my mother and father was in 1970. So much has happened me, my family, my community, my country since then, it's a lifetime. So many families just like mine, well reared and brought up to respect themselves and everybody else, caught up in history, a history not of their own making but a history that dealt us a hand that we had to play to the best of our ability. Ordinary families caught up in extraordinary times. A people that fought, when their backs were against the wall. A people history will show, that fight was hard and long. Who fought against huge odds and refused to lie down and be walked on nor be defeated. Backed to the hilt by the Irish population on the northern side of Britain's unwanted border, and an honourable minority south of the border, in the USA and Britain. A people that I have the highest respect and regard for. Our fight was a just fight, a necessary fight.

FORTY YEARS IN EXILE

I HAVE BEEN now a political exile from my native county Tyrone for over forty years. The summer of 1970 was the year I did best man for my eldest brother Seamus. The winter of 1970 was the last Christmas I had my Christmas dinner with my big happy family. To me it's a bit like the last supper! So this means that I have spent almost all of my adult life living amongst strangers, So what has this taught me? What has the greatest university of all taught me? The University of Life. It has taught me a lot.

An old story I heard comes to mind here. This man was just after getting off a train. The town was new to him. An old man was sitting on one of the station seats. The man approached him and sat down beside him, "What are the people like in this town" he demanded from the old man. "How long did you live in the last town you were in", was the old man's question. "A good few years" said the man. "And what were the people like in that town" he asked. They were all a shower of wasters" said the man. "Well" said the old man, "they will all be a shower of wasters in this town too". The man walked off. It wasn't the people in the towns that were the man's problem, the real problem was his attitude to them. How you treat the people that you meet along the road of this life, is fundamental to everything about life, and I would say that to treat people with fair play is the most important principal of all. I joined the civil rights movement in the north in the late 60's seeking fair play for my family and community, as thousands of others did. The continued denial of basic fair play to a whole section of the northern people, lead to one of the bloodiest and the longest political conflicts that this country has ever known. Ask the Palestinians of the Middle East, they will tell you the denial of fair play is the most hurtful thing of all. It is the absence of this basic civil right that cuts deepest into the human being. Ask the black people of South Africa or the black slaves of Southern America, or just look at the face of a child who is just after been chastised in the wrong - the look on that child's face tells it all. The absence of fair play, be it in family, a school, a workplace, a community, a country or between countries, it is a sure recipe for conflict. If everybody in this world was getting treated with the decency, the dignity, the respect that they are entitled to, by the laws of God, and the laws of man, then conflicts would be virtually nonexistent. I suppose that the basic lesson forty years of living away from home has taught me, is to treat everybody that you meet along the road of this life, with the decency, dignity and the respect that they are entitled to. Especially women and children, the old the weak and the vulnerable, those who are completely under your control, and those unfortunates who, for some unfathomable reason, seem to have drawn the short straw in life. Be good to them all, and God and this world will always be good to you. Be grateful for all the good that you have got out of life.

It was the great U.S. President Abraham Lincon that said "A person in this world is as happy as they set out to be". The world is a beautiful, but imperfect, place. I am a stonemason. I have worked with stone, marble, granite and slate. It is the very imperfections of these natural materials that is their beauty. Perhaps the world is the same.

WE WERE NEIGHBOURS
AND NEIGHBOURS CHILDREN

'I'll wear no criminal uniform, or meekly serve my time, that England might brand Irelands fight, eight hundred years of crime'. I have no apologies to make to anybody for joining the I.R.A. and fighting against the British administration in Ireland, against the corrupt northern state, and its British imposed border, as a young man. It was the British and the unionist state that created, over 50 years of misrule and corruption, The circumstances where conflict was inevitable. A people will only resort to armed conflict as a last resort. The nationalist Irish population of the north found themselves with their backs against the wall in 1969. When they were denied civil rights, burned out of their homes in Belfast and across the north, and were let down by the Jack Lynch government. They had no choice but to come out fighting. 'Out of the ashes arose the I.R.A. Provisionals!' The northern nationalist peoples' army, an army that was never a threat to the southern part of our country. This lie was used by dishonest southern politicians to undermine the provisional's 'fight for the north'. It was political change in the island of Ireland that they really feared. The reason why we survived 25 years of guerrilla warfare against a formidable enemy, was because we were 'of the people'. We weren't aliens or mercenaries or terrorists. We were all from good decent families. Sure we made mistakes, some terrible mistakes, but we were fighting a war. I was a bricklayer with a trowel and a brick in one hand, and suddenly, in what seemed like the blink of an eye, I had a rifle in one hand, and a bomb in the other. My trowel and brick were replaced by the weapons of war. We dragged one of the most powerful standing armies in the world to the negotiating table. They conceded, they could never beat us. The British Army generals stated that, when it came to the toughness of guerrilla armys they had fought anywhere in the world, the Provisional I.R.A. 'were top of the Premier League'. We were just ordinary young men and women, caught up in extraordinary times. We just did our best. Was our best good enough? Time and history will tell. I believe we have created the conditions where 800 years of conflict can be put to rest. The British army are withdrawn to barracks, the B specials, the U.D.R., the R.U.C., the U.D.A., the U.V.F. all gone. The orange order has no longer any political power. The hated sectarian 'protestant Parliament for a protestant people' is gone, The absolute claim of the six counties by the British parliament is gone. The people will have a right to vote in the future, whether to break the connection with Britain in the north. The six counties are now governed by London and Dublin with a power sharing administration in Belfast. Catholic Irish and protestant Irish now working together for the good of all, and where parity of esteem is now guaranteed. This is all within an internationally recognised agreement. That it took a 25 year Guerrilla conflict, with all its suffering, to achieve this, is tragic. All sides in this conflict suffered. The Irish, the British, the catholic, the protestant sides, and those on no sides at all. There is no blue print for war. No plan to follow, as when you build a building. A war is fought from day to day, and you just do your best to fight it to win, as humanely as possible. Mistakes will be made in the heat of the battle, and we made some bad mistakes, but mistakes they were. I can't ever recall a time when an I.R.A. unit went out to deliberately strike an innocent person. In my experience that never happened. I regret all the casualties of war on every side especially innocents. I regret that conflict was ever allowed to happen. It was not of our making. But I would fight again, if I was back in the same place in 1969. Some did stand idly, by but I wasn't one of them. I stood my ground, fought for what I believed in, as did my family and many other families right across the north and the south. I thank all the good people who looked after me through those hard tough long years. They were, and still are, the salt of the earth! I was proud to fight for them. But then, weren't we all neighbours and neighbour's children anyway?

The Man In The Glass

When you get what you want in your struggle for self
And the world makes you king for the day,
Just go to a mirror and look at yourself,
And see what that man has to say.

For it isn't your father or mother or wife.
Whose judgement upon you must pass;
The fella whose verdict matters the most in your life,
Is the one staring back from the glass.

He's the fellow to please, never mind all the rest,
For he's with you right up to the end,
And you've passed your most dangerous difficult test,
If the man in the glass is your friend.

Some people may think you a straight shooting chum
And call you a wonderful guy,
But the man in the glass says you're only a bum,
If you can't look him straight in the eye.

You can fool the whole world down the pathway of years,
And get pats on the back as you pass,
But your final rewards will be the heartaches and tears,
If you've cheated the man in the glass.

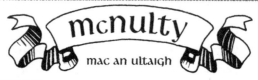

mcnulty
mac an ultaigh

he McNultys are the descendants of the Gaelic Irish sept, the Mac an Ultaigh, which means "Son of the Ulsterman". The Mac an Ultaigh were originally found in County Donegal, where they are still found in significant numbers. The McNultys had an uneasy relationship with the dominant O'Donnells, sometimes found in battle with them, and sometimes, against. Today, the name is also found in numbers in County Mayo, where it is expected that a branch of the Co. Donegal sept established after migrating south. Some noted of the name were, Bernard McNulty, founder member of the Fenians in America, he was also friend and associate of John Boyle O'Reilly, Irish American newspaper man and Fenian supporter whose family home although in ruin, is a monument near Dowth in County Louth; Thomas McNulty (1818-1899) of Oldcastle, Co. Meath, was appointed Bishop of Meath in 1864.

VARIANTS: Mc Anulty, Nulty, McKnulty.

ARMS: Argent, on a mount in base proper a lion gules and a buck of the second rampant combattant supporting a dexter hand couped at the wrist, of the second.

MOTTO: MERITO. "Deservedly".

NAME MEANING:
"Son of the Ulster man".

© 1995
Heraldry Names Ltd. Ballina Ireland
Text and Illustrations HNW 205